Harvey Washington Wiley

Cereals and cereal products

Harvey Washington Wiley

Cereals and cereal products

ISBN/EAN: 9783337732899

Printed in Europe, USA, Canada, Australia, Japan

Cover: Foto ©ninafisch / pixelio.de

More available books at **www.hansebooks.com**

BULLETIN No. 13.

U. S. DEPARTMENT OF AGRICULTURE.
DIVISION OF CHEMISTRY.

FOODS
AND
FOOD ADULTERANTS.

INVESTIGATIONS MADE UNDER DIRECTION OF

H. W. WILEY,
CHIEF CHEMIST,

WITH THE COLLABORATION OF K. P. McELROY, W. H. KRUG,
T. C. TRESCOT, W. D. BIGELOW, AND OTHERS.

PART NINTH.

CEREALS AND CEREAL PRODUCTS.

WASHINGTON:
GOVERNMENT PRINTING OFFICE.
1898.

LETTER OF TRANSMITTAL.

U. S. DEPARTMENT OF AGRICULTURE,
DIVISION OF CHEMISTRY,
Washington, D. C., January 11, 1898.

SIR: I transmit herewith, for your inspection and approval, the manuscript of part 9 of Bulletin No. 13 of this Division. It discusses the composition of cereals and cereal products and the adulteration thereof.

Respectfully,

H. W. WILEY,
Chief of Division.

Hon. JAMES WILSON,
Secretary.

ILLUSTRATIONS.

PLATES.

	Page.
Pl. XLVII.—Typical wheat starch	1193
XLVIII.—Typical maize starch	1193
XLIX.—Typical oat starch	1194
L.—Typical barley starch	1194
LI.—Typical rye starch	1194
LII.—Typical rice starch	1194
LIII.—Typical buckwheat starch	1194

FIGURES.

Fig. 1.—Farinometer in parts	1270
2.—Farinometer ready for use	1271
3.—Gluten tester in parts	1273
4.—Gluten tester ready for use	1273

CONTENTS.

	Page.
Cereal products	1171
Composition of cereal grains	1171
Barley	1172
Composition of proteids of barley	1173
Composition of unhulled barley	1173
Buckwheat	1174
Maize	1175
Maize proteids	1177
Variation of maize under different climatic conditions	1177
Oats	1178
Notes on analyses of oats	1179
Variation in composition of oats	1180
Proteids of the oat kernel	1181
Rice	1181
Proteids of rice	1183
Rye	1183
Proteids of rye	1184
Wheat	1185
Comparison of American and foreign wheat	1187
Variation of wheat with climate and soil	1188
Proteids of the wheat kernel	1190
Separation of the constituents of gluten	1191
The carbohydrates of the cereals	1192
Insoluble carbohydrates	1192
Starch	1192
The cellulose group	1195
Insoluble carbohydrates of wheat	1198
Soluble carbohydrates	1203
Sucrose	1204
Invert or reducing sugars, dextrin, galactin	1205
Raffinose	1207
Miscellaneous constituents of cereal grains	1207
Nitrogenous bases	1207
Ferments	1208
Diastase	1209
Composition of the ash of cereals	1209
Principal difficulties in procuring ash	1210
Description of samples of ash	1211
Mineral substances in the ash and their relations	1213
Preparation of cereals for food	1219
Grinding of cereals	1219
The milling of wheat	1219
The roller process	1219

CONTENTS.

	Page.
Preparation of cereals for food—Continued.	
Grades of flour	1234
Composition of wheat flours	1236
Heat of combustion of cereals	1243
Analyses of wheat flours	1253
Typical American flours	1263
Composition of typical French flours	1266
Viscosity of dough	1269
The use of farinometers	1269
Gluten tester	1272
An examination of flours by a new method of determining their quality	1274
Particles of debris in the flour	1275
Preparation for the microscope	1275
Results under the lens	1276
Microscopic examination of cellulose particles in flours	1276
Milling of Indian corn (maize)	1277
Microscopic character of Indian corn meal	1278
Composition of fine Indian corn flour	1279
Production of rye meal	1280
Ergot in rye flour	1281
Composition of rye flour	1281
Barley flour	1282
Buckwheat flour	1282
Discussion of buckwheat products	1284
Flour and meal substitutes	1285
Substitutes other than cereals	1285
Use of maize meal for wheat and rye flour	1286
Detection of corn meal in flour	1287
Use of potatoes for cereals	1288
Reports as to minerals and wood as substitutes	1289
Relative nutritive properties of wheat and Indian corn	1290
Experiments in feeding corn and wheat	1291
Comparative production of pork from wheat and maize	1292
Comparative nutritive value of the carbohydrates	1293
The action of sulphurous acid on flour	1293
Effect on fermentation	1294
Experiments in bread making with sulphured flour	1295
Method of testing flours practiced by the Vienna board of health	1295
Making and baking of bread	1296
Varieties of bread	1297
Processes of leavening	1298
Character of the yeast fermentation	1299
Experiments with yeast	1299
Spontaneous fermentation	1301
Method for making salt-rising bread	1301
Aeration by means of already formed carbon dioxid	1302
Chemical aerating agents	1303
Classification of baking powders	1304
Residues of baking powders	1310
Composition of bread	1312
Temperature of baking	1315
The percentage of moisture in the loaf	1315
Relation of flour to moisture in bread	1316
Relation of moisture to size and shape of loaf	1316
Summary of observations regarding moisture	1317

CONTENTS.

	Page.
Making and baking of bread—Continued.	
Loss during fermentation	1317
Chemical changes produced in the loaf during baking	1318
Classification of the breads of commerce	1318
Description of samples analyzed	1319
Analytical data	1321
Ether extract	1321
Fiber	1321
Comparison of bread with flour	1326
A typical American high-grade bread	1328
Rye bread	1328
Determination of fat in bread	1329
Imperfection of method for extracting fat	1329
Fat used in greasing pans	1330
Use of alum in bread	1330
The acidity of bread	1331
Adulterations	1332
Analyses of Russian "Hunger bread"	1332
Character of substitutes for flour in bread	1333
Comparative chemical examination of biscuit made from rye, and from rye and wheat	1334
The detection of egg yolk in breadstuffs	1335
The influence of mold on the composition of bread	1335
Bread made from the whole grain	1336
Shredded wheat biscuit	1336
Bread from whole-wheat flour	1337
Adulteration of bread	1338
Soap as an adulterant	1338
Gypsum as an adulterant	1339
Stannous chlorid as an adulterant	1339
Partially prepared, or breakfast, foods	1340
Description of partially prepared cereals and breakfast foods	1341
Study of the analytical data	1350
Indian corn products	1350
Wheat products	1350
Oat products	1351
Tapioca	1351
Macaroni, etc	1352
Barley products	1352
Miscellaneous products	1352
Biscuits	1353
Preparation	1353
Discussion of the analytical data	1358
Rolls	1359
Discussion of the data	1362
Cakes and like goods	1362
Discussion of the analytical data	1368
Stannous chlorid in ginger cake	1369

PREFATORY NOTE.

More than two years have elapsed since the publication of part eight of Bulletin 13. The delay in completing this bulletin has been due to several causes. Chief among these must first be mentioned the great amount of analytical work which has attended the preparation of the present part. A mere glance through the following pages will show anyone familiar with chemical processes the great amount of time which must necessarily have been consumed in securing the analytical data which follow. In addition to this, the appropriations which Congress has made for the prosecution of this work have been greatly diminished. From an annual appropriation of $15,000 a year the whole amount has been cut down until less than $5,000 a year have been available for our work. This has made it necessary to confine the chemical work to a few analysts, and thus increase the delay in the publication. The general conduct of all the work connected with this bulletin has been under the immediate supervision of the Chief of the Division of Chemistry, who has prepared the manuscript and arranged the analytical data connected with the work. Among the analysts who have been chiefly active in conducting the chemical investigations may be mentioned Mr. K. P. McElroy, who had charge of the ash analyses; Mr. W. H. Krug, who determined the fiber, ether extract, sugar, salt, and digestibility in the samples; Mr. T. C. Trescot, who made the determinations of the nitrogen; and Mr. W. D. Bigelow, who made a part of the determinations of the ash and moisture and all of the combustions in oxygen. Other members of the laboratory staff have assisted from time to time in the incidental work connected with the preparation of this bulletin.

It will be noticed by the reader that very little space has been given to analytical processes. The methods which have been employed are, in all cases save where exception is noted, those which are prescribed by the Association of Official Agricultural Chemists. It has not, therefore, been deemed wise to burden the pages of this bulletin by descriptions of methods which can be found officially set forth in other places. In those cases where departures have been made from the association methods the fact is stated, and new methods which have been employed and which are deemed of essential importance are described.

PREFATORY NOTE.

The chief object in view in the preparation of Part IX has been to establish as carefully as possible a standard of composition for typical cereal foods, not only as a contribution to our chemical knowledge of these bodies, but especially with a view to securing the proper starting point for the study of the nutritive properties of the bodies in question and as a basis for detecting adulterations. For this reason the number of samples purchased has been made as large as possible, and especial care has been observed in every detail of the examination.

It is believed that the data which the following pages contain, although subject to the errors of analysis and observation which occur in spite of ordinary care, can be relied upon by physicians, physiologists, and physiological chemists as a safe basis for deductions in respect of the character of cereal foods.

The analyses whose results are recorded in the following pages have extended over a period of more than four years. The examinations of flours had for their primary purpose the establishment of a standard of composition. These analyses were made chiefly in the years 1894 and 1895. At that time there was little occasion for supposing that wheat flours were adulterated to any great extent with the products of Indian corn, and for this reason those brands which were made by millers of national reputation were not examined for this adulterant.

It is hoped that the remaining parts of Bulletin 13, two in number, viz., a part devoted to infants' and invalids' foods and one to preserved meats, may follow without great delay. When, however, the reader considers the magnitude of the problem which was undertaken at the outset in the preparation of Bulletin 13, he will hardly expect an apology for the length of time the work has consumed.

H. W. WILEY.

FOOD AND FOOD ADULTERANTS.

PART IX.—CEREALS AND CEREAL PRODUCTS.

CEREAL PRODUCTS.

COMPOSITION OF CEREAL GRAINS.

The cereal grains and the preparations made therefrom form the most important part of human foods. This preeminence is evident both from an economic and dietary point of view. Among all civilized nations bread, in its broad sense, is the basis of human nutrition. All dietary standards cluster about it as the center and support of the system of nutrition. Not only is it the most important, but at the same time it is the cheapest of nutrients. Measured by actual nutritive power, there is no other complete ration which in economy can compare with bread.

Bread is here spoken of as a complete ration. By this is meant a ration which in itself contains all the essential elements of nutrition. In it are found the proteids in various forms, carbohydrates of different composition of which starch is the chief, fats and oils, phosphoric acid, lime, potash, and other mineral matters. There is no tissue of the body which can not be completely nourished with bread, especially if it be made of the whole wheat. In speaking of bread as a complete ration, it is not meant to imply that no other food is necessary. The demands of digestion in sentient animals are wider than mere nutrition. The element of taste and flavor is always a most important one. In man not only are the tissues to be nourished and replenished, but the taste must be ministered to and the palate flattered, in the interests of hygiene and gustatory demands. It is therefore necessary in the human dietary to regard bread as the foundation on which is to be erected a structure of diet which abundantly cares for the needs of the system, and at the same time, by its constant variation, conforms to the demands, maybe whims, of the gustatory nerve. Happily, in the case of bread, we have many sources from which it may be supplied. The principal cereals are wheat, maize, rye, barley, rice, oats, and buckwheat. The different kinds of potatoes have also served for bread making, and the banana and cassava root are likewise employed for this purpose. In fact, nearly every plant furnishing a fruit or product rich in starch has been utilized for bread making, and starch is therefore to be considered as the chief constituent of bread of all kinds.

Nearly related to bread in composition and in dietetic qualities are various compounds made with the flour of cereals and of other starchy materials. These products have many different names, most of them being included under the name biscuits, or crackers, and cakes of various descriptions. In addition to these, however, must be mentioned puddings, different preparations of oatmeal, etc., known as breakfast foods, and similar materials prepared in different ways and used under a great variety of names. The scope of the present investigation, therefore, is seen to be the determination of the composition and nutritive value of cereal products in general, of which bread is the chief and typical one; all the others, known by different names, being related thereto in the predominance of their chief constituents and in their general dietetic value. It is evident, as a preliminary study in the investigation of these products, that an accurate knowledge of the constitution of the cereals themselves is necessary. For many years this division has been engaged in investigations of the composition of cereals, and these investigations have been published as Bulletins 1, 3, 9, and 45, of the Chemical Division. In Bulletin No. 45, which contains the study of the cereals collected at the World's Columbian Exposition, a summary of the composition of the principal cereals has been published, and this summary is so important in the present investigation that it is advisable to insert it here.

BARLEY.

The mean composition of the samples of barley exhibited at the World's Columbian Exposition and analyzed by this division is as follows:

Weight of 100 kernels ....grams.. 4.533	Crude fiber............per cent.. 4.07
Moisture...............per cent.. 11.31	Ash...................do.... 2.44
Proteids................do.... 10.61	Carbohydrates, other than crude
Ether extract............do.... 2.09	fiber...............per cent.. 69.48

The composition of 14 samples of barley analyzed in this division is shown in the following table:

	Per cent.		Per cent.
Moisture...........................	6.47	Ether extract..................	2.67
Proteids soluble in 80 per cent alcohol................................	3.66	Sugar...........................	7.02
		Dextrin and soluble starch	3.55
Proteids insoluble in 80 per cent alcohol	7.86	Starch	62.09
		Crude fiber....................	3.81
Ash................................	2.87		

COMPOSITION OF THE PROTEIDS OF BARLEY.

According to Osborne (18th An. Rep. Conn. Ex. Sta.), the following proteids are found in barley:

Soluble proteids:		Total weight of seed.
Leucosin	per cent..	0.30
Hordein	do....	4.00
Edestin. } Proteose }	do....	1.95
Insoluble proteids	do....	4.50

The composition of the proteids which can be obtained in a pure state is shown in the following table:

Composition of barley proteids in pure state.

Constituent elements.	Leucosin.	Edestin.	Hordein.
	Per cent.	*Per cent.*	*Per cent.*
Carbon	52.81	50.88	54.29
Hydrogen	6.78	6.65	6.80
Nitrogen	16.62	18.10	17.21
Sulphur	1.47	} 24.37 {	0.83
Oxygen	22.32		20.87

In case the composition of the insoluble proteids is approximately that of the soluble, the total nitrogen content of the proteids of the barley is about 17.6 per cent. The factor for calculating the nitrogen to proteids in barley based on this figure is 5.68 instead of the common factor 6.25, employed in computing the proteids in the analyses made in this division and mentioned above. Since it has been the general custom to calculate the proteids by $N \times 6.25$ the data given will not be changed, but the recalculation can be easily made by anyone who desires to make use of the new factor.

As an illustration of the changes in composition which the new factor would require, the instance of a typical American barley cited below may be mentioned. The percentage of nitrogen corresponding to the proteids given is 1.76. This figure multiplied by 5.68 gives the product 10 for total proteids instead of 11. Since in this analysis the carbohydrates other than crude fiber are calculated by difference, the percentage given would be increased from 69.45 to 70.45 per cent. Numerically considered, the difference in the two sets of data is important.

COMPOSITION OF UNHULLED BARLEY.

From a comparative study of the recorded analyses of American barleys it is evident that a typical unhulled American barley has approximately the following composition:

	Per cent.		Per cent.
Moisture	10.85	Ash	2.50
Proteids	11.00	Carbohydrates other than crude fiber	69.55
Ether extract	2.25		
Crude fiber	3.85		

In this country barley is scarcely used at all as a material for bread-making, but more commonly for soup; therefore it is not probable that any of the samples whose composition is given farther on contains any barley flour whatever. The barley grain in this country is used almost exclusively for brewing and cattle feeding. When used for brewing purposes the refuse, known as brewers' grains, when properly dried and preserved, becomes a valuable cattle food, in which, however, there is a deficiency of carbohydrates as compared with the other constituents.

BUCKWHEAT.

Only a few samples of buckwheat have been subjected to analysis in this laboratory, and of these the mean composition of 10 of American origin follows:

Weight of 100 kernels ...grams.. 3.069	Crude fiber.............per cent.. 10.57
Moisture ....per cent.. 12.31	Ash.......................do.... 1.85
Proteids ....do.... 10.86	Carbohydrates, other than crude
Ether extract ....do.... 2.06	fiber ....per cent.. 62.34

Judged by the limited number of samples examined, a typical American buckwheat has approximately the following composition:

Weight of 100 kernels ....grams.. 3.00	Crude fiber.............per cent.. 10.75
Moisture ....per cent.. 12.00	Ash.......................do.... 1.75
Proteids ....do.... 10.75	Carbohydrates, other than crude
Ether extract ....do.... 2.00	fiber ....per cent.. 62.75

In the buckwheat it will be noticed that there is a large percentage of fiber; that is, of carbohydrates insoluble in the ordinary processes of analysis. This large percentage is due chiefly to the thick inner envelope which surrounds the kernel. In the process of grinding this hull is mostly removed, so that the buckwheat flour contains a smaller percentage of fiber than the grain itself. It is probable that of all the cereals and flours which are on our markets the buckwheat is the most extensively adulterated. It is only by a careful microscopic examination that the adulteration of buckwheat flour can be detected. Inasmuch as the flour of other cereals is very much cheaper, it becomes a matter of financial advantage to dealers to mix the buckwheat flour with that of cheaper materials. In this country buckwheat flour is used to a large extent in the baking of pancakes, which are eaten hot with sirup or honey. It therefore is a matter of considerable importance in the present investigation. The buckwheat flour gives a cake of somewhat dark color, owing to a mixture of a part of the hulls therewith, and this is a common index in the judgment of its purity. Certain rye flours, however, also give dark-colored cakes and breads; and therefore the appearance of this dark color is not always a certain indication of the purity of the sample. Even buckwheat flour when bolted through fine cloth gives an almost white cake. When, however, the buckwheat is mixed with flour made of wheat or maize the light color is, as a rule, the distinguishing feature, but such a light color is no positive proof of adulteration.

The separation of the proteids in buckwheat has not been recently made, and it is not possible, therefore, to give a statement of their different components, as in the case of barley and the other cereals. They doubtless consist of soluble and insoluble portions resembling in composition the typical proteids of those two classes.

MAIZE, OR INDIAN CORN.

The most important cereal, from an economical point of view and also from its dietary importance, which is grown in the United States is maize. In all parts of the country it forms a considerable percentage of the food of our people, and especially is this true in the Southern States, where corn bread, among parts of the population, is the chief bread food used. In various other forms, as hasty pudding (mush) and in other methods of preparation, it enters largely into our dietaries. Although important as a human food, the principal uses of maize are in cattle feeding, and in the manufacture of starch, of whisky, and of alcohol. On account of its great importance, a somewhat careful study of its composition in this place is justifiable. For the typical samples grown in the United States and collected at the World's Columbian Exposition at Chicago, the following represents the constitution:

Weight of 100 kernels...grams.. 38.979	Crude fiber............per cent.. 1.71
Moisture...........per cent. 10.93	Ash ....do.... 1.36
Proteids............do.... 9.88	Carbohydrates, other than crude
Ether extract........do.... 4.17	fiber ....per cent.. 71.95

The following table represents the maxima, minima, and means of the constituents of maize collected in all parts of the world:

Table of maxima, minima, and means of constituents of maize.

Kinds and numbers of samples.	Weight of 100 kernels.	Moisture.	Proteids.	Ether extract.	Crude fiber.	Ash.	Carbohydrates, excluding fiber.
	Grams.	Per cent.	Per cent.	Per cent.	Per cent.	Per cent.	Per cent.
Domestic corn:							
Maxima............	a 48.312	b 12.32	a 11.55	a 5.06	b 2.00	b 1.55	b 75.07
Minima............	c 10.608	b 9.58	b 8.58	b 2.94	d 1.00	a 1.19	a 68.97
Means.............	38.979	10.93	9.88	4.17	1.71	1.36	71.95
Foreign corn:							
Maxima............	e 46.487	f 12.60	g 11.55	e 4.85	f 2.20	g 1.80	e 71.85
Minima............	f 18.428	e 10.43	e 9.80	f 4.02	e 1.57	f 1.26	g 68.02
Means.............	28.553	11.71	10.72	4.51	1.87	1.54	69.65
Means of samples from the United States exhibited at the Columbian Exposition (18 analyses)	38.979	10.93	9.88	4.17	1.71	1.36	71.95
Means of foreign samples exhibited at the Columbian Exposition (2 analyses)	28.553	11.71	10.72	4.51	1.87	1.54	69.65

a Kentucky. c Wisconsin. e New South Wales. g Argentine Republic.
b Indiana. d New Hampshire. f Bulgaria.

Table of maxima, minima, and means of constituents of maize—Continued.

Kinds and numbers of samples.	Weight of 100 kernels.	Moisture.	Proteids.	Ether extract.	Crude fiber.	Ash.	Carbo-hydrates, excluding fiber.
	Grams.	*Per cent.*	*Per cent.*	*Per cent.*	*Per cent.*	*Per cent.*	*Per cent.*
	(a)	(b)	(c)	(b)	(b)	(c)	(b)
Means of former analyses of the Department of Agriculture:							
United States	36.474	10.04	10.39	5.20	2.09	1.55	70.69
Northern States	37.320	9.98	10.64	5.11	1.41	1.54	71.32
Southern States	40.659	8.96	10.95	4.94	1.72	1.37	72.06
Middle West	32.457	12.33	10.89	4.97	2.22	1.43	68.16
Far West	37.528	9.50	10.43	5.30	2.47	1.55	70.75
Pacific Slope	27.900	9.78	8.14	6.40	2.07	1.48	72.13
Jenkins and Winton (208 analyses)		10.90	10.50	5.40	2.10	1.50	69.60
König—Mean composition of samples from various localities:							
Miscellaneous origin (137)		13.35	9.45	4.29	2.29	1.29	69.33
Italian samples (24)		13.13	10.26	3.84	2.88	1.95	67.72
American samples (80)		10.02	10.17	4.78	1.67	1.40	68.63
Dent corn (149)		10.14	9.36	4.96	2.21	1.47	68.65
Sugar corn (27)		8.70	11.43	7.79	2.86	1.81	62.76
Southeastern Europe (19)		14.53	9.42	4.13	2.34	1.39	69.37
Southwestern Europe (8)		12.47	8.84	5.80	4.16	2.06	65.79

a 1211 analyses. *b* 114 analyses. *c* 202 analyses.

Comparing the means of the analyses of American samples with those of foreign origin, we are struck with the excess of moisture in the foreign samples. In those from southwestern Europe are found 4 per cent more moisture than in samples of domestic origin. Among the samples grown in the United States, those in the Middle West, viz, Iowa, Missouri, Nebraska, etc., contain the largest amount of moisture, while those grown in the arid regions have the smallest amount. Of the domestic samples exhibited at the World's Fair it was found that the mean content of water was 10.93 per cent, nearly 1 per cent higher than the mean of former analyses of the Department. The weight of 100 kernels was a little more than that before found, and this is not a surprising fact, inasmuch as it would be natural for exhibitors to send not only the largest ears but also the largest grains to the Exposition. The percentage of proteids in the domestic World's Fair samples was surprisingly low, being about 0.75 per cent less than was found in the samples examined a few years ago. On the other hand, the percentage of carbohydrates was about one point higher than that obtained in the former work. In the above table is found a convenient comparison of the means of maize analyses from all parts of the world.

The typical American maize should have approximately the following composition:

Weight of 100 kernels......grams.. 38.00
Moisture ....per cent.. 10.75
Proteids ....do.... 10.00
Ether extract ....do.... 4.25
Crude fiber.............per cent.. 1.75
Ash....................do.... 1.50
Carbohydrates, other than crude fiber ....per cent.. 71.75

MAIZE PROTEIDS.

The maize proteids have been studied by Chittenden and Osborne, who divide them as follows:

Globulins: Unnamed, myosin, vitelline.
Albumins: (1) Existing in small quantities, (2) existing in small quantities.
Zeins: (1) Soluble in alcohol, (2) insoluble in alcohol.

Of these bodies the albumins have not been obtained sufficiently pure to give the final data of composition. The other proteids have the following composition:

Composition of maize proteids.

Constituent elements.	Myosin.	Vitelline.	Unnamed globulin.	Soluble zeins.	Insoluble zeins.
	Per cent.	Per cent.	Per cent.	Per cent.	Per cent.
Carbon	52.66	51.71	52.38	55.26	55.15
Hydrogen	7.02	6.85	6.82	7.27	7.24
Nitrogen	16.76	18.12	15.25	16.09	16.22
Sulphur	1.30	0.86	1.26	0.59	0.62
Oxygen	22.26	22.46	24.29	20.77	20.77

The relative quantities of the different proteids have been lately definitely determined, but the two zeins comprise by far the largest part. As a result of Osborne's latest determination, it may be stated that the mean percentage of nitrogen in maize proteids is 16.057, equivalent to the factor 6.23. This is so near the old factor 6.25 as to make unnecessary any correction in the percentages of total proteids given above.

VARIATION OF MAIZE UNDER DIFFERENT CLIMATIC CONDITIONS.

Certain special varieties of early maturing maize, or sweet maize intended for table use when in the partially ripe state, may be detected by the large quantity of sugar which they contain, especially when the starch is still soft. In the earlier investigations of the Department, it was noticed that the percentage of crude fiber was somewhat larger in the West and South than in the North and East, and further that in samples grown on the Pacific coast there was a slight deficiency of proteids. Further investigations, however, would be necessary to determine whether or not this apparent increase in fiber be due to the accidental constitution of the sample or to the real influence of the soil and climate. It is reasonable to expect that in some slowly maturing varieties, such as would grow in the Southwest and South, the percentage of fiber in the grain would be greater than in the more rapidly maturing varieties growing in the East and North.

In the case of sugar or sweet corn Richardson found the mean composition of 19 samples to be the following:

	Per cent.		Per cent.
Moisture	8.44	Crude fiber	2.82
Proteids	11.48	Carbohydrates, other than crude fiber	66.72
Ash	1.97		
Ether extract	8.57		

This analysis shows that the sweet corn has a considerably larger percentage of oil than the field varieties, and there is a larger percentage of sugar in the carbohydrates. A study of all the analyses which have been made in this division reveals the fact that maize is one of the most invariable of the cereals, maintaining under the most different climatic conditions a most remarkable uniformity of composition, and varying chiefly in the size, color, and general physical characteristics of its kernels rather than in their composition. For detailed information in regard to the variations and general characteristics of different varieties of maize grown in different localities, Bulletins 1 and 45 of this Division may be consulted.

OATS.

In the United States the quantity of oats grown is very great, but only an inconsiderable portion of the whole is used for human food, and this chiefly in the form of oatmeal, used for making the so-called breakfast foods and other puddings. The investigations of this division, as recorded in Bulletin 9, show that the ratio of kernel to husk of oats grown in the United States is 73 to 27. In the Western States the proportion of kernel is relatively higher, and in the Southern States lower. One hundred samples of the hulls of oats, collected from all parts of the United States, were found to have the following mean composition:

	Per cent.		Per cent.
Moisture	5.22	Crude fiber	17.88
Proteids	2.48	Carbohydrates, other than crude	
Ash	5.59	fiber	68.83

In the above data any bodies soluble in ether are included with the carbohydrates, but the hulls contain only a small quantity of such substances.

A large number of samples of typical oats was collected at the World's Columbian Exposition, and the mean composition of the unhulled kernels grown in the United States, as determined by an examination of these samples, was as follows:

Weight of 100 kernels...grams..	2.918	Crude fiber............per cent..	12.07
Moisture............per cent..	10.06	Ash ....do....	3.46
Proteids............do....	12.15	Carbohydrates, other than crude	
Ether extract..........do....	4.33	fiber ....per cent..	57.93

The large quantity of crude fiber in the case of the oats is due to the heavy chaff surrounding the kernel. It will be of interest here to present, as in the case of maize, a comparative table showing the composition of oats, as determined by all recorded analyses. In presenting such tables it should be noted that the analysis of the World's Columbian Exposition samples should be given the preference in regard to determining the typical character of these cereals, on account of the facts that the samples themselves were presumably typical of the best varieties, and that the methods of analysis employed were the most recent and reliable. At the top of the table the numbers under "Domestic oats" and "Canada" represent the samples on exhibition at Chicago in 1893. A comparison of the results of these analyses with those heretofore made by this Department and in other places may be made from the table.

Table of maxima, minima, and means of constituents of oats.

Kinds and numbers of samples.	Weight of 100 kernels.	Moisture.	Proteids.	Ether extract.	Crude fiber.	Ash.	Carbohydrates, excluding fiber.
Domestic oats:	Grams.	Per cent.	Per cent.	Per cent.	Per cent.	Per cent.	Per cent.
Maxima	a 3.891	a 13.02	b 15.05	b 6.14	a 16.65	c 4.37	d 61.44
Minima	d 2.038	e 7.87	d 9.10	a 0.93	b 8.57	f 2.47	g 53.70
Means	2.918	10.06	12.15	4.33	12.07	3.46	58.75
Canada:							
Maxima	4.253	11.63	12.78	5.56	15.65	3.29	61.98
Minima	2.791	8.52	10.68	3.79	8.52	2.71	57.61
Means	3.364	9.46	11.83	4.73	11.39	2.92	59.69
Means of World's Fair samples (72 analyses)	2.995	9.96	12.07	4.42	11.92	3.35	58.28
Means of samples previously analyzed by Department of Agriculture, hulled (179 analyses)	h 2.507	6.93	14.31	8.14	1.38	2.15	67.09
Means of Jenkins and Winton (30 analyses)	....	11.00	11.80	5.00	9.50	3.00	59.70
König—Mean composition of samples from various localities:							
Miscellaneous (377)	....	12.11	10.66	4.99	10.58	3.29	58.37
Middle and north Germany (31)	....	12.45	10.82	5.30	10.25	3.29	53.23
Southern and southwestern Germany (16)	....	13.39	11.36	5.30	9.93	3.18	58.12
Austro-Hungary (14)	....	11.85	11.41	5.84	11.01	3.23	56.40
France (196)	....	13.50	9.52	3.46	9.18	3.26	62.47
United States (22)	....	12.11	10.11	6.24	9.33	2.99	68.61

a Washington.
b Kansas.
c Wyoming.
d Illinois.
e Ohio.
f Pennsylvania.
g Michigan.
h Unhulled.

NOTES ON ANALYSES OF OATS.

In discussing the comparative results contained in the above table, it will be noticed at once that the samples examined at the World's Fair contained much less moisture than those reported by König. These samples were almost wholly of domestic origin, and thus show that the oats follow the other cereals which have been mentioned in having a less quantity of moisture when grown in the United States. The percentage of crude fiber also appears to be somewhat larger than in other sets of samples. This may be due to the fact that naturally the largest and finest looking kernels would be selected for exhibition and the hulls of these kernels would be correspondingly developed. In the samples formerly examined by the Department of Agriculture we find the same striking deficit in moisture that has been noticed in the other cereals, and the consequent increase in the percentage of other constituents, notably proteids and ether extract. It must not be forgotten, however, that these samples can not be compared with the other sets in the series, because the hulls of the kernels were removed before the analyses were made. Taking into consideration all the data at hand, it may be said that the typical oats of the United States may be shown as follows:

Composition of typical unhulled oats.

Weight of 100 kernels	grams..	3.0
Kernels	do....	2.1
Hulls	do....	0.9
Moisture	per cent..	10.0
Proteids	do....	12.0
Ether extract	do....	4.5
Crude fiber	do....	12.0
Carbohydrates, other than crude fiber	do....	58.0

Variation of Composition of Oats.

In regard to the influence of soil and climatic conditions on the composition of oats, Richardson, in Bulletin No. 9, makes the following observations:

The chemical composition of the specimens appears from the preceding data to be rather surprising. It was reasonable to suppose that as oats deteriorate so readily, and are apparently so easily influenced by their environment, great variations would be found in their composition under different climatic conditions, as is the case with wheats. Brewer remarks in his census report that a hundred or more analyses would be requisite to set at rest all questions in regard to this grain, and that they would be an extremely valuable contribution to our knowledge of the comparative nutritive values of the oats grown in different portions of the United States and their relative economic values. One hundred and seventy-nine analyses have been made, and we learn that there is not that variation in the oat kernel itself which was expected to be due to climatic condition. The proportion of husk to kernel and the compactness of the grain prove to be the all-important factor, and the weight per bushel the best means of judging of the value of the grain.

The only peculiarities noticed are that the 18 specimens from the Pacific slope are poorer in proteids and richer in crude fiber than the averages for other parts of the country. The average for the hulls from the West show the presence of more ash than in those from the East, and more crude fiber, and, like the kernels, they are slightly deficient in proteids. * * *

An immense number of conditions seems, therefore, to affect the characteristics of this grain, and while in many ways, at first glance, it seems to be less changeable than one would expect, on examination it appears to be quite largely influenced by all the circumstances of its environment, and in a more irregular way than wheat.

Throughout all the averages it will be seen that oats are much drier than other grains, owing largely to their small size. In ash and fiber they are not exceptional.

The Proteids of the Oat Kernel.

Osborne has studied the composition of the proteids of the oat kernel, and found that there are three primary proteids, which are characterized by being soluble in alcohol, common salt solution, and alkali solution, respectively. The composition of the three proteids is shown in the following table:

Primary oat proteids.

Constituent elements.	Alcohol-soluble proteid; average of 5 analyses.	Salt-soluble proteid or globulin; average of 9 analyses.	Alkali-soluble proteid; average of 2 analyses.
	Per cent.	Per cent.	Per cent.
Carbon	53.01	52.19	53.56
Hydrogen	6.91	7.00	7.09
Nitrogen	16.43	17.86	16.20
Sulphur	2.26	0.65	0.90
Oxygen	21.39	22.30	22.25
Total	100.00	100.00	100.00

The average content of proteid matter in the oat kernel is about 14 per cent. Of this the proteids soluble in alcohol form about 1¼ per cent. The proteids soluble in salt solution form 1½ per cent, and the proteids soluble in alkali the remainder. From these data the proper factor for calculating the proteid matter in the oat kernel from the percentage of nitrogen is easily obtained, the mean percentage of nitrogen in the proteid being 16.4 per cent, and the factor being 6.10.

RICE.

This cereal may reach the analyst in three different states, viz, unhulled, hulled, and polished. He may also have occasion to examine the broken fragments used in polishing and hulling, the waste in manufacturing rice bran and other products. The most important of these products in the present connection is the polished rice as it is found in commerce, ready for preparation as food. In this country rice is not frequently used in the form of bread, but almost exclusively in the freshly boiled state, in puddings and other similar preparations. Rice is a cereal in which the starchy matters predominate, and in which there is a marked deficiency of proteids and oils as compared with other standard cereals. The composition of rice, as determined by the analysis of samples exhibited at the World's Columbian Exposition, and by standard authorities, is best shown in the table of maxima, minima, and means, as in the case of the other cereals which have been mentioned. In the following table the items marked I, II, and III represent data obtained at the World's Columbian Exposition, while the means of all the samples there analyzed are given in another part of the table.

Table of maxima, minima, and means of constituents of rice.

Kinds and numbers of samples.	Weight of 100 kernels.	Moisture.	Proteids.	Ether extract.	Crude fiber.	Ash.	Carbohydrates, excluding fiber.
	Grams.	*Per cent.*	*Per cent.*	*Per cent.*	*Per cent.*	*Per cent.*	*Per cent.*
I. Rice in the hull (foreign):							
Maxima	a 3.250	b 11.52	b 8.40	b 2.04	b 11.47	a 4.66	a 65.70
Minima	b 2.842	a 9.03	a 8.23	a 1.44	b 9.45	b 3.26	a 65.01
Means	2.979	9.88	8.32	1.71	10.62	4.12	65.35
II. Unpolished rice (foreign):							
Maxima	c 2.826	c 12.57	c 10.50	c 2.26	c 1.00	c 1.22	c 77.84
Minima	c 2.260	c 10.92	c 7.27	c 1.62	c 0.87	c 1.04	c 73.35
Means	2.466	11.88	8.02	1.96	0.93	1.15	76.05
III. Polished rice (foreign):							
Maxima	b 2.633	b 13.15	b 10.33	c 0.54	a 0.56	a 0.65	c 81.66
Minima	a 1.560	c 11.32	c 5.42	c 0.04	a 0.27	c 0.28	b 75.62
Means	2.132	12.34	7.18	0.26	0.40	0.46	79.36
Mean composition of polished rice, etc., as given by Jenkins and Winton:							
Polished rice (10 analyses)	....	12.40	7.40	0.40	0.20	0.40	79.20
Rice bran (5 analyses)	....	9.70	12.10	10.90	9.50	10.00	49.90
Rice hulls (3 analyses)	....	8.20	3.60	0.70	35.70	13.20	38.60
Rice polish (4 analyses)	....	10.00	11.70	7.30	6.30	6.70	58.00
Mean composition of rice, etc., as given by König:							
Unhulled rice (3 analyses)	....	11.99	6.48	1.65	6.48	3.33	70.07
Hulled rice (41 analyses)	....	12.58	6.73	1.88	1.53	0.82	76.46
Polished rice (9 analyses)	....	12.52	7.52	0.84	0.48	0.64	78.00
Means of World's Fair samples:							
Unhulled rice (4 analyses)	2.929	10.28	7.95	1.65	10.42	4.09	65.60
Unpolished rice (6 analyses)	2.466	11.88	8.02	1.96	0.93	1.15	76.05
Polished rice (14 analyses)	2.132	12.34	7.18	0.26	0.40	0.46	79.36

a Guatemala. b Johore. c Japan.

The mean composition of the different classes of rice as shown by the analyses of the World's Fair samples is almost the same as that shown by the work of other analysts collated as indicated above. A typical unhulled rice has about the following composition:

Weight of 100 kernels	grams..	3.00	Crude fiber	per cent.. 9.00
Moisture	per cent..	10.50	Ash	do.... 4.00
Proteids	do....	7.50	Carbohydrates, other than crude	
Ether extract	do....	1.60	fiber	per cent.. 67.40

A typical hulled rice, but unpolished, has about the following composition:

Weight of 100 kernels	grams..	2.50	Crude fiber	per cent.. 1.00
Moisture	per cent..	12.00	Ash	do.... 1.00
Proteids	do....	8.00	Carbohydrates, other than crude	
Ether extract	do....	2.00	fiber	per cent.. 76.00

A typical polished rice has a composition represented by the following numbers:

Weight of 100 kernels ....grams..	2.20	Crude fiber..............per cent..	0.40
Moisture................per cent..	12.40	Ash......................do....	0.50
Proteids..................do....	7.50	Carbohydrates, other than crude	
Ether extract.............do....	0.40	fiber ....per cent..	78.80

PROTEIDS OF RICE.

No modern studies of the proteids of rice have been made, and, in the lack of detailed description of the different proteids which the rice contains, the whole proteid matter may be calculated, as is usual, by multiplying the percentage of nitrogen by 6.25.

RYE.

Rye is not used to any great extent by the native citizens of the United States as a source of bread making. In Europe it is one of the most important constituents of bread, and is used to some extent by our naturalized citizens.

Typical samples of rye were obtained at the World's Columbian Exposition, and the figures obtained by their analysis are compared with other reliable data in the subjoined table. The data under the captions "domestic" and "foreign" represent the Columbian samples, as given in Bulletin 45 of this division.

Table of maxima, minima, and means of constituents of rye.

Kinds and numbers of samples.	Weight of 100 kernels.	Moisture.	Proteids.	Ether extract.	Crude fiber.	Ash.	Carbohydrates excluding fiber.
	Grams.	Per cent.	Per cent.	Per cent.	Per cent.	Per cent.	Per cent.
Domestic:							
Maxima................	a 4.201	a 11.45	a 18.99	b 2.30	c 2.50	a 2.41	d 75.36
Minima................	a 1.932	a 9.54	d 8.40	a 1.16	a 1.65	a 1.71	a 63.61
Means	2.493	10.62	12.43	1.65	2.09	1.92	71.37
Foreign:							
Maxima................	e 3.417	f 14.10	f 12.25	e 1.61	f 2.25	f 1.95	e 74.74
Minima................	f 2.031	e 10.74	e 9.28	f 0.37	e 1.75	e 1.88	f 69.08
Means	2.724	12.42	10.77	0.99	2.00	1.92	71.91
Means of World's Fair samples:							
Domestic samples (18)....	2.493	10.62	12.43	1.65	2.09	1.92	71.37
All samples (20)..........	2.516	10.77	12.26	1.58	2.08	1.92	71.42
Means of previous analyses by the Department (57 samples)	2.070	8.67	11.32	1.94	1.46	2.09	74.52
Means given by Jenkins and Winton (6 samples)	....	11.60	10.60	1.70	1.70	1.90	72.50
Means given by König:							
Miscellaneous (173)........	....	11.15	10.81	1.77	1.78	2.06	70.21
Spring rye (11)............	....	12.00	12.90	1.98	1.71	1.93	68.11
North Germany (27)	....	14.84	11.01	1.70	2.17	1.97	69.78
South Germany (36)......	....	12.31	12.04	1.98	2.73	1.91	67.97
Sweden (3)................	....	14.29	8.50	2.29	1.47	2.11	71.34
All Germany (63)	....	13.37	11.52	1.84	2.45	1.94	68.88

a Illinois.   b New York.   c New Hampshire.   d Oregon.   e Spain.   f Brazil.

We see again, in the comparison of the means, the greater dryness of the United States ryes. This is, as has been the case heretofore in the cereals already mentioned, especially marked in the analyses made a few years ago by the Department. In the World's Fair samples the difference is less marked, the percentage of moisture being almost as high as in the foreign samples.

The United States ryes are also distinguished by their smaller kernels. Even the samples on exhibition in Chicago, which were presumably those of the finest and plumpest kernels, were not nearly so large as the kernels of the foreign samples. They were, however, distinctly larger and heavier than the kernels analyzed here a few years ago.

In the percentage of proteids the United States samples are fully equivalent to those of foreign origin, and in their mean composition their other constituents do not differ greatly from those of standard varieties abroad. The cultivation of rye is not very extensively practiced in the United States, and that which is grown is used chiefly for the manufacture of whisky and for cattle food, and not for bread making, as is the case in Europe.

A typical American rye has approximately the following composition:

Weight of 100 kernels....grams.. 2.50
Moisture...............per cent.. 10.50
Proteids...................do.... 12.25
Ether extract..............do.... 1.50
Crude fiber ....per cent.. 2.10
Carbohydrates, other than crude fiber ....per cent.. 71.75
Ash.......................do.... 1.90

PROTEIDS OF RYE.

The proteids of the rye kernel have been recently investigated by Osborne (18th Annual Report, Conn. Experiment Station, pages 147 and following), and as a result of these studies it has been established that the commonly employed factor, namely, 6.25, which has been used for calculating proteids for rye from the percentage of nitrogen, is too large. Owing to the presence of a gum which interferes with the processes of filtration, it has not been found practicable so far to secure the separation of the proteid matter with such detail as has been accomplished in some other cereals; in other words, it has not been found possible, so far, to separate the globulin, albumins, and proteose. In general, the proteids of rye may be classified as follows: Proteids insoluble in dilute salt solution; proteids soluble in dilute salt solution. The latter class may be subdivided as follows: A proteid gliadin, soluble in alcohol; a proteid leucosin, soluble in water; a proteid edestin, soluble in salt solution; proteids representing globulin, albumins, and proteose, soluble in dilute salt solution. Of the total proteid matter in rye, it is found that 71.07 per cent are soluble in a 5 per cent common salt solution, followed by alcohol. An attempt was made to extract the proteids remaining in the flour, after exhaustion, with dilute salt solution and with dilute alcoholic potash. The gum present in the flour, however, dissolved in the alkaline solution and rendered it impossible to purify the preparations. Since the other proteids found in rye, however, are similar to those found in wheat, with the exception of gluten, Osborne concludes that the nonidentified proteid is not identical with the glutenin of the wheat.

The proteids of rye, in so far as they have been separated in a pure state, have the following composition:

Composition of proteids of rye.

Constituents.	Carbon.	Nitrogen.	Hydrogen.	Sulphur.	Oxygen.
Leucosin	52.97	16.66	6.79	1.35	22.23
Gliadin	52.75	17.72	6.84	1.21	21.48
Edestin	51.19	18.19	6.74		23.88

The sample of rye flour on which Osborne worked contained only 1.52 per cent of nitrogen, while the average of the World's Fair samples contained 1.99 per cent. It is fair to presume that in a normal rye flour the distribution of the various proteids is proportional to that found in the sample examined by Osborne. The relative proportion of proteids in the sample examined by Osborne and in the typical sample containing 1.96 per cent of nitrogen is given below:

Proportions of proteids in rye.

Constituents.	Osborne's sample.	Typical sample.
	Per cent.	Per cent.
Insoluble in salt solution	2.44	3.14
Gliadin, soluble in alcohol	4.00	5.16
Leucosin, soluble in water	0.43	0.55
Edestin and proteose, soluble in salt solution	1.76	2.27
Total	8.63	11.12

It appears from the above investigations that the protein of the rye kernel contains an average of 17.6 per cent of nitrogen, and the factor for converting the nitrogen of rye into protein is 5.68 instead of 6.25. Judged by this standard, a typical American rye, instead of having 12.25 per cent of protein, would have only about 11.15 per cent, and the percentage of carbohydrates would be raised from 71.75 to 72.85.

WHEAT.

Wheat is the typical bread-making cereal. It differs essentially from the other cereals in the character of its proteid content. The proteids of wheat are composed chiefly of two bodies, gliadin and glutenin, which together form the body, gluten, which gives its characteristic properties to wheat flour. More detailed information concerning these bodies is found under the section devoted to wheat proteids.

The products of wheat are used as human foods in many forms. There are nearly a hundred different grades of food materials made from wheat by the patent-roller process of milling.

Next to maize, wheat is the most important of the cereal products of this country. It is grown in every part of the Union, but only to perfection in the more northern states. When sown in the autumn, it is called winter wheat; sown in the spring, it is spring wheat. The kernels of winter wheat are, as a rule, larger and softer than those of the spring variety. Spring wheat, as a rule, contains more gluten than the winter varieties.

The mean composition of wheat, domestic and foreign, is shown in the following table. Under domestic, Canada and foreign are given the composition of the samples collected at the World's Columbian Exposition in 1893:

Table of maxima, minima, and means of constituents of wheat.

Kinds and numbers of samples.	Weight of 100 kernels.	Moisture.	Proteids.	Ether extract.	Crude fiber.	Ash.	Carbohydrates, excluding fiber.	Wet gluten.	Dry gluten.
	Grams.	Per ct.	Per ct.	Per ct.	Per ct.	Per ct.	Per ct.	Per ct.	Per ct.
Domestic:									
Maxima	a 6.190	b 14.53	c 17.15	d 2.50	d 3.72	a 2.35	e 76.05	e 39.05	e 14.65
Minima	c 2.125	b 7.11	f 8.58	f 0.28	b 1.70	f 1.40	g 66.67	f 12.33	f 4.70
Means	3.866	10.62	12.23	1.77	2.36	1.82	71.18	26.46	10.31
Canada:									
Maxima	5.335	13.98	16.10	2.32	3.12	2.00	75.36	38.94	15.24
Minima	3.242	9.38	8.23	0.41	1.75	1.38	65.92	6.38	2.29
Means	4.054	11.69	12.25	1.80	2.26	1.69	70.31	25.13	9.76
Foreign:									
Maxima	h 5.723	h 12.97	i 14.52	i 2.26	i 2.80	i 2.04	h 76.14	j 32.57	j 12.33
Minima	i 2.250	i 8.52	h 8.58	h 0.73	h 1.87	k 1.67	i 67.01	h 18.72	h 7.00
Means	4.076	11.47	12.08	1.78	2.28	1.73	70.66	25.36	9.82
Means of World's Fair samples:									
Domestic samples (165)	3.866	10.62	12.23	1.77	2.36	1.82	71.24	26.46	10.31
Canadian samples (62)	4.054	11.69	12.25	1.80	2.26	1.69	70.31	25.13	9.76
All foreign samples (62)	4.076	11.47	12.08	1.78	2.28	1.73	70.66	25.36	9.82
All samples (227)	3.940	10.85	12.20	1.74	2.35	1.81	71.09	26.28	10.22
Means of previous analyses by the Department:									
Domestic (147)	3.653	9.97	10.53			2.06			
United States and British America (407)	3.644	10.16	12.15			1.92			
Colorado (155)	4.235	7.54	12.54	2.29	1.64	1.82	74.17	33.80	11.07
Means given by Jenkins and Winton:									
Spring (13)		10.40	12.50	2.20	1.80	1.90	71.20		
Winter (262)		10.50	11.80	2.10	1.80	1.80	72.00		
Means given by König:									
Samples of miscellaneous origin (428)		13.37	12.51	1.70	2.56	1.79	68.01		

a Wyoming.   d Pennsylvania.   g Iowa.   j Spain.
b Kansas.   e Illinois.   h Australia.   k Bulgaria.
c Nebraska.   f Oregon.   i Argentine Republic.

Table of maxima, minima, and means of constituents of wheat—Continued.

Kinds and numbers of samples.	Moisture.	Proteids.	Ether extract.	Crude fiber.	Ash.	Carbohydrates, excluding fiber.
	Per ct.	Per ct.	Per ct.	Per ct.	Per ct.	Per ct.
Means given by König—Continued.						
Samples from northeast and middle Germany (90)	14.01	10.93	1.65	2.12	1.92	70.01
Samples spring wheat (81)	14.75	11.23	2.03	2.26	2.52	68.61
Samples from south and west Germany (52)	13.18	12.29	1.71	2.82	1.85	67.96
Samples spring wheat (30)	13.80	14.95	1.56	......	2.19	67.93
Samples from Austria-Hungary (18)	11.72	12.66	1.99	3.39	1.75	66.84
Samples from Russia—spring wheat (39)	12.65	17.65	1.58	......	1.66	65.74
England (22)	13.41	10.99	1.86	2.90	1.67	69.21
Scotland (16)	11.37	10.58	1.73	......	1.55	72.77
France (70)	15.20	12.64	1.41	2.00	1.66	68.92
Denmark (4)	13.95	9.36	2.34	2.19	1.34	71.40
Spain (9)	13.37	12.45	1.92	......	1.80	......
Africa (34)	11.80	11.18	1.83	1.82	1.76	70.04
Asia (8)	12.57	11.09	2.10	1.94	1.46	70.84
Australia (4)	13.37	10.16	1.39	......	......	......
North America (504)	9.92	11.60	2.07	1.70	1.79	69.47
North America, spring (40)	9.36	12.92	2.15	1.72	1.86	67.98

In the means taken from König, as given above, the amount of moisture as found is given. The means of the other constituents, however, in order to secure a proper comparison, are calculated on the supposition that the mean content of moisture is the same as that in the chief or miscellaneous table, namely, 13.37 per cent.

In the discussion of the comparative results, it will be noticed first, as with other cereals, that the content of moisture in the domestic samples is low, being about 1 per cent less than in the Canadian samples, and eight-tenths of 1 per cent less than in all the foreign samples. This remarkable dryness of cereal products appears, therefore, to be a characteristic of those grown in the United States, although the difference is not so marked in the case of wheat as it is in some other cereals. In general, the size of the grains of the domestic samples is less than that of the Canadian and foreign wheats, but in the World's Fair samples, as might be expected, the kernels were a little larger than those examined in previous work of the Department.

COMPARISON OF AMERICAN AND FOREIGN WHEAT.

In respect of proteids, the American wheats, as a rule, are quite equal to those of foreign origin. This is an important characteristic when it is remembered that both the milling and food values of a wheat depend largely on the nitrogenous matter which is present. It must not be forgotten, however, that merely a high percentage of proteids is not always a sure indication of the milling value of a wheat. The ratio of gluten to the other proteid constituents of a wheat is not always constant, and it is the gluten content of a flour on which its bread-making qualities chiefly depend. The percentage of moist gluten gives, in a rough way, the property of the glutinous matter of absorbing and holding water under conditions as nearly constant as can be obtained. In general, it may be said that the ratio between the moist gluten and the dry gluten in a given sample is an index for comparison with other substances in the same sample. Upon the whole, however, the percentage of dry gluten must be regarded as the safer index of quality. In respect to the content of glutinous matter, our domestic wheats are distinctly superior to those of foreign origin. They are even better than the Canadian wheats in this respect. It may be fairly inferred that while our domestic wheats give a flour slightly inferior in nutritive properties to that derived from foreign samples, it is nevertheless better adapted for baking purposes, and this quality more than compensates for its slight deficiency in respect of nutrition, a deficiency, indeed, which is so small as to be hardly worth considering.

Variation of Wheat with Climate and Soil.

In this connection, attention should be called to the great influence of climate upon the quality of wheat. The best wheats grown in the United States are produced in the central northern part of the country, while the poorest are grown in the Southern States. The influence of climate and soil upon the quality of wheat has been fully pointed out by Richardson in Bulletins Nos. 1, 3, and 9 of the Chemical Division of the Department of Agriculture. The following quotation from page 25, Bulletin No. 9, will illustrate the above statement:

From observations in this and previous reports, it may be said that of all grain wheat is probably the most susceptible to its environment.

Oats in certain directions are more variable, but in their general character are more permanent, as will appear in subsequent pages. The inherent tendency to change which is found in all grains is most prominent in wheat. It may be fostered by selection and by modifying such of the conditions of environment as it is in the power of man to affect.

The most powerful element to contend with is the character of the season or unfavorable climatic conditions. The injury done in this way is well illustrated in Colorado, and it would seem advisable in such cases to seek seed from a source where everything has been favorable, and begin selection again.

It must be borne in mind that selection must be kept up continuously, and that reversion takes place more easily than improvement. It took but one season to seriously injure Professor Blount's wheats, but it will be two or more years before they have recovered from that injury. Hallett, in England, was able to make his celebrated pedigree wheat by selection, carried on through many years, but the same wheat grown by the ordinary farmer under unfavorable conditions for a few years without care has reverted to an ordinary sort of grain.

The effect of climate is well illustrated by four specimens of wheat which are to be seen in the collection of the Chemical Division. Two of these were from Oregon and Dakota some years ago, and present the most extreme contrast which can be found in this variable grain. One is light yellow, plump, and starchy, and shows on analysis a very small per cent of albuminoids; the other is one of the small, hard, and dark-colored spring wheats of Dakota, which are rich in albuminoids. Between these stand two specimens from Colorado, which have been raised from seed similar to the Oregon and Dakota wheat. They are scarcely distinguishable except by a slight difference in color. The Colorado climate is such as to have modified these two seed wheats, until after a few years' growth they are hardly distinguishable in the kernel.

All localities having widely different climates, soils, or other conditions produce their peculiar varieties and modify those brought to them.

The result of these tendencies to change and reversion from lack of care in seed selection or other cause has led to the practice of change of seed among farmers. A source is sought where either through greater care or more favorable conditions the variety desired has been able to hold its own. Sometimes this change is rendered necessary by conditions which are beyond the power of man to modify. As an example, No. 10 of Professor Blount's wheats, known as "Oregon Club," a white variety from Oregon, has been deteriorating every year since it has been grown in Colorado, whereas if the seed had been supplied every season directly from Oregon the quality would have probably remained the same. In extension of this illustration the fact may be mentioned that the annual renewal of the seed from a desirable and favorable source often makes it possible to raise cereals where otherwise climatic conditions would render their cultivation impossible through rapid reversion. This is particularly the case with extremes in latitude, the effect of which is not founded so much upon the composition of the crop as on the yield and size of the grain. In the South, the warmer climate, together of course with poorer soil and cultivation in many instances, reduces the yield.

A typical American wheat of the best quality should have approximately the following composition:

Weight of 100 kernels....grams.. 3.85	Ash ....per cent.. 1.75
Moisture ....per cent.. 10.60	Carbohydrates other than crude
Proteids ....do.... 12.25	fiber ....per cent.. 71.25
Ether extract..............do.... 1.75	Dry gluten................do.... 10.25
Crude fiber ....do.... 2.40	Moist gluten.............do.... 26.50

To bring into a comparative view the means of the data obtained for American cereals exhibited at the World's Columbian Exposition, the following general table is given containing the data above mentioned, with the exception of those relating to rice, together with the approximate typical composition taken from the preceding pages:

Mean data calculated from the analyses of samples exhibited at the World's Columbian Exposition.

Constituents.	Barley.	Buck-wheat.	Maize.	Oats.	Rye.	Wheat.
Weight of 100 kernels ....grams..	4.19	3.12	38.98	2.92	2.49	3.87
Moisture ....per cent..	10.80	12.15	10.93	10.06	10.62	10.62
Proteids.........................do....	10.69	10.75	9.88	12.15	12.43	12.23
Ether extract....................do....	2.13	2.11	4.17	4.33	1.65	1.77
Crude fiber ....do....	4.05	10.75	1.71	12.07	2.09	2.36
Ash ....do....	2.44	1.89	1.36	3.46	1.92	1.82
Carbohydrates other than crude fiber per cent.............................	69.89	62.33	71.95	58.75	71.37	71.18

Approximate typical composition of domestic samples taken from the data given in the preceding pages.

Constituents.	Barley.	Buckwheat.	Maize.	Oats.	Rye.	Wheat.
Weight of 100 kernels .... grams..	4.00	3.00	38.00	3.00	2.50	3.85
Moisture .... per cent..	10.85	12.00	10.75	10.00	10.50	10.60
Proteids .... do....	11.00	10.75	10.00	12.00	12.25	12.25
Ether extract.................... do....	2.25	2.00	4.25	4.50	1.50	1.75
Crude fiber .... do....	3.85	10.75	1.75	12.00	2.10	2.40
Ash .... do....	2.50	1.75	1.50	3.50	1.90	1.75
Carbohydrates other than crude fiber per cent..................	69.45	62.75	71.75	58.00	71.75	71.25

PROTEIDS OF THE WHEAT KERNEL.

Osborne and Voorhees have lately made a study of the proteids of the wheat kernel, and found it necessary to revise to a certain extent the data previously existing on this subject. (American Chemical Journal, volume 15, pages 392 and following.)

It is found that the proteids of the wheat kernel are best classified as follows:

(1) A globulin, soluble in saline solutions, and not coagulable at temperatures below 100° C.

(2) An albumin, which is coagulated at 52° C., and differs from animal albumin in several important particulars.

(3) A proteose, which is extracted from the wheat kernel by dilute saline solutions after removing the globulin by dialysis and the albumin by coagulation. It is probably derived from other proteid matters present in the seed by the action of the reagents employed for isolating it.

(4) A proteid, gliadin, soluble in dilute alcohol, and forming nearly half of the whole proteid matter of a kernel.

(5) A proteid, glutenin, which is insoluble in water, dilute saline solutions, and dilute alcohol, and forming with gliadin nearly the whole proteid content of the wheat kernel. The gluten of the wheat, which is one of its most important constituents, is composed of gliadin and glutenin in almost equal proportions. The gliadin forms the sticky substance of the gluten, while the glutenin imparts to it its solidity. Gluten can not well be formed from its constituents by the action of pure water, as gliadin, one of the chief constituents of gluten, is quite soluble in pure water, and thus is easily removed. The presence of the mineral salts of the wheat, however, is sufficient to form with distilled water a medium in which the gluten is scarcely soluble, and in this medium the two unite to form the gluten, which is so important a constituent in the formation of bread. It is probable, according to Osborne and Voorhees, that no fermentative action occurs in the formation of gluten, but it is produced by the simple, mechanical, and chemical action mentioned above.

SEPARATION OF THE CONSTITUENTS OF GLUTEN.

In a whole-wheat flour containing 10 per cent of protein, the relative quantities of the chief kinds of proteids mentioned above are about as follows:

	Per cent.
Globulin	0.70
Albumin	0.40
Proteose	0.30
Gliadin	4.25
Glutenin	4.35
	10.00

The composition of the wheat proteids is given in the following table:

Composition of wheat proteids.

Constituents.	Carbon.	Hydrogen.	Nitrogen.	Sulphur.	Oxygen.
	Per cent.	Per cent.	Per cent.	Per cent.	Per cent.
Globulin	51.03	6.85	18.39	0.69	23.04
Albumin	53.02	6.84	16.80	1.28	22.06
Proteose	51.86	6.82	17.32		24.00
Gliadin	52.72	6.86	17.66	1.14	21.62
Glutenin	52.34	6.83	17.49	1.08	22.26

The average content of nitrogen in the proteid matter of wheat is about 17.6 per cent, and the proper factor, therefore, for computing the total proteid matter from the percentage of nitrogen found is 5.68 instead of 6.25, the one usually employed. To convert data obtained by the factor 6.25 to the corresponding data for the factor 5.68 it is sufficient to multiply by 0.9.

In the data for wheat flours, which are given further on, the computation is made for the factor 5.70, and in this case the data for the factor 6.25 are multiplied by 0.912 for the proper conversion.

SEPARATION OF THE CONSTITUENTS OF GLUTEN.

Fleurent makes use of the following process for separating the constituents of gluten after it has been formed by kneading the flour with cold water, which also washes out the starch and fragments of débris:

According to the theory of Osborne and Voorhees, the gluten is formed during this process from its elements, glutenin and gliadin, preexisting in the flour. The gluten obtained by the usual method of kneading with water is divided into fragments of the size of a pea and placed in flasks having ground glass stoppers, where it is mixed with potash lye containing 3 grams of potash per liter, a liter of the solution being used for each 200 grams of the moist gluten. Some glass beads are also added to facilitate the disaggregation of the mass. The flask thus charged is placed upon a shaking table and shaken continuously for some time, or it may be shaken by hand until the fragments of gluten are completely disaggregated. When the fragments of gluten are reduced to a homogeneous condition alcohol is added to the flask in sufficient quantity to make a total of 70 per cent of alcohol in the solution. The alcohol is left in contact with the contents of the flask for a few hours, and, with occasional shaking, at the end of this time the mixture is exactly saturated with dilute sulphuric acid. A precipitate of glutenin is produced, which subsides rapidly, carrying with it any suspended matter which the liquid may have contained. The precipitate is washed several times by decantation with 70 per cent alcohol. The supernatant liquors and the washings are mixed and preserved. The precipitate is taken up with a solution of potash in 70 per cent alcohol, containing 3 grains of potash per liter. The potash is then saturated with an excess of carbon dioxid, and there remains an insoluble product which consists of gluten-casein or glutenin. After this has been separated by filtration the alcoholic filtrate is neutralized with dilute sulphuric acid, by which there is obtained a precipitate which resembles the conglutin of the lupines. The conglutin of wheat forms from 2 to 8 per cent of the total amount of gluten present. The first alcoholic liquor obtained by washing the first precipitate is evaporated at a low temperature to drive off the alcohol and rendered slightly acid by dilute sulphuric acid, by which an abundant precipitate of gluten-fibrin—that is, gliadin—is obtained. The respective proportions of the two bodies in gluten are about as follows: Glutenin, from 18 to 25 per cent of the total gluten; gliadin, from 60 to 80 per cent of the total gluten. The gliadin, according to Fleurent, is the true agglutinating matter, and not the glutenin, and the reason the proteids of the other cereals do not form a sticky dough is because the quantity of gliadin is comparatively small, ranging from 8.17 per cent of the total amount of proteids in barley to 47.50 per cent in maize.[1]

THE CARBOHYDRATES OF THE CEREALS.

By reason of the fact that the principal carbohydrate of cereals is starch, and that the remaining carbohydrates, small in quantity, are practically the same in all, it has been thought advisable to give a résumé of our present knowledge of these carbohydrates in a separate section rather than to describe those belonging to each one under its own caption. By following the plan just indicated a great deal of repetition can be avoided.

INSOLUBLE CARBOHYDRATES.

There are several constituents of cereals which may be classified as insoluble carbohydrates. These are starch, cellulose, pentosans, and galactans.

STARCH.

Cereal grains are composed largely of starch, the quantity ranging from 60 to more than 80 per cent of the entire weight of the dry hulled kernels. The starch is collected in almost a pure state in the inner

---

[1] Comptes rendus, Vol. 123, p. 327.

BUL. No. 13, DIV. OF CHEMISTRY.   PLATE XLVII.

FIG. 1. WHEAT STARCH X 350.
FROM BULLETIN 13, PART 2, PLATE 26.

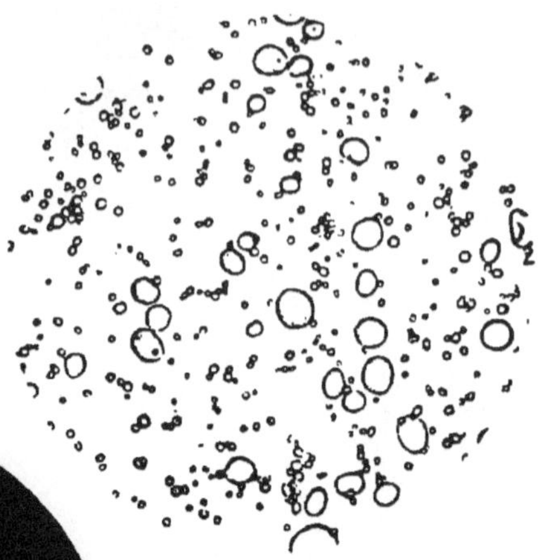

FIG. 2. WHEAT STARCH X 180.
FROM GRIFFITH'S PRINCIPAL
STARCHES USED AS FOOD.

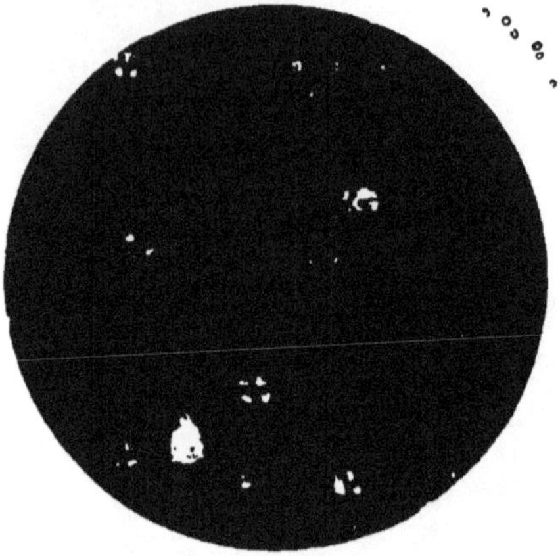

FIG. 3. WHEAT STARCH, POLARIZED LIGHT X 145.
FROM BULLETIN 13, PART 2, PLATE 17.

FIG. 4. WHEAT STARCH X 300.
FROM TSCHIRCH AND OESTERLES ANATOMISCHER ATLAS DER PHARMAKOGNOSIE UND NAHRUNGSMITTELKUNDE.

BUL. No. 13, DIV. OF CHEMISTRY.　　　　　　　　　　　　　　　PLATE XLVIII.

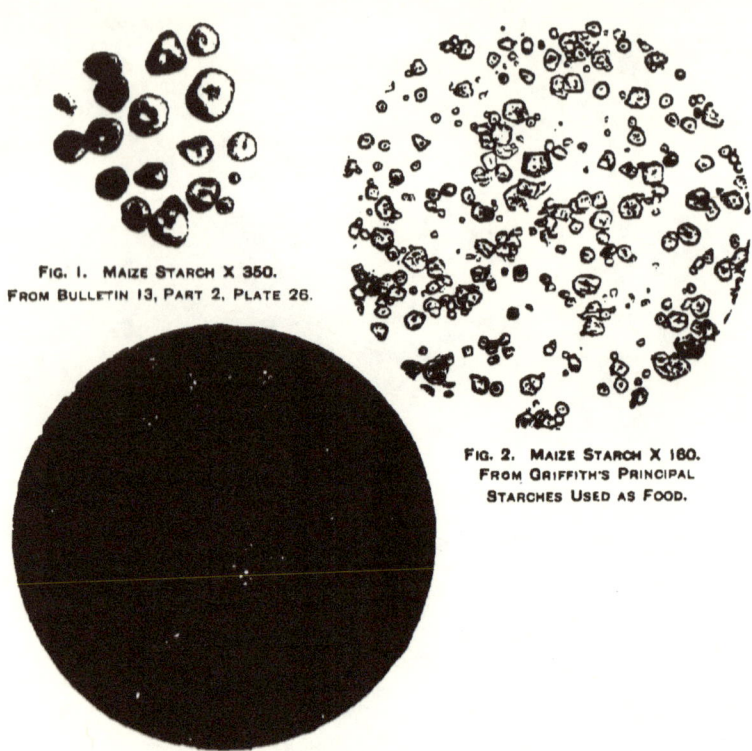

FIG. 1. MAIZE STARCH X 350.
FROM BULLETIN 13, PART 2, PLATE 26.

FIG. 2. MAIZE STARCH X 160.
FROM GRIFFITH'S PRINCIPAL
STARCHES USED AS FOOD.

FIG. 3. MAIZE STARCH, POLARIZED LIGHT X 145.
FROM BULLETIN 13, PART 2, PLATE 17.

FIG. 4. MAIZE STARCH X 300.
FROM TSCHIRCH AND OESTERLE.

TYPICAL MAIZE STARCH.

portion of the grain, smaller portions being found in the coats, and only a trace, or none at all, in the germs.

The starches of the cereals have many common properties. They are, as far as can be determined, chemically identical, and are polymers of the simple molecule $C_6H_{10}O_5$. On account of the great insolubility of the starch grains it has been found almost impracticable to determine the actual molecular size of the starch particle. Determinations of the molecular weight have given numbers greater than 30,000, and it is difficult to say, with any degree of exactitude, to what extent the condensation of the simple carbohydrate molecule mentioned is carried. If the molecular weight of starch be 32,000, the starch molecule is produced by the condensation of about 200 of the simple carbohydrate molecules indicated above. In the absence, however, of any exact information on the subject, it is preferable to write the symbol of starch $(C_6H_{10}O_5)_n$.

The starch of all the cereals is detected by the same qualitative chemical action, and yields, upon hydrolysis, either by means of a ferment or by an acid, the same products. The starch kernels of different cereals, however, differ greatly in size and shape, in their deportment toward enzymes, and to a certain extent in their deportment toward polarized light. A brief description, with illustrations of the kernels of the different cereals, will be useful here.

DESCRIPTION OF THE CEREAL STARCHES.

The starches of the cereals have been carefully studied in this division by Richardson and others, and fully described in Bulletin No. 13, part 2. The following descriptions, as well as the illustrations accompanying them, are taken chiefly from that source. As an article of human food, wheat starch should come first on the list.

Wheat starch.—The granules of wheat starch differ greatly in size, varying from 0.05 to 0.01 mm. in diameter. There seem to be, in fact, two kinds of granules in wheat starch, both of them shaped like circular disks, but one class much larger than the other, with very few of an intermediate size. The hilum of the starch is almost invisible, and the rings which characterize it are not prominent. The typical forms of wheat granules, showing the two sizes, are seen in Pl. XLVII.

Maize starch.—The granules of maize starch are of more uniform size than those of wheat, varying from 0.02 to 0.03 mm. in diameter. Now and then a few are seen which are much smaller. In general they differ in shape from the wheat granules, and some are found to be polyhedral, with rounded angles. They resemble the granules of rice starch, but are larger. Under polarized light they appear as brilliant objects, but under the microscope, with ordinary illumination, they give only the faintest sign of rings, but show a well-developed hilum, which is at times star-shaped, or like an irregular cross, and at others resembles a circular depression. The maize starch granule is a type of the angular, as the wheat is of the spherical or spheroidal form. The characteristic appearance of maize starch kernels is shown in Pl. XLVIII.

Oats starch.—The granules of oats starch tend to adhere together in large masses, the surfaces of which resemble somewhat the base of honeycomb. These masses are of very different sizes, ranging from 0.12 to 0.02 mm. in length. They are easily broken up by grinding or pressure, and therefore are not found in great abundance in commercial meals. The single starch granules of oats vary from 0.02 to 0.015 mm. in diameter. The granules do not polarize well, and show neither rings nor hilum. Typical granules and aggregates thereof are shown in Pl. XLIX.

Barley starch.—The granules of this starch are very similar to those of wheat, but do not vary so much in size. The small granules, however, are even smaller than in wheat. Their average diameter is 0.05 mm. The rings of the granules are more distinct than in wheat, and often very small particles are found adhering to the larger ones in a characteristic manner. The appearance of typical barley starch granules is shown in Pl. L.

Rye starch.—The granules of rye starch are quite variable in size, some of them not exceeding 0.02 mm. in diameter, while the largest may reach from 0.06 to 0.07 mm. in diameter. They have no distinguishing characteristics, save the extremes in size, and in the fact that in some cases an irregular cross occupies the position of the hilum. They may be taken easily for wheat starch on the one hand, and on the other some of them very closely resemble rice starch. (See Pl. LI.)

Rice starch.—The granules of rice starch resemble those of maize more than any other of the starches mentioned, but in general are smaller. They are also more irregular in shape, and the hilum is often star-shaped or elongated, while in the granules of maize starch it is more of the nature of a circular depression. In general, the granules of rice starch may be distinguished from those of maize because of their smaller size and of their more polygonal form and well-defined angles. Often several granules of rice starch are found united. Typical rice granules are shown in Pl. LII.

Buckwheat starch.—The granules of buckwheat starch are very characteristic. They consist of chains or groups of angular granules, with a well-defined nucleus, and without rings. The contour of buckwheat starch granules is more angular than that of any common cereal, and it is this angular construction which enables the observer to distinguish them from other starches. The size of the granules is quite uniform, varying from 0.01 to .015 mm in diameter. The appearance of typical buckwheat starch granules is shown in Pl. LIII.

APPEARANCE OF STARCH GRANULES WITH POLARIZED LIGHT.

Under polarized light starch granules usually appear with a cross, which is very distinct and often characteristic.

The starch granules for this purpose are mounted in balsam and show

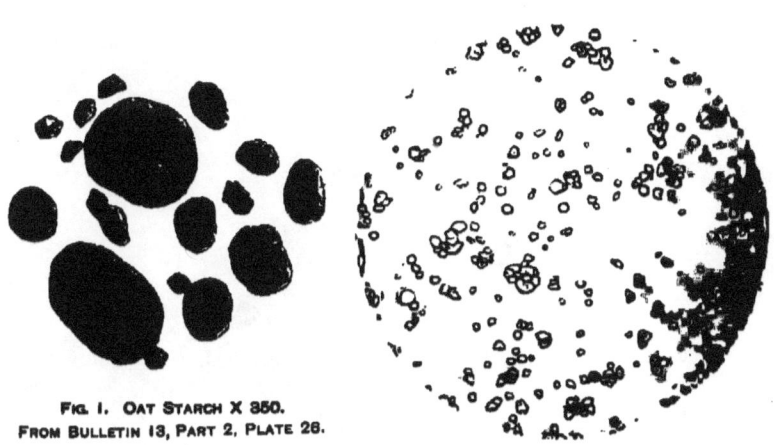

FIG. 1. OAT STARCH X 350.
FROM BULLETIN 13, PART 2, PLATE 26.

FIG. 2. OAT STARCH X 160.
FROM GRIFFITH'S PRINCIPAL STARCHES USED AS FOOD.

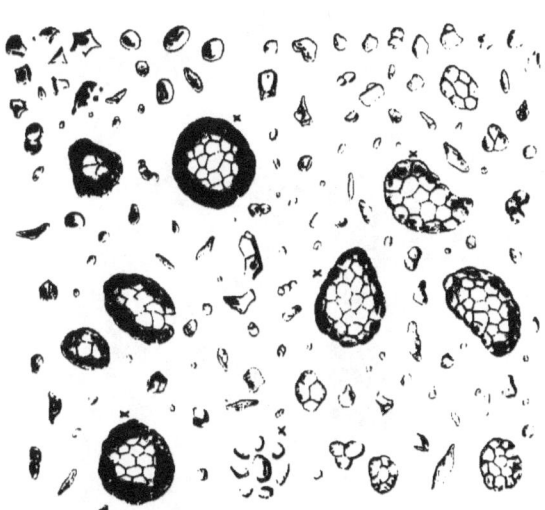

FIG. 3. OAT STARCH X 300.
FROM TSCHIRCH AND OESTERLE.

A. Hoen & Co. Lith. Baltimore.

TYPICAL OAT STARCH.

BUL. No. 13, DIV. OF CHEMISTRY. PLATE L.

FIG. 1. BARLEY STARCH × 350.
FROM BULLETIN 13, PART 2, PLATE 26.

FIG. 2. BARLEY STARCH × 160.
FROM GRIFFITH'S PRINCIPAL
STARCHES USED AS FOOD.

FIG. 3. BARLEY STARCH × 300.
FROM TSCHIRCH AND OESTERLE.

A. Hoen & Co. Lith. Baltimore.

TYPICAL BARLEY STARCH.

BUL. No. 13, DIV. OF CHEMISTRY. PLATE LI.

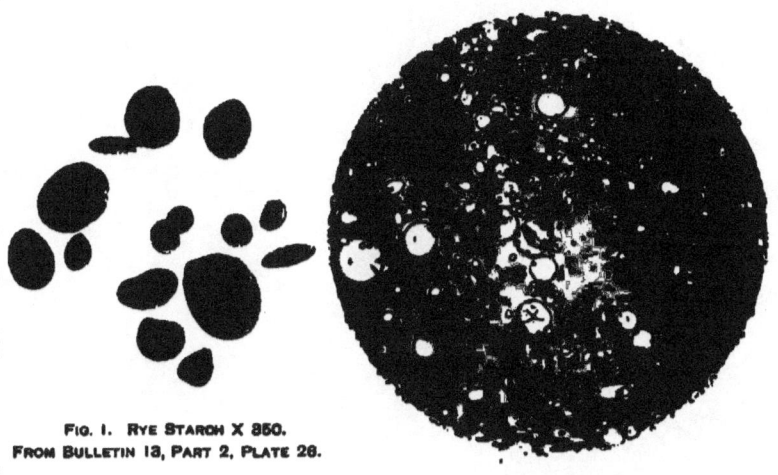

FIG. 1. RYE STARCH X 350.
FROM BULLETIN 13, PART 2, PLATE 28.

FIG. 2. RYE STARCH X 160.
FROM GRIFFITH'S PRINCIPAL
STARCHES USED AS FOOD.

FIG. 3 RYE STARCH X 300.
FROM TSCHIRCH AND OESTERLE.

TYPICAL RYE STARCHES.

BUL. No. 13, DIV. OF CHEMISTRY.   PLATE LII.

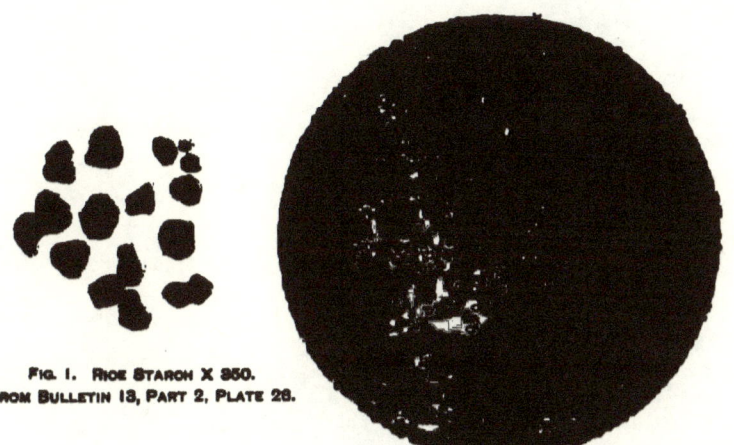

FIG. 1. RICE STARCH X 350.
FROM BULLETIN 13, PART 2, PLATE 28.

FIG. 2. RICE STARCH X 160.
FROM GRIFFITH'S PRINCIPAL
STARCHES USED AS FOOD.

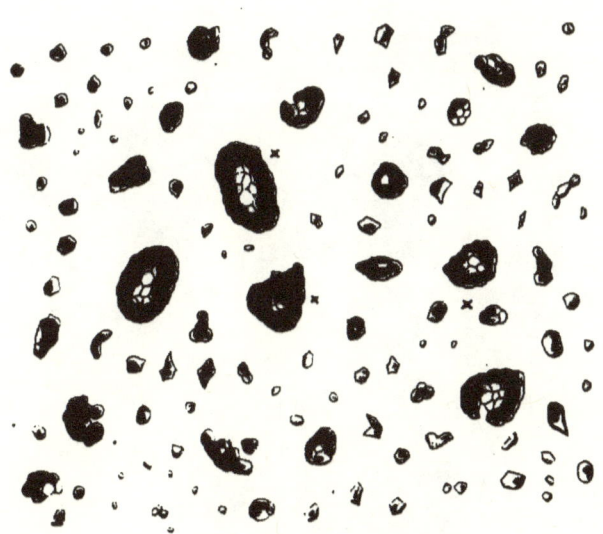

FIG. 3. RICE STARCH X 300.
FROM TSCHIRCH AND OESTERLE.

Fig. 1. Buckwheat Starch × 350.
From Bulletin 13, Part 2, Plate 26.

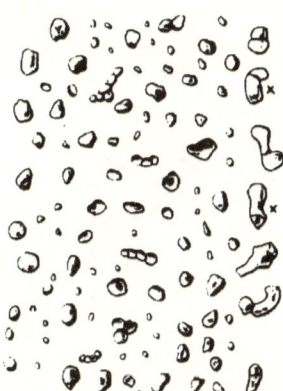

Fig 2. Buckwheat Starch × 300.
From Tschirch and Oesterle's Anatomischer Atlas der Pharmakognosie und Nahrungsmittelkunde.

TYPICAL BUCKWHEAT STARCH.

few characteristics with ordinary illumination. The nucleus of the granule when viewed with polarized light is indicated by the intersection of the cross. By interposing a selenite plate a beautiful play of colors is secured on rotating the analyzer. This fact may be useful in analysis.

These characteristic appearances are shown in the accompanying illustrations.

DEPORTMENT WITH SACCHARIFACIENT ENZYMES.

In a paper read before the Russian Academy of Science in 1875 Leuberg and Georgiewsky[1] showed that potato starch is much more readily attacked by the enzyme of the saliva than are the common cereal starches. This observation has been confirmed by other observers.[2] With diastase this difference is less marked but still important. The blue coloration which a paste of potato starch gives with iodine disappears in a few minutes when treated with saliva, while it may persist for several hours in the case of wheat starch. This difference in deportment shows a great difference in the resistance of the several starches to the action of the ferments. This difference may be due to the strucure of the starch granule or to the fact that the coloration produced by iodine varies with the origin of the starch.

THE CELLULOSE GROUP.

Interesting both from a chemical and dietetic point of view is that class of organic matter which constitutes the woody part of plants, viz, the cellulose group. It is included in the ordinary expression of analytical data with that miscellaneous collection of carbohydrate bodies designated as nitrogen-free extract.

Various names have been given to the different bodies composing this mixture, but these names have but little definite chemical signification, because of the great difficulty which has been experienced in securing a definite separation of the several components. The terms cellulose, hemicellulose, lignin, and fiber have been applied to these component parts of the woody substance of plants, and while authorities do not in all cases agree on the use of these terms, yet in general it may be said that it is possible to define, by means of them, the principal parts of woody matter with a fair degree of satisfaction. The term "cellulose group" is used to designate all that part of plant substance free of nitrogen which is composed of the carbohydrate bodies exclusive of pentosans, soluble carbohydrates, and starch.

The term cellulose is applied to that part of the cellulose group which resists the action of dilute boiling acids and is insoluble in ammonia and soluble in cuprammonium. In other words, it is pure cellulose, corresponding to the formula $C_6H_{10}O_5$. Those portions of the cellulose group which pass into solution when boiled with dilute mineral acids

---

[1] Berichte, vol. 9, p. 76.   [2] Stone, Bul. 34, O. E. S., Dept. of Agr., p. 39.

with the formation of reducing sugars are characterized by the term hemicellulose.

This class of bodies evidently comprises a large number of individual substances, inasmuch as the sugars which are formed by hydrolysis with dilute boiling mineral acids include mannose, galactose, arabinose, xylose, and dextrose. The term hemicellulose therefore embraces at least the substances mannan, galactan, araban, xylan, and dextrosan, if this term may be allowed to designate that class of hemicelluloses which furnishes dextrose by hydrolysis. The term "wood gum" has been applied by Hoffmeister[1] to those carbohydrate bodies which are extracted by 5 per cent sodium hydroxid solution from a fiber not previously freed of incrusting bodies. As will be seen further on, if the fiber be first extracted with ammonia to free it from these incrusting bodies and then the residue extracted with 5 per cent sodium hydroxid solution, the matters which are abstracted are regarded by Hoffmeister as belonging to the hemicelluloses. The term cellulose is reserved by Hoffmeister for the carbohydrates which are insoluble in dilute acids, and which are found in the cell walls. He designates as cellulose gum the product which goes into solution when the residue, after treating the fiber with chlorin or other similar reagents, is submitted to the action of cold dilute sodium hydroxid.[2] For a more detailed explanation of these carbohydrate bodies the article by E. Schulze in the Landwirthschaftliche Jahrbücher for 1894, page 13, may be consulted. It is seen at once that a great number of terms have been applied in the designation of these materials, and while later investigations have shown a certain restriction in the use of these terms to more definite groups of bodies, it is not yet possible, on account of the difficulty of complete separation, to reach a system of nomenclature which is definite and satisfactory. For the present, therefore, we may regard the cellulose group as being composed essentially of the following components:

(1) Carbohydrate bodies yielding sugars on hydrolysis with dilute acids (preferable term, hemicellulose); chief members of the group, araban and xylan; less important members, mannan, galactan, dextran.

(2) Carbohydrate bodies insoluble in boiling dilute mineral acids and dilute alkalies and ammonia, and soluble in cuprammonium (preferable term, cellulose); varieties of cellulose not well known.

(3) Carbohydrate bodies insoluble in boiling dilute mineral acids and dilute alkalies and in cuprammonium, but soluble with more or less difficulty in ammonia (preferable name, lignin), composed of humus-like bodies, soluble in dilute ammonia and cellulose-like bodies, the whole capable of being almost completely decomposed by successive treatments with ammonia and cuprammonium, the residue after such repeated treatment containing chiefly mineral matters with some organic matter, the nature of which is not well known.

---

[1] Landwirthschaftlichen Versuchsstationen, vol. 39, p. 462.
[2] Landwirthschaftliche Jahrbücher, 1894, p. 15.

The above is a condensed synopsis of our present knowledge concerning the chief classes of the carbohydrate matters composing the cellulose group or the woody fiber of plant substances.

QUANTITATIVE SEPARATION OF CELLULOSES.

Hoffmeister[1] agrees with Tollens in applying the term hemicelluloses to that class of insoluble carbohydrate bodies, other than the starches, dissolved by boiling dilute acids, and also includes bodies soluble in sodium hydroxid. The term, therefore, includes not only the pentosans, which are the more soluble in soda lye, but also to a certain extent some of the true celluloses—hexosans. He reviews the common methods of separation, and especially the chlorination method of Cross and Bevan, and finds that all the known methods fail to separate definitely the cellulose bodies into groups of like kind; as, for instance, the pentosans separated by any of the methods are always found to contain some hexosans, and the residual celluloses are never obtained quite free from pentosans and lignin. The conventional method of determining crude fiber in food analysis can not be practically replaced by any of the methods for quantitative separation of the celluloses, except at a loss of time in analysis, which is scarcely worth while. Hoffmeister proposes a method of separation which evidently is open to the same objections as those urged against the other methods, but which at least, with the exception of extraction with ammonia, can be carried out without any great loss of time. The material which is to be freed from starch, if any be contained therein, by the action of malt extract, is ground, after drying and extraction with ether, to the very finest possible powder. Weighed quantities of this powder are treated as follows: The material is extracted by repeated treatment with hydrochloric acid or with ammonia. After thoroughly mixing and shaking, the material is allowed to stand until the solid matters have subsided and the supernatant liquor is removed by pouring or siphoning. After this treatment has been continued for several hours the residue is at once, without drying, treated at room temperature with a 5 or 6 per cent sodium hydroxid solution. This is allowed to stand for two days, with frequent shaking. At the end of this time, after all the solid matter is deposited, the supernatant solvent is removed as above. The residue is brought upon the filter and washed with hot water. The extract in sodium hydroxid is neutralized with hydrochloric acid, treated with a sufficient quantity of alcohol, and the precipitate collected upon a filter.

Great difficulties of filtration may be encountered, which may be lessened to some extent by increasing the quantity of alcohol. The material extracted by sodium hydroxid and precipitated by alcohol after thorough washing with alcohol is dried and weighed, and estimated as hemicellulose. The residue left after extraction with sodium

---

[1] Landw. Versuchs-Sta., Vol. XLVIII, p. 401. Abstract.

hydroxid is treated with cuprammonium (Schweitzer's reagent) until no more of it passes into solution. The material dissolved is precipitated with alcohol, washed, dried, and weighed, and regarded as cellulose. The residue is washed, dried, and weighed as lignin. The several precipitates in this process are not tested for protein, and it is probable that a considerable quantity of protein will be found in them. The final residue, called lignin, is still a compound body. If it be treated in a continuous extraction apparatus for several days with ammonia all superficial lignin (incrusting substance) goes into solution, coloring the ammonia brown. The residue, treated with cuprammonium, yields a pure cellulose. In the remainder lignin or incrusting substance can again be detected, showing the intimate manner in which the lignin and cellulose are associated.

The exhaustion of the incrusting substance with ammonia requires days, sometimes weeks and months, and therefore the process has little practical value. A special form of apparatus is used, which, with the aid of folded strips of filter paper, admits the dilute ammonia to all parts of the finely ground mass.

The material dissolved in ammonia is recovered by evaporating the solvent.

Cuprammonium dissolves not only the cellulose, but also the pentosans. This is shown in a very striking manner by treating the residue after extraction with ammonia with cuprammonium. The soluble matter thus obtained contains varying quantities of pentosans, according to the nature of the substance. The material extracted by ammonia from woody substances, as has already been remarked, imparts to the ammonia a dark color. On evaporation on the water bath a vanilla-like odor is also distinguished. The dry residue, after evaporation of the ammonia, is insoluble in water, but is soluble in ammonia, and is thrown out of solution by acids. This substance exhibits in a marked degree the character of humic acids, and doubtless belongs to this category.

Another body has been separated from the lignin or vegetable fiber; it is easily soluble in alcohol, but has only been obtained so far in an amorphous condition. In the dry state it is in the form of a yellow powder. Its melting point lies between 200° and 210°, and on elementary analysis it appears to have the empirical formula $C_6H_7O_2$. In cereal grains the bodies described above are found chiefly in the fibrous envelopes of the kernels, and on milling are secured chiefly in the bran.

INSOLUBLE CARBOHYDRATES OF WHEAT.

Sherman[1] has made an investigation of the insoluble carbohydrates other than starch contained in wheat. Inasmuch as these insoluble carbohydrates are practically all in the bran, the investigations were made upon this substance. The bran was successively extracted with

---

[1] J. Am. Chem. Soc., vol. 19, p. 291. Abstract.

water, saline solution, malt extract, 2 per cent ammonia, cold, and boiling 0.1 per cent sodium hydroxid. By this treatment, it is stated, fatty and resinous matter, all the soluble carbohydrates, and nearly all the proteid matter were removed. The extract treated with sodium hydroxid solution yielded the principal part of the pentosans, giving the characteristic red coloration with phloroglucin in hydrochloric acid and affording furfuraldehyde when distilled with an acid.

The term hemicellulose is used by Sherman to designate the carbohydrate matter, obtained by boiling in dilute acids, from vegetable cells free from starch. The hydrolysis of the hemicelluloses was effected by boiling for thirty minutes with 1.25 per cent sulphuric acid, and the resulting solution was boiled with 2 per cent sulphuric acid for about six hours until its copper-reducing power no longer increased. The reducing power of the sugars obtained was found to be 91.2 per cent of of that of pure dextrose. The sulphuric acid solution, after complete hydrolysis, was tested for mannose with phenylhydrazine acetate; for galactose, by evaporation with nitrous acid, and for levulose, with resorcin in hydrochloric acid. None of these bodies was present. Pentoses were present in large quantities. The dextrose was distinguished by the preparation of its osazone. The osazones of the pentoses and of dextrose are separated by boiling water, the pentose osazones being quite readily soluble, and the dextrose osazones being quite insoluble in this reagent. The result of the experiment with the osazones showed that no dextrose, or at least not more than a trace, was present. It is concluded from this that wheat bran, after treatment as above, yields only pentoses on hydrolysis with sulphuric acid.

CHARACTER OF THE RESIDUE.

The residue left on hydrolysis with sulphuric acid was washed with water and alcohol and dried. In the dry state it contained nearly 0.7 per cent of ash, nearly 0.3 per cent of nitrogen, and yielded, on distillation with hydrochloric acid, nearly 12 per cent of furfuraldehyde. When treated with chlorin and then boiled with sodium sulphite it gave a deep magenta color, characteristic of lignin. It also gave the red color when treated with phloroglucin, which is the qualitative test for pentosans. No coloration was obtained on boiling with aniline sulphate, showing the absence of oxycellulose.

DEPORTMENT WITH FERRIC CHLORID AND POTASSIUM FERRICYANID.

Fresh aqueous solutions containing in 100 c. c. 1.6 grams of ferric chlorid and 3.3 grams of potassium ferricyanid, respectively, were mixed in equal volumes. The fiber was immersed in this solution for some time; washed and dried at 105°. The immersion before washing should be continued for an hour at least, and better for sixteen hours. In every case a large increase in weight was obtained, showing that the fiber of wheat bran, like the typical lignocellulose of jute, has the power of fixing a considerable amount of cyanid.

COMPOUNDS WITH CHLORIN.

This compound was prepared according to the method of Cross and Bevan by boiling 75 grams of the bran with 1 per cent sodium hydroxid solution, washing, pressing to remove the greater part of the water, and exposing the moist fiber for one hour to chlorin gas free of hydrochloric acid. The fiber, during the passage of the chlorin, is suspended in alcohol. The alcoholic solution is removed by pressure and found to be of a deep golden yellow color. On concentrating and pouring into water, a part of the substance dissolved by the chlorin alcohol is separated. In all, about 1 gram of this precipitate was obtained, which contained 26.7 per cent of chlorin. Wheat bran, therefore, contains to some extent that character of lignin compound peculiar to jute which gives the above reaction.

SEPARATION OF THE CELLULOSE.

Three methods of separating cellulose were tried:

(1) *Schulze's method.*—In this method 30 grams of the wheat fiber are treated at ordinary temperature with a solution of 25 grams of potassium chlorate in 350 c. c. of nitric acid of 1.10 specific gravity for seven days, with occasional stirring. Enough nitric acid is added to increase the strength to 1.13 specific gravity, and the digestion is continued for another seven days. At the end of this time the mixture is kept at 40° for two hours, filtered, washed free of acid, and treated on the filter with cold 2 per cent ammonia as long as the filtrate is colored. Finally, the residue is washed with water and alcohol. Thirty-four per cent of the fiber was dissolved by this treatment. The residue still contained 7 per cent of furfuraldehyde.

(2) *Method of Cross and Bevan.*—Thirty grams of fiber are boiled for thirty minutes with 800 c. c. of 1 per cent sodium hydroxid, the mixture poured on a filter, washed with water until free from alkali, pressed as free of water as possible, placed loosely in a covered beaker, and exposed to the action of chlorin gas for an hour, with occasional stirring. At the end of this time it is thrown on a filter and washed with water until all free acid is removed, heated to boiling with 600 c. c. of 2 per cent sodium sulphite, and sufficient sodium hydroxid solution added to make 0.2 per cent of the whole. The boiling is continued for five minutes longer, the solution filtered while heated, and the residue washed until the washings are neutral and colorless. The final washing is made with alcohol and the residue dried and weighed. This treatment dissolves 33.5 per cent of the total fiber.

(3) *Solution in alkalies.*—Lange's method of dissolving the cellulose in alkalies was employed, as described in Principles and Practice of Agricultural Analysis (vol. III, p. 104).

It is probable that the insoluble carbohydrates of the other cereals are composed essentially of the same bodies. The general composition of the wheat bran as ascertained by Sherman is as follows:

	Per cent.
Total soluble carbohydrates calculated as dextrin	7.2
Starch	17.7
True pentosans	17.5
Lignin and allied substances	11.6
Cellulose (as defined above)	8.5
Ether extract, protein, and ash	33.4
Undetermined	4.1

SUMMARY OF RESULTS.

The chief results of this investigation may be briefly stated as follows:

1. As determined by the analysis of the osazones, only the pentoses, xylose, and arabinose result from the hydrolysis of the hemicellulose. This is, therefore, practically identical with the free or normal pentosans which the wheat contains.

2. The preparation of cellulose from the fiber insoluble in dilute acid was found to be best effected by means of alkali and chlorin as described by Cross and Bevan.

The dilute boiling alkali removes matter which appears to contain a condensed form of pentosan, since it yields furfurol on distillation and gives a red color with phloroglucin reagent, but does not yield any notable amount of reducing sugar on boiling with dilute sulphuric acid.

The lignin not removed by dilute alkali forms with chlorin an alcohol-soluble compound containing 26.7 per cent of chlorin corresponding to the "lignone chlorid," $C_{19}H_{18}Cl_4O_9$, of Cross and Bevan.

3. The cellulose obtained as just mentioned, or by fusion of the fiber with strong alkali (Lange's method), contains furfuraldehyde-yielding bodies whose deportment toward reagents indicates the presence of penta-anhydrid, probably in combination with a part of the hexa-anhydrid or normal cellulose.

When dissolved in sulphuric acid, diluted, and hydrolyzed, a small quantity of dextrose only was obtained as osazone.

4. The property of dyeing in a solution of ferric chloride and potassium ferricyanid is possessed in a marked degree by the wheat fiber, and the reaction has been found useful in testing the purity of "cellulose" residues. In this respect, as in the formation of the lignone chlorid, the lignified tissue of wheat resembles that of jute, the typical lignocellulose.

5. No notable amount of oxycellulose has been found in any of the preparations from the wheat fiber.

6. The relations of the constituents under consideration may be represented as follows:

A. Starch granules. ⎫
B. Outer seed-coat. ⎭ Separated automatically.
    a. Free pentosans. ⎫
    b. Lignified tissue. ⎭ Associated in position but not chemically combined.
        Cellulose............................
            baa. Hexa-anhydrids. ⎫ Apparently in ⎫
            bab. Penta-anhydrids. ⎭ combination. ⎬ In chemical combination.
        bb. Lignin............................⎭

Undefined substances, apparently of a condensed nature, associated with and doubtless allied to the lignin.

7. The determination of starch has been carefully studied and the methods now available are quite satisfactory. An approximate separation of free pentosans, lignin and its allies, and cellulose may be effected by means of the method proposed in this paper.

8. Thus determined, the digestibility of the components in a case where wheat bran had been fed alone was found to be: Starch, 100 per cent; free pentosans, 66.2 per cent; lignin and allied substances, 36.7 per cent; cellulose, 24.8 per cent.

9. From the analyses given in this paper and the best available results of other experimenters, the proportions present in normal mature wheat, air-dried, are calculated as follows:

Average percentages of insoluble carbohydrates in air-dried wheat.

	Per cent.
Starch	54.0 to 59.0
Free pentosans	3.5 to 4.5
Lignin and its allies	2.0 to 2.5
Cellulose	1.6 to 2.1
Insoluble carbohydrates	61.1 to 68.1

These data have been confirmed by investigations made in this division, with the exception that the mean percentage of starch as determined by the latest methods is somewhat higher than given by Sherman.

Pentosans.—The occurrence of a body in wheat bran capable of yielding a peculiar oily body caused Döbereiner in 1831 to adopt the name furfurol (furfuraldehyde) for this oil.[1] Traces of this body are also obtained, according to the earlier writers, from sugars and starches.

Emmet got furfurol by distilling sugar, starch, gum, and wood with sulphuric acid when the temperature was not carried to the carbonizing point.[2]

Fownes states as the result of his investigations that furfurol is derived chiefly from the cell walls of vegetable substances.[3]

Fownes obtained furfuraldehyde freely by distilling bran and flour with an acid.

---

[1] Ann. Pharm., vol. 3, p. 141.
[2] Silliman's Journal, vol. 32, p. 140.
[3] Gmelin's Handbuch, English translation, vol. 10, p. 370.

Steinhouse suggested the use of hydrochloric acid for obtaining furfurol from bran by a process entirely analogous to that now employed in chemical analysis. He objected to the use of this acid, however, because it was found in the distillate with the oil. For obtaining large quantities of furfurol he used 16 kilograms of bran, and 5 of sulphuric acid diluted with 10 of water.[1]

Babo used zinc chlorid as the distilling reagent, and thereby obtained furfurol from bran.[2]

These earlier investigations of furfuraldehyde, however, did not lead to the isolation and characterization of the true source of the supply. The presence of a gum-like body in wheat germs, yielding furfuraldehyde, was established by Richardson in this division in 1885–86, and a preparation of several grams of this material made at that time is still in our possession. Shortly after this the researches of Tollens and his pupils and others showed the quantitative relation existing between the production of furfuraldehyde and the pentosan bodies, and laid the foundation of the approximately exact estimation of the latter. It then became possible to determine, for the first time, the quantity of pentose forming bodies (araban, xylan) in the bran and other parts of the cereal grains.

In this laboratory the percentage of pentosans in the following cereals has been found to be: Wheat, 5.80 per cent; rye, 8.10 per cent; oats (unhulled) 13.65 per cent; barley (hulled) 6.50 per cent. These percentages are calculated on the samples as ground, containing 11.33, 11.71, 9.26, and 12.20 per cent of water, respectively.

Stone found 4.54 per cent of pentosans in winter wheat, 3.94 per cent in spring wheat, and 4.99 per cent in maize.[3]

SOLUBLE CARBOHYDRATES.

In 1817 Proust[4] found 5 per cent of sugar and 4 per cent of dextrin in barley, and Thomson[5] soon thereafter reported 4 per cent of sugar in the same substance. Peligot[6] reported 7.2 per cent of dextrin in barley, and Boussingault the same quantity in wheat. Sace[7] in 1857 reported 6 per cent sugar in wheat. De Saussure stated that wheat contained 2.44 per cent of sugar and 3.46 per cent of dextrin. Mitscherlich[8] in 1844 stated that the unsprouted grains of cereals contained neither sugar nor dextrin. Soon thereafter Mulder[9] stated that these seeds contained dextrin but no sugar. Hermbstaedt, Einhof, and Stein

---

[1] Gmelin, op. cit., p. 371.
[2] Ann. Pharm., vol. 85, p. 100.
[3] Bulletin 34, O. E. S., pp. 14, 16.
[4] Ann. de chem. et de phys., vol. 5, p. 337.
[5] Op. cit. supra, vol. 6, 216.
[6] Op. cit. supra, 3e Serie, vol. 29, p. 1.
[7] Traité de chim., vol. 4, p. 508.
[8] Lehrb. de. Chem., edition of 1844, p. 368.
[9] Chim. des bieres, p. 26.

gave,[1] respectively, the following data for sugar and dextrin in barley: Sugar, 4.7 and 5.2 per cent; dextrin, 4.5, 4.6, and 6.5 per cent.

Lermer found no sugar in barley, but 6.63 per cent of dextrin, while Pillitz and others report 2.71 per cent of sugar and 1.96 per cent of dextrin in barley, and 1.60 per cent of sugar and 1.76 per cent of dextrin in wheat.

Kühnemann, who tabulated the literature of the subject prior to Lermer's time, examined malt and obtained two crystallizable sugars, one of which reduced copper salts—probably maltose. He concluded, however, that the other substance he secured, which resembled dextrin in being precipitated by alcohol, was not a true dextrin. With the isolation of pure sucrose from cereals by the last-named investigator the period of exact investigation of the soluble carbohydrates of these bodies may be regarded to have begun.

Sucrose.

The presence of this sugar in cereal kernels has long been known. The first recorded determination of soluble sugars in cereals is found in an account of some researches by Banister[2] in 1880. Banister states that the saccharine matters extracted from the grains of cereals behave like cane sugar, being inverted with the same facility and not until then reducing a solution of copper salt. Banister found the following quantities of sugar, which he supposed from its deportment to be cane sugar, in the cereals named.[3]

Percentage of sucrose in cereals.

	Per cent.		Per cent.
Winter wheat	2.57	Maize	1.94
Spring wheat	2.24	Rye	4.30
Barley	1.34	Rice	0.38

The occurrence of sugars in cereals is mentioned in earlier articles, and indeed Kühnemann[4] in 1875 stated that he had isolated from 0.6 to 1 per cent of sucrose in germinated barley.

In 1883 Richardson,[5] in this division, called attention to the large quantity of sugar in wheat germs. Richardson found that this sugar did not reduce copper salts until after inversion; that it was strongly dextrorotatory, and less so after inversion. These properties show that it was a mixture of sucrose and raffinose, with perhaps a small quantity of dextrin or maltose.

---

[1] Mulder, Chim. des bieres, p. 30; Berzelius, Lehrb. d. Chemie, 1838, vol. 7, p. 551; Polytech. Centralbl., 1860, p. 494.

[2] These data were published in the second part of the South Kensington Art Handbook on the adulteration of foods, and are repeated in the Chemical News of December 11, 1885.

[3] Chem. News, Dec. 11, 1885, p. 293.

[4] Berichte, vol. 8, p. 202.

[5] Bul. 4, p. 47.

Later, it was found in this laboratory by Richardson and Crampton[1] that this sugar contained about 85 per cent of sucrose, and a fine preparation of a very pure sucrose was secured. The rest of the sugar was found to possess the properties of raffinose, but this sugar was not separated in a pure state at that time.

O'Sullivan[2] found from 0.8 to 1.6 per cent of sucrose in barley and less than 0.5 per cent in wheat.

In malt he found 4.7 per cent of sucrose. He infers that during germination there is a considerable increase in the quantity of the sugar.

Tollens and Washburn[3] detected and determined sucrose in maize and Schulze and Frankfurter[4] in wheat, rye, oats, and buckwheat. Frankfurter[5] has found 17 per cent of sucrose in wheat germs.

Stone found from 0.48 to 0.51 per cent of sucrose in wheat, 3.51 per cent in sweet maize, and from 0.24 to 0.27 per cent in common maize.

In this laboratory Krug has lately determined the percentage of sucrose in a few of the cereals, with the following results: Wheat, 0.33; rye, 0.42; oats, 0.17; barley, 0.18 per cent.

The data obtained by Stone and Krug are doubtless more nearly correct than those given by earlier investigators.

INVERT OR REDUCING SUGARS, DEXTRIN, AND GALACTIN.

It is doubtful whether reducing sugars are present in fresh unsprouted cereal grains. Most observers have found that fresh ground cereal grains give an aqueous extract which does not reduce alkaline copper solutions, or at most reduces them in a very slight degree. In old cereals or in flours kept for some time at room temperatures the reducing sugars found in the aqueous extract may arise from the activity of an unorganized ferment (invertase, diastase, etc.). O'Sullivan[6] found a reducing sugar in barley extract which he was unable to identify by its optical and reducing qualities. The quantity of this sugar obtained from 200 grams of barley meal was only 0.73 gram. A similar body in respect of reducing power was observed in wheat. Wheat yielded to O'Sullivan a trace of a fermentable, nonreducing sugar of a moderately high levo-rotatory power, but there is doubt of the actual existence of such a body in the fresh grain. Frankfurter[7] was able to detect a trace of reducing sugar, however, in the germs of wheat.

Stone[8] found small quantities of invert sugar in winter wheat, but none in spring wheat. None was found in maize. He also detected weighable quantities of dextrin in both cereals, in amount equal to about 0.25 per cent. With the possible exception of barley, it is believed that maltose is not found in fresh cereals. After germina-

---

[1] Berichte, vol. 19, p. 1180.
[2] J. Chem. Soc. Trans., vol. 49, p. 64.
[3] Berichte, vol. 22, p. 1047.
[4] Berichte, vol. 27, p. 62.
[5] Versuchsstat, vol. 47, p. 464.
[6] J. Chem. Soc. Trans., vol. 49, p. 60.
[7] Versuchsstat, vol. 47, p. 457.
[8] O. E. S. Bul. 34, pp. 14–16.

tion, however, it is probable that other cereals than barley may have a part of their starch converted into maltose.

In most samples of cereal grains and flours made from them traces of invert or reducing sugar may be found. Whether these preexist in the fresh grain or are the result of the action of the enzymes it is difficult to say. In addition to this there are found also weighable traces of dextrin, or, as claimed by Girard [1], galactin.

In the common method of separating the carbohydrates soluble in water from the freshly ground grain or flour it must not be forgotten that precautions are not usually taken to prevent the action of the natural enzymes, which all cereal flours contain, during the time of extraction. Under the conditions in which ordinary aqueous extraction is practiced these enzymes may become active, and consequently a portion of the soluble materials secured may be due to this source. In order to avoid the action of the enzymes Girard proposes to conduct the extraction at a very low temperature, viz, at about 0° C. This low temperature is secured by conducting the extraction in a vessel which is surrounded by pounded ice. In these conditions the water in contact with the finely ground flour is reduced almost to the temperature of zero. At this temperature, with the help of a mechanical stirrer all the matter which will pass into solution can be practically extracted in about four hours, and the action of the enzymes being arrested, only the actual soluble matter in the flour of ground grain at the time the extraction is begun is secured. It is probable, therefore, that the values given by analysts in general to represent the quantity of matters in a flour soluble in water are too high. According to Girard, the precipitate which is produced in the aqueous extract from a flour secured as above described on the addition of alcohol is not dextrin, but galactin. In some instances he has detected nearly 1 per cent of this substance, a matter not only of importance scientifically, but also in baking. Girard also has found a considerably larger quantity of sucrose than Krug found in the aqueous extract of finely ground wheat. The quantities of invert or reducing sugars found by him reach as much as 0.2 per cent in some instances. The following table gives the names and quantity of substances soluble in water in four samples of wheat:

Substances in wheat soluble in water.

Constituents soluble in water.	Sample No. 1.	Sample No. 2.	Sample No. 3.	Sample No. 4.
	Per cent.	Per cent.	Per cent.	Per cent.
Glucose or reducing sugar	0.21	0.16	0.20	0.09
Sucrose	0.86	1.20	1.70	0.08
Nitrogenous matter and diastase	1.10	1.02	1.02	1.28
Galactin	0.52	0.59	0.78	0.99
Mineral matters	0.36	0.32	0.30	0.22
Not determined	0.07			

[1] Comptes rendus, vol. 104, April 26 and May 3, 1897.

NITROGENOUS BASES.

I will add here the quantities of invert or reducing sugar, sucrose, and dextrin or galactin obtained by Krug in this laboratory on the samples named in the table.

Table showing the percentages of invert sugar, sucrose, and dextrin or galactin in cereals and cereal products.

Name.	Invert sugar.	Sucrose.	Dextrin.
	Per cent.	Per cent.	Per cent.
Wheat	0.027	0.330	0.160
Rye	.008	.416	.220
Oats	.031	.173	.260
Barley	.017	.177	.140
Wheat flour	.014	.101	.190
Graham flour	.038	.382	.210
Buckwheat flour	.000	.060	.006
Self-raising wheat flours	.000	.056	.080
Miscellaneous wheat flours	.003	.098	.130
Common market wheat flours	.021	.288	.210
Bakers' and family flours	.027	.190	.220
Patent wheat flours	.002	.085	.200

RAFFINOSE.

Richardson and Crampton,[1] as already stated, found from 15 to 18 per cent of sugar in the germs of wheat, of which the chief part, from 80 to 90 per cent, consisted of cane sugar. The rest behaved in a manner analogous to raffinose, but they did not succeed in getting this sugar in an isolated state, and were of the opinion that a new kind of sugar was present.

O'Sullivan[2] obtained raffinose from barley by evaporating an alcoholic extract of the meal, dissolving the sirup obtained in the least possible quantity of alcohol, and adding a little ether. After some time quite pure crystals of raffinose were separated.

Later, in 1893, Schulze and Frankfurter[3] secured a nearly pure preparation of raffinose from the germs of wheat, but the percentage amount of it is not stated.

The sugars were separated from the germs by hot alcohol and were subsequently precipitated by strontium hydroxid. Frankfurter[4] has found 6.89 per cent raffinose in wheat germs.

MISCELLANEOUS CONSTITUENTS OF CEREAL GRAINS.

NITROGENOUS BASES.

The nitrogen contained in cereal grains is not all in the form of proteids. A part of it exists in the form which is commonly known as amido nitrogen, forming compounds which are not nutritious nor digestible.

---

[1] Berichte, vol. 19, p. 1180.
[2] J. Chem. Soc., Trans., vol. 49, p. 70.
[3] Berichte, vol. 27, p. 64.
[4] Versuchsstat, vol. 47, p. 464.

In 1885 the first of these amido compounds found in cereal grains, allantoin, was isolated from wheat germs in this laboratory by Richardson and Crampton.[1]

Associated with allantoin Frankfurter[2] has found also asparagin.

Two other nitrogenous bases, cholin and betain, have also been isolated from the wheat germ by Frankfurter and Schulze.[3] Sprouted barley germs also contain these bases. In addition to these, a small quantity of xanthin-like bodies was detected by the same investigators.

FERMENTS.

The cereal grains contain either ferments which are capable of acting upon proteid matters and starches, or else the elements from which these ferments can be produced under the influence of warmth and the vital activity of the plant. A body from which the ferments are evolved is known as zymogen, and the unorganized ferments themselves are called enzymes. The most important of these is a substance which has already been mentioned, namely, diastase.

Kjeldahl[4] has isolated a ferment from germinated barley identical in its action with invertase, and therefore capable of converting sucrose into invert sugar.

It is quite probable, therefore, that the grains of all the cereals contain these ferments of a proteid nature, less active in the nongerminated grain and developed to the highest activity during the process of germination. It is also probable, as indicated by Brown and Morris, that there may be slight differences in the character of these ferments.

In the separation of enzymes or zymogen from vegetable material it is customary to extract the fine-ground material with glycerol or glycerol-water, and subsequently precipitate the extracted matter with alcohol. The ferment is then purified by repeated precipitations with alcohol of its aqueous solution, and the salts which it contains are thoroughly removed by dialysis. With the exception of diastase, the unorganized ferments of the cereal grains have not been thoroughly studied. Frankfurter[5] isolated a ferment from wheat germs capable of dissolving fibrin. This ferment, however, could not be obtained without previous heating of the germ for two days to 40°. This ferment, therefore, does not exist in the free state in fresh wheat germs which have not been exposed to this temperature. Since, however, in this country wheat is often exposed to a temperature approaching 40° in the fields, it is not improbable that it might be found in such wheats without previous heating. The wheat evidently contains a zymogen which, under the action of heat, develops the ferment.

---

[1] Berichte, vol. 19, p. 1180.
[2] Versuchsstat, vol. 47, p. 453.
[3] Berichte, vol. 26, p. 2151.
[4] Bourquelot, Les ferments solubles, p. 9.
[5] Versuchsstat, vol. 47, p. 455.

DIASTASE.

Kirchoff,[1] in 1814, was the first to observe that germinated barley contained a substance which was capable of hydrolyzing starch, but he mistook it for gluten. The ferment itself was first isolated by Payen and Persoz[2] in 1833, and named diastase by them.

The word "enzyme" as a general characterization of soluble ferments was proposed by Kühne[3] in 1878.

Kjeldahl[4] has found diastase in the nongerminated barley.

Brown and Morris[5] recognize two kinds of diastase, viz, of secretion and displacement. The diastase which is produced by the vital activity of germinating grains is analogous to that of the secreted digestive ferments, and hence belongs to the first-named class. The second class of diastatic ferments is much more largely distributed in the vegetable kingdom, and it is found in nongerminated grains. The first kind of diastase, when in contact with starch particles, corrodes them as if mechanically, and the starch granules which have been subjected for a short time to their action have the appearance of having been gnawed. The second kind of diastatic ferments acts more generally on the starch granule without producing any mark of disaggregation or corrosion, the starch granule diminishing in volume little by little without changing its form suddenly until complete solution takes place. This variety of diastase acts very slowly on the solid starch or on the starch paste, but rapidly converts soluble starch into sugar.

Osborne,[6] who has made the most extensive study of the chemical properties of diastase which has yet been published, thinks it probable that this substance is a true proteid, or closely resembles it. According to his view, it is either an albumin, a combination of an albumin with a proteose, or a proteose. It is probable that it is most closely related to the albumin which is known as leucosin.

COMPOSITION OF THE ASH OF CEREALS.

The mineral matters of cereal grains are left after incineration in combination with carbon dioxid and with phosphoric, sulphuric, hydrochloric, and silicic acids. In the unburned grains the mineral matters doubtless exist partly in combination with some of the acids named above, and also to a great extent as salts of the organic acids. On ignition the compounds of the organic acids and bases are reduced to carbonates. All of the phosphorus, sulphur, and chlorin which are found in the inorganic state in the ash may not have existed as such

---

[1] Memoirs read at the Academie of Sciences at St. Petersburg, December 30, 1814. Bourquelot, op. cit. supra, 12.
[2] Ann. de chim et de phys. (2), vol. 43, p. 73.
[3] Untersuchungen der Phys. Inst. Heidelberg, 1878, p. 291.
[4] C. r. des travaux du lab. de Carlsberg, 1879, p. 138.
[5] J. Chem. Soc., Trans., 1890, p. 505.
[6] 18th Report Conn. Agr. Exp. Station, p. 206.

in the original grains, but a portion of each of these is found in organic combination; for instance, a part of the phosphorus doubtless exists as lecithin and neuclein, and a large part of the sulphur is found in combination with the proteid matter. The chlorin exists mostly in the inorganic state in combination with sodium, but nearly the whole of the sulphuric acid which is found in the ash is derived from the sulphur of the proteids. A study of the composition of the ash of the cereals from the purely chemical side is not altogether satisfactory. The difficulties attending the determination of the ash ingredients are very considerable, and the fact that the final form in which they are obtained is quite different from that in which they exist in the cereal grains, diminishes to a great extent the value of the information which the analytical data afford. In the data which follow the ash was burned without the addition of any substance to help secure complete combustion. The method recommended by the Association of Official Agricultural Chemists was strictly followed; viz, the charring of the material at a low temperature, the extraction of the char with hot water to remove the soluble ash therein, and the final combustion of the carbonaceous residue at as low a temperature as possible until an ash fairly free of carbon was secured. While this method can be applied with a fair degree of success to small quantities of cereal flours, and for the purpose of determining simply the percentage of ash therein, the attempt to apply it to considerable quantities for the purpose of securing an amount of ash necessary for the complete analysis is attended with difficulties.

Principal Difficulties in Procuring Ash.

The chief of these difficulties are the following:

In the first place, in the absence of any oxidizing material a part of the sulphur may escape oxidation to sulphuric acid. The amount of sulphates, therefore, contained in the ash is often much less than would be expected from the total sulphur in the grains.

In the second place, the ash of cereals is apt to be excessively acid on account of the large quantity of phosphoric acid which it contains. As a result the acid phosphates rather than the neutral phosphates predominate among the mineral salts. It is difficult to burn finely divided carbon in contact with acid phosphates without a reduction of a portion of the phosphorus and a consequent loss thereof. For the same reason the organic phosphorus is apt to escape oxidation, and a portion of it may be lost as volatile compounds. If the temperature be allowed to rise the least degree above the lowest redness a certain amount of the reduced phosphorus combines with the platinum of the dish in which the combustion takes place, and the result is the loss of the dish.

In the third place, the acid phosphates or free phosphoric acid, even at very low temperatures, decompose any alkaline chlorids which may be present, with the consequence that the chlorin of the ash may escape. In several instances no chlorin was found, and yet it is not

THE ASH OF CEREALS. 1211

probable that any cereal grain exists without at least a trace of chlorin. While the amount of chlorin in any case is very small, and the error which would be introduced into the analysis by its loss is proportionately negligible, yet the existence of such a state of uncertainty is at least annoying to the analyst.

In the fourth place, there is the great difficulty of burning a considerable quantity of cereal grains to secure an ash reasonably free of carbon. At best the ashes are of a light-gray color, and in some cases, owing to the excess of carbon, inclined to black. The application of sufficiently high temperature to secure complete oxidation produces serious changes in the composition of the ash, rendering complete oxidation difficult, and the resulting ash unsatisfactory for analytical purposes. It is only necessary for one to look at the data in tables of ash analysis to show how wide are the variations for almost every constituent found therein. It is believed that these variations are due chiefly to differences in composition, but to some extent they may be attributed to faults of analysis and changes produced in the mineral matters of the ash during incineration rather than to any such wide variations in the natural constituents of the substance. In large numbers of analyses the mean data may represent very nearly the average constitution of the ash, but in individual analyses the variations may be quite pronounced.

DESCRIPTION OF SAMPLES OF ASH.

The samples of ash, the analyses of which are given in the following tables, were obtained by the incineration of composite samples of the cereals exhibited at the World's Columbian Exposition.

Wheat.—Sample No. 16000 is the ash derived from 7 typical samples of Canadian wheat.

No. 16001 is the ash from 4 samples of wheat from the Argentine Republic.

No. 16002, 1 sample of rye from Minnesota.

No. 16003, 16 samples of rye from different parts of the United States.

No. 16004, 1 sample of rye from Brazil.

No. 15996, 28 samples of barley from the United States.

No. 15995, 19 samples of barley from Canada.

No. 15998, 45 samples of oats from the United States.

No. 15997, 12 samples of oats from Canada.

No. 15999, 1 sample of oats from Great Britain.

No. 16010, 18 samples of maize from the United States.

No. 16011, 2 samples of maize from the Argentine Republic.

No. 16012, 1 sample of maize from Bulgaria.

No. 16013, 1 sample of maize from New South Wales.

No. 16006, 1 sample of rice from Johore.

No. 16008, 2 samples of rice from Guatemala.

No. 16009, 1 sample of rice from Bulgaria.

1212   FOODS AND FOOD ADULTERANTS.

No. 16007, 6 samples of rice from Japan.
No. 16005, 8 samples of buckwheat from the United States.

In each group, for the purpose of comparison, are given the means of the analyses of the ashes of that group as given in Wolff's work on ash analysis. In regard to the comparison between the data given and those copied from Wolff's book attention should be called to the fact that Wolff's analyses, from which the data were copied, were made more than twenty-five years ago. Although the methods of examination have not been greatly changed in that time, yet there has been a sufficient modification of them to render of slightly less value the comparisons of late with old analyses.

Cereals: Composition of pure ash.

Serial No.	Kind of grain.	K_2O.	Na_2O.	CaO.	MgO.	Fe_2O_3.	P_2O_5.	SO_3.	Cl.	SiO_2.
	WHEAT.	Per ct.	Per ct.	Per ct	Per ct.	Per ct.	Per ct.	Per ct.	Per ct.	Per ct.
16000	Canada	24.03	9.55	3.50	13.24	0.52	46.87	0.01	0.00	2.28
16001	Argentina	14.06	2.04	5.73	16.88	0.57	58.38	0.02	0.00	2.32
	Mean of Wolff's analyses—									
	Winter wheat	31.16	2.25	3.34	11.97	1.31	46.98	0.37	0.22	2.11
	Spring wheat	29.99	1.93	2.93	12.09	0.51	48.63	1.52	0.48	1.64
	RYE.									
16002	Minnesota	27.60	4.64	5.56	11.73	5.23	41.81	0.52	0.58	2.45
16003	Other parts of United States	43.20	2.83	5.29	16.54	0.42	27.63	0.87	0.00	3.22
16004	Brazil	25.18	4.67	6.04	10.05	2.19	34.20	1.84	0.00	17.30
	Mean of Wolff's analyses	31.47	1.70	2.63	11.54	1.63	46.93	1.10	0.61	1.88
	BARLEY.									
15996	United States	24.15	6.42	2.44	8.23	0.33	35.47	0.22	0.56	22.30
15995	Canada	26.76	9.36	4.27	7.87	0.35	24.63	0.71	0.47	20.69
	Mean of Wolff's analyses	20.15	2.53	2.60	8.62	0.97	34.68	1.09	0.93	27.54
	OATS.									
15998	United States	15.91	4.38	4.09	7.18	0.20	24.34	0.48	1.02	42.64
15997	Canada	20.74	2.16	5.93	9.41	0.30	22.36	0.56	0.62	38.06
15999	Great Britain	19.22	5.95	5.00	7.05	0.63	29.61	0.81	0.86	31.03
	Mean of Wolff's analyses	16.38	2.24	3.73	7.06	0.07	23.02	1.36	0.58	44.33
	MAIZE.									
16010	United States	33.92	7.72	3.18	17.99	0.50	35.25	0.44	0.00	1.00
16011	Argentina	30.75	10.55	2.69	17.15	0.31	36.66	0.33	0.00	1.56
16012	Bulgaria	27.61	3.34	3.90	17.10	0.37	45.06	0.06	0.00	1.76
16013	New South Wales	30.47	4.93	3.27	14.21	0.54	44.54	0.68	0.00	1.34
	Mean of Wolff's analyses	27.93	1.83	2.28	14.98	1.26	45.00	1.30	1.42	1.88
	RICE.									
16006	Unhulled	20.84	13.98	4.48	9.60	0.89	43.21	0.24	0.80	6.14
16008	Polished Guatemala	22.45	8.89	5.64	9.80	0.49	45.13	0.50	0.95	6.66
16009	Polished Bulgaria	14.59	7.70	3.31	10.42	0.70	46.44	0.60	1.00	16.14
16007	Unpolished Japan	25.82	6.38	4.22	19.69	0.39	36.95	0.39	0.00	6.16
	Mean of Wolff's analyses, shelled	21.73	5.50	3.29	11.20	1.23	53.68	0.62	0.10	2.74
	BUCKWHEAT.									
16005	United States	35.15	2.26	6.62	20.55	1.68	24.09	3.59	0.67	5.54
	Mean of Wolff's analyses	23.07	0.12	4.42	12.42	1.74	48.67	2.11	1.30	0.23

THE ASH OF CEREALS.

MINERAL SUBSTANCES IN THE ASH AND THEIR RELATIONS.

The most important constituents of the ash of cereals from an agricultural point of view are the potash and phosphoric acid. The most important constituents from the nutrient or physiological point of view are the lime, soda, and phosphoric acid. In regard to the other constituents of the ash, namely, the magnesia, iron, sulphuric acid, chlorin, and silica, it may be said that they play a less important rôle in nutrition. Soda is more important from a physiological point of view, since it is well known that herbivorous animals consuming large quantities of potash require more soda than is found in their food. Common salt thus becomes a necessity in the nutrition of those animals, affording, according to some authorities, a means whereby the excess of potash may be removed as chlorid. It is also seen that the phosphoric acid is in far larger proportion than would be necessary to unite with the lime present to form the tricalcium phosphate, of which the mineral matter of bone is chiefly composed.

Mineral matters have quite a different rôle in the building of plant tissues from that which they play in the building of animal tissues. In general, it may be said that the plant assimilates the mineral matters in the inorganic state and elaborates them in the form of organized bodies, in which condition the mineral matters are chiefly valuable in animal nutrition. From the standpoint of vegetable physiology, therefore, the rôle which mineral matters play is different from that which they assume in the animal system.

THE PART OF MINERAL SUBSTANCES IN NUTRITION.

A few words in detail in regard to the rôles of some of the principal mineral matters in plant and animal nutrition are necessary to a correct conception of the value of the mineral ingredients of foods.

Iron.—It has long been supposed by physiologists that the iron plays an important part in vegetable growth in being an indispensable component of the chlorophyl cells. Investigations in the last few years, especially those made by Molish,[1] show that iron is not a constituent of the coloring matter of the chlorophyl cells. At present, therefore, iron can not be regarded as an essential constituent of the vegetable organism. The rôle which it plays as a mineral matter in general will be mentioned further on.

Lime.—Lime is undoubtedly an important element of plant growth. Water cultures of plants show that in the absence of lime the full development of the plant can not be secured. Its universal presence in plants in large quantities can not be regarded as merely accidental. Its chief rôle in vegetable growth is doubtless to act as a neutralizing agent for the organic acids which are produced, especially as derivatives of the carbohydrates. Oxalic acid is extremely poisonous to the

---

[1] Die Pflanze in ihre Beziehungen zum Eisen, Jena, 1892.

plant, and as this is one of the acids which is developed in the degradation of carbohydrates, its presence would greatly hinder or even prevent the growth of the plant unless some substance were present to neutralize it. Calcium is one of the best of these substances, since it forms with the oxalic acid a practically insoluble compound rendering the acid harmless. Lime doubtless has other functions, but this may be regarded as one of its chief.

Magnesia.—The constant association of lime and magnesia in plants is an evidence of the fact that magnesia is also an important constituent of plant substances. Magnesia is doubtless associated with phosphorus and lime in favoring the formation of protein in the plant tissues. It is found especially in large quantities in the grains of plants where the proteid is largely accumulated.

Potash.—This, among the mineral substances, is the most important constituent of plant tissue, with the possible exception of phosphorus. As phosphorus seems to be associated especially with the formation of protein, so potash is found to be associated with the production of carbohydrates. It is especially active in the production of the soluble carbohydrates like sucrose. In those plants which produce sucrose in large quantities, such as the sugar beet, potash plays a most important function. It is probable that its activity in the formation of carbohydrates is not the sole function of potassium in plant growth, but its less important functions have not been carefully made out.

Sulphur.—Sulphur is indispensable in the formation of protein, and it is therefore essential to the metabolic processes of the plant cells, whereby inorganic carbon, nitrogen, hydrogen, oxygen, and sulphur are built up into the complex forms assumed by the vegetable proteids.

Silica.—It is frequently stated that silica has an important function in serving to give solidity and strength to plant tissues. This is certainly a mistake. It is impossible to say, with our present knowledge, whether or not silica has an important function in plant growth, or whether its occurrence in plants is an accident due to the fact that the plants grow in a medium containing very abundant quantities of this substance. The metabolic processes which render the silica of the soil soluble and secure its transportation through the plant are not well understood.

Soda.—Soda and potash are so intimately related chemically that it is not strange to find them associated in the mineral constituents of plants. Some high authorities are of the opinion that soda may to some extent take the place of potash in the growth of plants, but this idea has not received sufficient corroboration experimentally to warrant its adoption. Soda doubtless has some use in satisfying the hunger of plants for mineral substances in general, but that it plays any specific rôle in vegetable physiology, or that it can replace potash as an essential element of plant food has not been demonstrated.

Nitrogen.—Nitrogen forms, with potash and phosphorus, the trio of inorganic substances which are regarded as those most essential to plant growth. It is now the generally accepted opinion that nitrogen enters the plant only in the inorganic state, and from this condition is elaborated into the complex organic forms in which it is found in the mature plant. There is, however, some experimental evidence, quite weighty in its character, going to show that nitrogen may be used by plants in a partially organic state as amid nitrogen, or at least in a partially oxidized state, as ammonia or ammonia salts. It is undoubtedly true, however, that almost the whole of the nitrogen which is elaborated by plants in their tissues is fed to them in the form of nitric acid. The nitrogen of plants is found almost exclusively as protein, constituting the plant proteids. Only small quantities of nitrogen are found in the amid or ammoniacal or nitric forms in mature plants.

Phosphorus.—Phosphoric acid is perhaps the most valuable of all the mineral foods of plants. Phosphorus is absorbed almost exclusively in the form of phosphoric acid or phosphates, mostly calcium phosphate. In the processes of plant activity the phosphorus is separated largely from the calcium phosphate, and is found in the perfected organism of the plant, chiefly in combination with potassium, as far as its mineral form is concerned. A large quantity of the phosphorus, however, passes into the organic form, chiefly lecithin, in which state it is a highly important and essential constituent of many parts of the plant, and especially of the seeds. It is believed that this organic phosphorus plays an important rôle in animal nutrition.

It is certain that phosphorus plays a highly important rôle in the vital organism aside from its usefulness in the building of bones. With nitrogen it shares the distinction of being an essential of fundamental cell activity. This is true not only of the vegetable, but of the animal organism. Phosphorus is quite as indispensable as water or air to vegetable or animal life. The primordial cell in which the chemical changes which condition animal and vegetable metabolism take place lives and exercises its function only in the presence of phosphorus, whether that phosphorus be presented to it in the organic or inorganic form. With most of the vegetable cells inorganic phosphorus seems to be entirely sufficient for forming organic compounds, of which lecithin is the most important, while with the animal cells it is probable that the phosphorus is best utilized in the organic state. In vegetable cells phosphorus is the indispensable element upon whose activity the transformation of inorganic into organic nitrogen depends. Whenever the primordial cells are placed in an environment entirely free of phosphorus, although all the other conditions of their growth are supplied, they refuse to multiply, and soon die of inanition. The nerve tissues of the animal body, including the brain, contain also large quantities of phosphorus, and, as in the case of the bones, it is an essential constituent thereof. The brain contains about 0.75 per cent of phosphorus. Other tissues of the body contain less than this, as, for instance, the skin, which contains only 0.15 per cent, while, strange to say, those tissues whose functions are so nearly allied to those of the bones, namely, the tendons, contain the least phosphorus of any of the animal tissues. There are some plants, notably those of a leguminous nature, which have the property of oxidizing atmospheric nitrogen and thus furnishing the nitrogenous vital principle which is necessary to their growth, even if it be absent in the soil. Phosphorus, not existing in the gaseous form, must be supplied to plant growth in the soil itself. It therefore may be said to be the essential vital element on which all vegetable growth is conditioned. In nutrition the rôle of phosphorus is intimately associated with that of the proteids. By oxidation of the proteid matter in the system it is changed into other forms of nitrogenous matter. Its destruction, as evidenced by the formation of urea, and its incorporation in other tissues, as, for instance, the muscular tissues of the body, take place in intimate union with the phosphorus in the vital cells.

Physiological chemistry shows that the growing and active cells are those which use the larger quantities of phosphorus. It is known that the blood which leaves the more energetic organs of the body, such, for instance, as the liver, is more completely exhausted of its phosphorus than the blood which leaves the capillaries, where the cell activity is less vigorous. This fact shows that the maximum cell activity of the vital organs is associated with the largest consumption of phosphorus. It is quite certain, therefore, that every rational system of nutrition will pay special attention to the proper supply of phosphorus. Fortunately, as has before been intimated, nature has placed a more than abundant supply of phosphorus in the cereal grains; so that it is possible in the process of milling to remove a certain portion, perhaps the greater portion, of the phosphorus and still leave a sufficient quantity to supply abundantly the ordinary needs of the mature body. In the case of children, however, where the demand for phosphorus is relatively greater than with grown persons, great care should be exercised not to supply them with a food in which the content of phosphorus has been reduced to too low a degree. For this reason bread made of the whole cereal grain is doubtless to be preferred for the nutrition of children to the fine flour breads of commerce. In the proportion that bread is the chief constituent of food, just in that proportion should attention be paid to the content of phosphorus in the ash for the purpose of avoiding a depreciation of its nutritive qualities to an extent which would render it insufficient to the proper nourishment not only of the bones and the tissues of the body requiring phosphorus, but of the primordial cells whose functional activity would be diminished or destroyed by withholding a sufficient amount of phosphatic food.

EXCESS OF MINERAL MATTERS.

It is evident, however, that a large part of the mineral constituents of cereals is not required for the nourishment of the body. Feeding experiments have confirmed this theoretical view, and the ash of food materials has the lowest coefficient of digestion of any constituent thereof, with the possible exception of cellulose. It must not be inferred from this, however, that the presence of these bodies in cereals is purely adventitious. The fact that the bodies mentioned in the table are constantly found in cereal products is sufficient indication that they naturally belong there. Although they may not directly nourish the body and are, after ingestion with the food, voided largely as waste products, yet they evidently have a function which is of great importance. Their presence gives to the food a relish and flavor which it would not otherwise have, and hence makes it more appetizing and palatable. In other words, they doubtless serve to a limited extent the same purpose as ordinary condiments. If it were possible to extract from cereal foods all their mineral constituents without altering the nature of the other ingredients, it would doubtless be found that the pleasant flavor of the food would be greatly diminished. In grinding and reducing to merchantable flour a considerable portion, as a rule more than half, of the mineral ingredients is removed in the waste products of the meal. Enough is left, however, not only to supply the need of the body for mineral constituents, but also for the condimentary purposes mentioned above.

MINERAL HUNGER.

A further important function of the mineral ingredients of plants from the point of view of vegetable physiology is manifested in the fact that a certain bulk quantity of mineral matter is essential to the production of organic matter. In general this quantity is not less than 2 per cent of the entire weight of the plant. All kinds of mineral matter found in plants help to satisfy this mineral hunger.

Relation of soda and potash.—It has been claimed by some that soda and potash are complementary in the composition of vegetable materials. A study of the data of the analyses of the ash of cereals affords no reason for believing such a theory to be true. The content of potash in the ash of the cereals is reasonably constant, but the content of soda apparently depends on local conditions, arising doubtless from the different quantities of common salt and other sodium compounds present in the soil. There is no observed regularity in the relations existing between the soda and the potash in the ash of cereals. Sometimes a high content of soda is associated with a high content of potash, and vice versa. The great variation in the content of soda is revealed by an inspection of the table on page 1212. As has been previously stated, herbivorous animals require more soda than is normally contained in their food.

The ash of wheats.—In all cases in the preceding table the data given are calculated for the pure ash. By the term pure ash is meant in each case the crude ash as obtained on combustion free of carbon dioxid, carbon, and sand. In the ash of wheats we have quite a constant content of phosphoric acid. In the samples of the ash of Canadian wheat the content of phosphoric acid is nearly 47 per cent, while the mean of the analyses given by Wolff for spring wheat is nearly 47 per cent and for winter wheat a little over 48½ per cent. A remarkable variation in the composition of the ash of wheats is shown in the sample from Argentina, where the potash was remarkably low and the phosphoric acid remarkably high. An ash of such a composition as this would be remarkably acid in its properties. In respect to potash the data are also quite uniform, with the exception of the sample from Argentina, which apparently is abnormal in its ash constituents.

In lime are found considerable variations. Magnesia is present in the ash of wheat in about four times as great an amount as lime. Magnesia is not regarded as an essential fertilizing material, but it is in one sense a nutrient. Its presence in such constantly large quantities can not be regarded as a mere incident of environment. It is probable, therefore, that its value as a plant constituent has been underestimated, and that it acts in plant growth in much the same manner as lime itself.

The low content of sulphuric acid in the samples from Canada and Argentina doubtless arose from a loss of the sulphur during ignition.

The ash of rye.—The content of phosphoric acid in the ash of rye is somewhat less than in that of wheat. In no case does the content of phosphoric acid in the rye ashes analyzed in this division reach the mean given by Koenig. In respect of phosphoric acid it is seen that the ash in the samples from Minnesota and from Brazil is below Wolff's mean, while the ash from other parts of the United States shows a content of potash considerably greater than that mean. Lime in our analyses is higher than in wheat, and magnesia about the same.

The ash of barley.—On account of the barley being ground with the hulls a marked contrast in the constitution of the ash with that of wheat and rye is observed, namely, in the increase in the percentage of silica. This increase naturally would diminish the percentage of the other constituents, and both the phosphoric acid and the potash suffer a severe decline as compared with the two preceding classes. The lime and the magnesia are also less in quantity.

The ash of oats.—The oats examined were also ground with the hulls, and thus show a heavy percentage of silica in the ash, and a corresponding depression in the content of phosphoric acid, potash, and other mineral constituents, although in the case of lime the quantity is almost the same as that in the ashes of wheat and rye.

The ash of maize.—There are several important points to be considered in a study of the data pertaining to the maize ash. In the first place, it is seen that this ash is almost entirely free of silica. Of all the cereals maize ash has the least proportion of silica. The content of phosphoric acid and of potash is practically the same as that in wheat. The con-

PREPARATION OF CEREALS FOR FOOD.

tent of lime is less than that of wheat, and the content of magnesia greater. There is a greater disproportion between the content of lime and magnesia in the ash of maize than in that of any other of the cereals. The deficiency of silica in the ash of maize appears to be supplied by the magnesia and not by the lime.

The ash of rice.—The ash of rice is in sharp contrast with that of maize in respect of its content of silica. Even the polished rices have a very high content of silica, which gives rise to the suspicion that the polishing may be done with a quartz powder or some similar material which remains to some extent adherent to the rice grains. The content of phosphoric acid and potash in the ash of rice is not greatly different from that of other standard cereals.

The ash of buckwheat.—There is a marked discrepancy between the analytical data obtained in this division and those given by Wolff, especially in the content of silica and phosphoric acid. The two sets of data are not comparable. This may have arisen from differences in the analytical methods, or from actual difference in the constitution of the samples examined.

PREPARATION OF CEREALS FOR FOOD.

GRINDING OF CEREALS.

Before using the cereals for food they are, as a rule, reduced to a fine powder called flour or meal. In common language the term meal is usually applied to the coarser ground or unbolted mill products of cereals, while the term flour is reserved for the fine-ground, bolted products. The operation of grinding may vary from the simple process of crushing the material to a fine powder, forming a single product, to the elaborate processes of modern milling, in which a cereal, for example wheat, is separated into a large number of products of different physical properties and varying chemical composition. The simplest form of milling is that process by which the cereal as a whole is reduced to a fine powder.

THE MILLING OF WHEAT.

Until within 25 years wheat was ground chiefly between stones and the resulting product was passed through bolting cloths of different degrees of fineness, by which the ground material was separated into two or three grades, the outer covering of the cereal forming the bran and the interior portions being separated into flour, shorts, and middlings.

THE ROLLER PROCESS.

The introduction of the roller process of milling has permitted a more perfect separation of the different parts of the wheat and the practically entire separation of the bran and germ from the starchy products of the grain. The starchy portions, moreover, are separated into flours of different degrees of nutritive value and different properties for baking purposes. Of all the cereals wheat is the one which is subjected to the most elaborate processes of milling. In the case of Indian corn, rye, oats, buckwheat, and other cereals, the milling processes are not so elaborate and the kinds of materials produced much less numerous than in the case of wheat. In the high-grade modern milling of wheat the whole number of products which are formed from the time the wheat enters the mill until the finished products are offered for sale is from 80 to 100. Of course it is understood that these products are not all placed upon the market for sale, but they are products from which succeeding products are made. An interesting study of the modern milling process was made some years ago in this Division, under the supervision of Mr. Clifford Richardson, and the various products of roller milling of wheat were subjected to separate chemical examinations. Inasmuch as the bulletin containing this information is entirely out of print it is advisable to reproduce the data relating to the milling products. Preliminary to a description of the several products a general description of the process of roller milling is desirable.

STRUCTURE OF WHEAT GRAIN.

An examination of the structure of the grain will enable us to understand the difficulties to be met in the chemical examination and milling, and the way in which the different products which have been analyzed are obtained.

If a blade of wheat were much thickened and the two halves folded back upon themselves a transverse section of it would represent a similar section of the grain—that is to say, the two lobes would meet, forming what is known in the grain as the crease, within which would be inclosed and hidden a portion of the outer covering. This explains how difficult it is in preparing the wheat for milling to remove all the foreign matter which this crease contains. On the exterior of the grain there is found toward one end a collection of hairs, and at the other end appears the embryo, or germ. A longitudinal section shows both of these undesirable additions to the floury matter of the grain. Aside from its exterior appearance the wheat grain is essentially an embryo, composed of the germ, together with a supply of food, and the endosperm, or floury matter, surrounded by several membranes or coats of greater or less importance. On the exterior is the first membrane or cuticle, a very thin coating, easily removed by rubbing. Next follows a more important, because thicker, portion of the outer covering, consisting of two layers of cellular tissue, the epicarp and endocarp. These three membranes together form the outer covering of the grain, and from one of them, the epicarp, spring the hairs which are found on one end. These envelopes are colorless and very light, constituting only from 3 to $3\frac{1}{2}$ per cent of the whole, and are more or less easily removed by friction. From an examination of a section of the grain it is seen that within the crease this removal is of course impossible; so that while the preparation of the wheat for milling may remove the hairs and much of the cuticle and dirt it can not completely free it from them. It is this inherent difficulty that the roller mills attempt to overcome by splitting the grain along the crease and afterwards cleaning it with brushes.

Under these outer coverings are three membranes, known as the testa or episperm, the tegmen, and the embryous envelope. The testa is a compact structure, and carries the coloring matter of the bran. The tegmen is an extremely thin membrane not easily seen except where it becomes thickened just under the testa in the heart of the crease. It is not of importance from a milling point of view. The testa and tegmen form about 2 per cent of the grain.

The embryous membrane is a continuation of the embryo around the endosperm or floury portion of the grain. It is composed of cells which are often erroneously termed gluten cells, but the true gluten cells are scattered through the endosperm. The cells of the embryous membrane contain little or no gluten, and as they are a continuation of the embryo it must be nearly as undesirable to allow them in the finished flour as to allow the germ itself.

The endosperm is by far the largest portion of the grain, and it is that part which it is the object of all milling processes to separate from the rest of the wheat and grind to flour.

It consists of large cells containing the granules of starch and the gluten. At the exterior, nearer the embryous membrane, it is much harder than in the center and contains much more gluten. In all methods of gradual reduction, therefore, the center is of course reduced first, and, being very starchy, is only fit for a low-grade flour, while the richest part of the endosperm, being harder and closely attached to the tough bran coats, is to a certain extent lost, or so mixed with small pieces of the bran as to injure the color of the flour, furnishing what is known as bakers' grades.

CHANGE IN MILLING PROCESSES.

By the old-fashioned low-milling process, or grinding between stones placed very close together and afterwards bolting the product, it was impossible to obtain a flour entirely free from deterioration. The advance to high milling with stones far apart, allowing the middlings which were produced to be purified before grinding to flour, was a step which made it possible to make from winter wheat an excellent and pure flour. When, however, spring wheat with its hard and brittle outer coats became important commercially, it was necessary to resort to the roller methods of milling, which, in conjunction with peculiar purifying machinery, furnishes a flour free from all undesirable impurities.

DESCRIPTION OF THE DIFFERENT MILL PRODUCTS OF WHEAT.

1. *Wheat as it enters the mill.*—The whole wheat grain mixed with cockle, oats, and other foreign seed, as it comes from the thrasher.

2. *Wheat prepared for the rolls.*—The foreign seeds have been removed, with the exception of a few grains of cockle and oats. The cockle is therefore to be found in subsequent parts of the process. The hairs have been largely rubbed off, together with portions of the cuticle. Some hairs are, however, still left, and portions of the cuticle remain attached and semidetached, especially toward the crease. The grain as a whole presents a changed and much cleaner appearance.

3. *Cockle and screenings.*—Among the impurities there are found principally cockle, a species of polygonum, and oats, together with broken pieces of wheat, dirt, chaff, etc.

4. *Scourings removed by cleaners.*—These consist almost entirely of cuticle and hairs, but portions of epicarp with the hairs still adherent and of endocarp are present. Treatment with iodine reveals a small amount of endosperm or starch, and shows that the inner part of the outer coats of the grain are the most highly nitrogenous. The contrast between the embryous membrane and endocarp and the epicarp and cuticle is prominent. The embryous membrane is recognized by its roundish cells; the endocarp by its transverse cells, twice as long as broad and packed closely and regularly, like cigars, which has given it the name of cigar coat; and the epicarp by its very long and irregular cells arranged longitudinally, the cuticle being of a similar sort.

5. *First break.*—The grain is split along the crease normally into two halves, but also frequently into fours, or even more irregularly. The glistening, hard, floury endosperm makes its appearance for the first time. Comparatively little flour or dust is made.

6. *Chop from first break.*—This consists principally of endosperm, but small portions of bran and germ are present, the former including the various outer coats.

7. *Second break.*—In this break the greater part of the endosperm is separated from the bran and is seen as large, well-shaped middlings, together, of course, with some small stuff and dust.

8. *Chop from second break.*—This is chiefly endosperm, with somewhat less bran than the previous chop. Whole chops and parts are numerous. The endosperm is of all sizes, but the greater portion is of large angular fragments. The bran includes portions of all the outer coverings, while dusty matter and starch grains are quite abundant.

9. *Third break.*—The endosperm is so completely separated in this break that it only remains in scattered patches upon the bran, and the embryous membrane is quite visible.

10. *Chop from third break.*—The middlings or particles of endosperm are much finer, and there is more dust. Small portions of germ are plentiful. The branny particles are similar in nature to those in the chop from second break, but smaller, and there is more dust of a nitrogenous kind.

11. *Fourth break.*—Only to be distinguished from No. 9 by the slightly cleaner bran.

12. *Chop from fourth break.*—Not very different in appearance from 10, except that it is composed of more finely divided particles.

13. *Fifth break.*—Still cleaner bran than 11. It still holds a very appreciable portion of endosperm.

14. *Chop from fifth break.*—This chop contains a great deal of branny matter, including pieces of epicarp, endocarp, and embryous membrane. The endosperm is very fine and much mixed with germ. Of course in all these products portions of the testa and tegmen are present, but they are not easily seen except in careful preparations.

15. *Sixth break.*—Barely distinguishable from bran.

16. *Chop from sixth break.*—Very largely made up of small pieces of branny material and germs. The endosperm which is present is very fine.

17. *Bran.*—This is composed practically of epicarp, endocarp, and embryous membrane, the cells of the latter having been very little disturbed. There is still a little cuticle and endosperm left, but they have mostly disappeared in previous operations.

18. *Shorts.*—These are made up of all the different parts of the grain in rather a finely ground condition, some of the branny particles having endosperm still adherent to them.

19. *Middlings, uncleaned, No. 1.*—These are the largest sized middlings, and consist of themselves in clean, angular fragments of endosperm, but they are mixed with considerable shorts and many whole and broken germs. They are the most impure of the five, and an analysis will show this fact.

20. *Middlings, uncleaned, No. 2.*—All the particles are finer than in the previous middlings and less germ and bran is present, which will produce a corresponding change in their chemical composition.

21. *Middlings, uncleaned, No. 3.*—Still finer than No. 2 and less bran and germ.

22. *Middlings, uncleaned, No. 4.*—Finer than No. 3 and less bran and germ.

23. *Middlings, uncleaned, No. 5.*—The finest of all the middlings, with almost no bran and germ. The effect of cleaning will be small.

24. *Middlings, cleaned, No. 1.*—Many of the lighter particles of bran removed, but there is much remaining, as well as of the germ.

25. *Middlings, cleaned, No. 2.*—The bran is to a large degree removed in cleaning these middlings, but the germ, of course, remains.

26. *Middlings, cleaned, No. 3.*—The bran is almost all gone.

27. *Middlings, cleaned, No. 4.*—These middlings are practically quite clean and pure endosperm—only here and there a particle of bran or germ.

28. *Middlings, cleaned, No. 5.*—Quite clean and very small in size.

29. *First middlings, reduction on smooth rolls.*—The germ is flattened and the endosperm reduced in size.

30. *Chop from first reduction of middlings.*—This sample appears to be misplaced, as it contains much bran and germ.

31. *Second middlings, reduction on smooth rolls.*—A sample of this reduction was not furnished.

32. *Chop from second reduction of middlings.*—This chop contains a few particles of bran and germ.

33. *Third middlings, reduction on smooth rolls.*—The germ is prominent in its flattened condition.

34. *Chop from third reduction of middlings.*—The bran and germ have been almost entirely removed.

35. *Fourth middlings, reduction on smooth rolls.*—Like the middlings themselves, merely reduced in size.

36. *Chop from fourth reduction of middlings.*—Here and there a small particle of bran is seen.

37. *Fifth middlings, reduction on smooth rolls.*—Resembles, of course, the middlings cleaned, No. 5.

38. *Chop from fifth reduction of middlings.*—This is not as white as the chop from the fourth reduction, as it contains bran and germ in small quantities.

39. *Flour from the first reduction.*—The grains of endosperm are clean and sharp.

40. *Flour from the second reduction.*—The grains are not as sharp as those from the first reduction.

41. *Flour from the third reduction.*—Very much like the flour from the second reduction, but perhaps a little lumpier.

42. *Flour from the fourth reduction.*—More coherent and yellower than previous flours.

43. *Flour from the fifth reduction.*—There is no specimen of this flour.

44. *Tailings from middlings, purifier No. 1.*—These tailings are coarse. They contain much bran, mixed with germ, and a considerable amount of large middlings.

45. *Tailings from middlings, purifier Nos. 2, 3, and 4.*—Much finer than the previous tailings and freer from germ and endosperm.

46. *Tailings from middlings, purifier No. 6.*—Largely composed of fine endosperm, mixed with bran and germ.

47. *Tailings from the first reduction.*—These are made up of about equal parts of fine endosperm, and of bran and germ.

48. *Tailings from the second reduction.*—These are finer than the first tailings, and contain more germ. There are also present pieces of endosperm, flattened like the germ.

49. *Tailings from third reduction.*—Still finer, with much flattened endosperm, and less grain and bran.

50. *Tailings from fourth reduction.*—Very finely divided and flattened endosperm, with only about 10 per cent of bran and germ. This should be very evident in the analysis.

51. *Tailings from fifth reduction.*—Coarser than the fourth tailings, and like the third in quality.

52. *Repurified middlings.*—Coarse pieces of endosperm, with much bran and germ.

56. *Bakers' flour.*—Slightly yellow in color. The grains lack distinctness, making the flour lumpy.

57. *Patent flour.*—A clear white grain.

58. *Low-grade flour.*—The grain is soft and the flour dark and lumpy. Particles of bran and germ are prominent.

59. *Break flour.*—Physically like the bakers' grade in appearance, but particles of bran and germ are present, making it of less value.

60. *Stone flour.*—This flour is white, of a fair grain, with a very little bran.

62. *Flour from first tailings.*—A very good, free grain, but a little branny.

63. *Flour from third tailings.*—A free grain, but quite branny and yellow.

64. *Flour from second tailings.*—This flour resembles that from the first tailings, but contains more bran and is yellower.

70. *First germ.*—This is made up of the finest particles of germ and contains the largest proportion of middlings and bran.

71. *Second germ.*—The largest particles of germ, with little bran and endosperm.

72. *Third germ.*—A medium between the two former.

74. *Bran-duster flour.*—This is black in color, and lumpy. It has little grain and a small portion of bran.

77. *Stone stock No. 2.*—A good middling, with a little bran and germ.

78. *Stone stock No. 3.*—This is not as good as No. 2, and holds more bran and germ.

83. *Tailings from sixth break.*—This is made up of about half barley-shaped and flattened pieces of endosperm, the rest being bran, with a little germ.

84. *Tailings from first centrifugal reel.*—Largely flattened endosperm; the rest germ, with a little bran.

85. *Tailings from second centrifugal reel.*—These are largely bran and flattened endosperm with a little germ.

86. *Tail end of the tailings.*—As would be expected, almost entirely bran, with a little adherent endosperm and a small amount of germ. The embryons membrane is still in place; in fact, during the whole process there is very little of it removed from the bran, and were it the chief source of gluten there would be very little in any of the products. This, however, is not the case. It contains little or no gluten, being merely a continuation of the germ and having a similar composition.

87. *Dust from No. 1 middlings.*—This is mostly cuticle, epicarp, and hairs, with smaller amounts of the more interior parts of the grain.

88. *Dust from the dust-catcher.*—This is all light, fluffy matter, and is made up of small particles from all parts of the grain.

Analyses of the products of roller milling.

	Name.	Moisture.	Ash.	Ether extract.	Carbohydrates.	Fiber.	Protoids. N×6.25.	Nitrogen.	Phosphoric acid.	Ratio of nitrogen to phosphoric acid.	Gluten.	
											Moist.	Dry.
		P. ct.	P. ct.	P. ct.	P. ct.	P. ct.	P. ct.	P. ct.	P. ct.	P. ct.	P. ct.	P. ct.
1	Wheat as it enters the mill..........	9.66	1.91	2.61	69.94	1.70	14.18	2.27	0.82	2.77	Not deter.	
2	Wheat prepared for the rolls....	9.07	1.79	2.74	70.37	1.68	14.35	2.30	0.82	2.80	32.31	11.88
3	Cockle and screenings	9.03	2.65	4.32	66.12	4.23	13.65	2.18	0.78	2.80	Not deter.	
4	Scourings removed by cleaners	9.27	3.68	3.73	70.19	1.58	11.55	1.85	0.76	2.43	Not deter.	
5	First break	8.23	1.73	2.68	71.56	1.62	14.18	2.27	0.91	2.49	31.92	11.69
6	Chop from first break...........	12.52	0.88	2.08	70.44	1.13	12.95	2.07	0.46	4.50	34.10	12.27
7	Second break	8.37	2.04	2.47	71.47	1.65	14.00	2.24	0.98	2.20	32.78	11.80
8	Chop from second break...........	12.78	0.57	1.68	71.82	0.55	12.60	2.04	0.34	5.94	36.88	12.56
9	Third break	9.92	2.55	5.25	65.10	2.13	15.05	2.41	1.33	1.81	32.09	12.04
10	Chop from third break...........	12.70	0.78	1.86	71.10	0.78	12.78	2.04	0.42	4.86	37.19	13.00
11	Fourth break.....	8.18	3.30	4.09	66.20	3.00	15.23	2.44	1.44	1.07	27.88	10.54
12	Chop from fourth break...........	12.35	1.47	2.87	67.90	1.23	14.18	2.27	0.75	5.05	30.52	11.64
13	Fifth break.......	7.62	5.16	4.91	61.76	4.80	15.75	2.52	2.53	0.98	Not deter.	
14	Chop from fifth break...........	11.91	1.90	4.16	64.46	1.73	15.75	2.52	1.01	2.49	27.97	11.82
15	Sixth break.......	7.66	5.68	5.34	59.42	5.60	16.28	2.60	2.95	0.81	Not deter.	
16	Chop from sixth break...........	11.84	3.29	4.92	59.09	3.18	17.68	2.83	1.66	1.70	24.04	10.69
17	Bran.............	10.91	5.50	5.03	56.21	5.98	16.28	2.60	2.78	0.94	Not deter.	
18	Shorts	10.94	3.41	4.67	60.28	3.90	16.80	2.69	1.62	1.66	Not deter.	
	Middlings uncleaned:											
19	No. 1..........	12.71	1.27	2.73	68.78	1.03	13.48	2.16	0.64	3.39	29.68	10.57
20	No. 2..........	12.18	1.04	2.16	70.49	0.83	13.30	2.13	0.54	3.94	32.99	11.49
21	No. 3..........	12.27	0.70	1.80	71.52	0.58	13.13	2.10	0.36	5.83	35.52	12.21
22	No. 4..........	12.47	0.68	1.75	70.69	0.58	13.83	2.21	0.40	5.52	45.62	15.60
23	No. 5..........	12.34	0.61	1.75	70.24	0.53	14.53	2.32	0.33	7.03	43.82	14.86
	Middlings cleaned:											
24	No. 1..........	12.67	1.07	2.12	70.16	0.85	13.13	2.10	0.59	3.56	34.00	11.16
25	No. 2..........	9.93	0.65	1.90	74.09	0.65	12.78	2.04	0.33	6.18	Not deter.	
26	No. 3..........	12.36	0.59	1.70	71.67	0.55	13.13	2.10	0.24	8.75	44.43	14.99
27	No. 4..........	12.51	0.52	1.77	71.57	0.33	13.30	2.13	0.29	7.34	51.93	17.85
28	No. 5..........	12.35	0.51	1.62	70.74	0.43	14.35	2.30	0.23	10.00	46.15	14.87
	Middlings, reduction on smooth rolls:											
29	First middling	12.64	0.82	2.50	70.80	0.58	12.60	2.02	0.46	4.39	31.20	11.57
30	Chop from first middling	12.74	0.72	1.99	71.72	0.58	12.25	1.96	0.40	4.90	32.10	10.91
32	Chop from second middling	12.48	0.57	1.68	71.24	0.38	13.65	2.18	0.34	6.41	41.36	13.65

¹Second middling not sent.

THE MILL PRODUCTS OF WHEAT. 1227

Analyses of the products of roller milling—Continued.

	Name.	Moisture.	Ash.	Ether extract.	Carbohydrates.	Fiber.	Proteids. N×6.25.	Nitrogen.	Phosphoric acid.	Ratio of nitrogen to phosphoric acid.	Gluten. Moist.	Gluten. Dry.
	Middlings, reduction on smooth rolls—Cont'd.	P. ct.	P. ct.	P. ct.	P. ct.	P. ct.	P. ct.	P. ct.	P. ct.	P. ct.	P. ct.	P. ct.
33	Third middling	12.29	0.61	1.86	71.91	0.55	12.78	2.04	0.34	6.00	36.70	11.81
34	Chop from third middling	12.73	0.79	2.01	71.29	0.58	12.60	2.02	0.43	4.70	34.58	11.68
35	Fourth middling	11.43	0.56	1.86	73.12	0.43	12.60	2.02	0.34	5.94	37.00	12.23
36	Chop from fourth middling	11.72	0.50	1.76	72.56	0.33	13.13	2.10	0.27	7.78	42.06	12.32
37	Fifth middling	12.21	0.65	2.08	71.85	0.43	12.78	2.04	0.40	5.10	36.25	11.97
38	Chop from fifth middling	11.47	0.50	2.03	72.66	0.50	12.78	2.04	0.37	5.57	40.84	13.11
	Flour from reduction of middlings:											
39	No. 1	12.03	0.39	1.58	73.70	0.25	12.05	1.93	0.24	8.04	31.51	10.97
40	No. 2	12.42	0.44	1.60	72.55	0.33	12.60	2.02	0.24	8.42	37.04	12.07
41	No. 3	11.54	0.38	1.36	75.24	0.28	11.20	1.79	0.19	9.42	32.54	10.99
42	No. 4	11.58	0.46	1.42	72.92	0.38	13.30	2.13	0.20	10.65	37.90	12.52
	Tailings from middlings purifiers:											
44	No. 1	12.33	3.30	4.96	60.06	3.25	16.10	2.55	1.61	1.60	Not deter.	
45	Nos. 2, 3, and 4	11.59	3.00	3.92	Not deter.		14.53	2.32	1.39	1.67	12.28	7.62
46	No. 6	12.00	0.90	2.37	60.10	1.10	14.53	2.32	0.40	4.73	39.88	14.37
	Tailings from reduction:											
47	No. 1	11.78	3.26	5.03	60.32	2.63	16.98	2.72	1.82	1.47	13.04	5.47
48	No. 2	10.35	3.38	4.37	59.87	2.08	19.95	3.19	1.68	1.90	Not deter.	
49	No. 3	11.72	2.35	4.37	63.27	1.66	16.63	2.66	1.34	1.98	Not deter.	
50	No. 4	12.09	0.88	4.16	68.47	0.40	14.00	2.24	0.48	4.67	35.73	13.34
51	No. 5	12.12	2.29	3.85	63.93	1.18	16.63	2.66	1.35	1.97	1.89	0.67
52	Repurified middlings	11.72	2.11	3.67	65.99	1.63	14.88	2.38	1.21	1.98	28.17	10.74
	Finished flour:											
56	Bakers'	12.18	0.62	2.00	69.99	0.33	14.88	2.38	0.31	7.68	51.21	16.97
57	Patent	11.48	0.39	1.45	73.55	0.18	12.95	2.07	0.18	11.50	36.14	10.85
58	Low grade	12.01	1.99	3.86	63.26	0.93	17.95	2.74	1.16	2.36	10.01	4.26
59	Break flour	12.48	0.58	1.87	69.44	0.23	15.40	2.46	0.31	7.94	51.38	15.87
60	Stone flour	12.04	0.49	1.61	72.85	0.23	12.78	2.04	0.27	7.55	38.21	11.74
	Flour from tailings:											
62	No. 1	12.55	0.62	2.93	70.25	0.35	13.30	2.13	0.30	7.10	39.13	12.85
63	No. 3	12.50	0.85	2.79	70.20	0.53	13.13	2.10	0.45	4.67	37.78	12.68
64	No. 2	11.20	0.76	2.63	72.28	0.48	13.65	2.18	0.39	5.59	43.25	13.87
68	Cockle chop	12.45	2.79	4.34	64.01	3.63	12.78	2.04	0.06	2.37	Not deter.	

[1] Flour from fifth middling not sent.

1228   FOODS AND FOOD ADULTERANTS.

Analyses of the products of roller milling—Continued.

	Name.	Mois-ture.	Ash.	Ether ex-tract.	Carbo-hy-drates.	Fiber.	Pro-teids. N×1.25.	Nitro-gen.	Phos-phoric acid.	Ratio of nitro-gen to phos-phoric acid.	Gluten.	
											Moist.	Dry.
		P. ct.	P. ct.	P. ct.	P. ct.	P. ct.	P. ct.	P. ct.	P. ct.	P. ct.	P. ct.	P. ct.
69	Cockle bran	7.71	3.46	3.84	65.46	9.03	10.50	1.68	0.83	2.02	Not deter.	
70	First germ	8.69	3.42	9.35	53.28	1.23	24.13	3.86	1.83	2.11	Not deter.	
71	Second germ	8.75	5.45	15.61	35.19	1.75	33.25	5.32	2.57	1.98	Not deter.	
72	Third germ	7.68	4.94	13.75	39.25	1.50	32.88	5.26	2.56	2.05	Not deter.	
74	Bran duster flour	11.78	1.17	2.70	70.20	0.50	13.65	2.18	0.66	3.30	58.59	13.72
	Stone stock:											
77	No. 2	12.15	0.40	1.64	72.91	0.25	13.65	2.18	0.19	11.58	47.55	15.32
78	No. 3	12.01	0.55	2.12	71.76	0.43	13.13	2.10	0.28	7.50	46.39	15.15
	Tailings:											
83	From sixth break	11.64	2.29	4.06	64.31	1.95	15.75	2.52	1.23	2.05	16.45	6.17
84	From first cen-trifugal reel	11.42	2.15	3.44	66.56	1.20	15.23	2.44	0.98	2.49	6.58	2.39
85	From second centrifugal reel	11.07	2.85	4.73	61.82	2.20	17.33	2.79	1.47	1.88	Not deter.	
86	Tail end of the tailings	11.36	3.87	5.23	Not deter.		15.75	2.52	1.75	1.44	10.74	4.41
87	Dust from No. 1 middlings	11.03	1.83	2.73	64.86	5.20	14.35	2.30	0.55	4.18	25.78	10.31
88	Dust from dust catcher	11.53	1.17	2.64	69.01	1.65	14.00	2.24	0.55	4.07	35.05	13.00

NOTES ON THE ANALYSES.

The foregoing analyses of the various products of roller milling afford data for a careful study of the changes which take place at different stages of manufacture. These changes have been discussed by Mr. Richardson in Bulletin No. 4 of this division, and his notes thereon follow:

The wheat as it enters the mill is subjected to a series of operations which removes dirt, foreign seed, the fuzz at the end of the berry, and a certain portion of the outer coats, through the agency of a run of stones and brushes. The result of this operation is to lower the amount of inorganic matter or ash and to increase or decrease the other constituents but slightly, the proteids being a few tenths of a per cent greater in amount. The point from which a convenient start may be made is at the first break.

The chop from the first rolls is very marked in its difference in composition from the original wheat. It of course has less fiber, and also, it is seen, less ash, oil, and albuminoids; in fact, it is starchy. It contains more moisture, owing to the fact that its comminution has allowed it to absorb the moisture from the air, and in general it will be observed that the coarser or more fibrous a specimen is the less water it contains, while the finer material holds more. For example, the percentages of moisture in several portions of the grain are as follows:

	Per cent.
Original grain	9.66
Ready for the break	8.23
Chop from first break	15.52
Fifth break	7.62
Bran	10.91

The heat caused by the friction of the process, of course, is an active agent, as may be seen on comparing the original grain and that ready for the break. The question of the relation of the various products to humidity is, however, considered in greater detail in another portion of this bulletin.

The starchy chop from the first break is carried off to the various purifying and grading machines, but for the present it will be left, as it is desirable to follow the breaks to the end.

The tailings from the first scalper, consisting of the wheat grain split open along the crease, which serve to feed the second break after the cleaning which they undergo, vary but little from the wheat which goes to the first break. There are slight differences which must be attributed to the difficulty of selecting and preparing for analyses samples of the product of the different breaks, the finer chop having a tendency to sift out from the lighter bran, but they are not great enough to vitiate the conclusions. In the first break so little is done, except to crack open the wheat and clean it for the following rolls, that only a small change should be expected.

The chop from the second break is more from the center of the wheat grain. It contains less ash, fat, and proteids than any of the break products, and includes, as was shown by our preliminary investigation, the greater portion of the endosperm.

The tailings supplying the third break already show, owing to the greater amount of chop produced on the second break, a marked increase in those constituents which are peculiar to the outer portions of the grain; that is to say, there has been a marked increase in ash, fiber, and proteids. This increase becomes still more apparent from break to break until the bran alone is left, which contains more ash and fiber than any other product of the wheat. The several chops increase in a like manner, the last or sixth break chop holding more proteids than the bran, and even any other of the resulting material. This is probably due to the comminution of the bran in the last break; and consequently, as will be seen, the middlings from this chop are richer in nitrogen than any other, although not the richest in gluten, owing to the proportion of bran and germ which they contain.

Having followed the grain through the breaks to the bran, the products of the purification of the chop remain to be studied.

The shorts, or branny particles removed from the chop or from the middlings by aspirators, contains much less fiber and ash than the bran, although it is of similar origin; that is to say, derived from the outer coats of the grain. The analyses point to an origin from those portions of the coat which contain less ash and fiber.

The middlings are graded into five classes, and in their original uncleaned state they differ chemically in the fact that from No. 1 to No. 5 there is a regular decrease in ash, fiber, and fat, while No. 5 is richer in proteids than the other. This would be expected from our preliminary examination, which showed a decrease in bran from beginning to end, and from the fact that No. 5 was the purest endosperm.

After cleaning the same relations hold good, but owing to the removal of the branny particles there is in all cases a loss of ash constituents and fiber. The effect of cleaning is more apparent in Nos. 1 and 2, where more bran is removed.

The reduction of the middlings on smooth rolls changes the composition but slightly, and the flours which originate from this process are very similar to the middlings from which they are produced. That from the fourth reduction is richer in nitrogen, as would, doubtless, also be the case with the fifth, although no analysis was made.

The tailings from the middlings purifiers present the usual characteristics of by-products, which owe their existence to the outer part of the grain with its high percentages of ash and fiber, and in this case also of nitrogen. It is remarkable, however, that the tailings marked No. 6 contain only one-third as much ash as the others, but this is explained by the fact that they are largely composed of endosperm.

The tailings from the different reductions are nearly alike in composition, with two exceptions: Those from the fourth contain little ash, fiber, and nitrogen. Like No. 6 of the purifier tailings, they consist largely of endosperm. Those from the second reduction contain much germ, and are therefore richer in nitrogen than the rest.

The repurified middlings, as might be expected, contain much more ash, oil, and fiber than the original, and there is also an increase in nitrogen, but not in gluten, owing to the large amount of bran they contain.

Analyses of the three grades of flour as furnished to the market follow. From a cursory glance it might be said that the low-grade flour was the best, as it contains the most proteids, but its weakness is discovered in the fact that it has only 4 per cent of gluten. The bakers' flour contains more ash, oil, fiber, proteids, and gluten than the patent, but owing to the increased amount of the first three constituents mentioned, it is proportionately lacking in whiteness and lightness. The two flours have each their advantageous points.

Several other grades of flour—break flour, stone flour, and flours from the first, second, and third tailings—are all very similar, and, as far as chemical analysis is concerned, good. The preliminary examination has, however, shown certain defects in each. The break flour is richer in proteids and gluten than any other, and if it were pure and its physical condition were good it would be of value.

The roller process is distinguished for the completeness with which it removes the germ of the grain during the manufacture of flour by flattening and sifting it out. This furnishes the three by-products, which are known as first, second, and third germ. They consist of the germ of the wheat mixed with varying proportions of branny and starchy matter, the second being the purest. They all contain much ash, oil, and nitrogen, and if allowed to be ground with the flour blacken it by the presence of the oil, and render it very liable to fermentation, owing to the peculiar nitrogenous bodies which it carries. A more complete analysis appears in another place.

The flour from the bran dusters is much like that from the tailings, and like the stone stocks from a chemical point of view. This merely shows that chemical evidence should not alone be taken into consideration, for the bran-duster flour is a dirty, lumpy by-product, while the stone stocks are valuable middlings. Analyses of various tailings are next in the series, and need no comment. Those of the dust from middlings and dust-catchers are rather surprising, in that they both contain much gluten and the first one much fiber, but this is due to their containing both bran and endosperm.

To follow the gluten through the process it is necessary to go back to the breaks. The amount in the various chops does not vary greatly. There is an apparent anomaly, however, in the fifth and sixth breaks, where no gluten was found in the feed but much in the chop. This is owing to the fact that the feed has become at this point in the process so branny that by the usual method of washing to obtain the gluten it does not allow of its uniting in a coherent mass and separating from the bran.

Among the middlings, both uncleaned and cleaned, the fourth is the richest in gluten, and the result of the process of cleaning is to increase the amount, although slightly diminishing the nitrogen. This is due to the removal of the branny matter, which, though rich in nitrogen, is poor in gluten.

In the products of the reduction on smooth rolls, the chops from the higher middlings are the richest, and if the analyses of the flours were complete, No. 4 would probably contain more than the lower numbers.

The tailings are, as has been already said, remarkable, not so much because No. 1 has no gluten, but in the fact that Nos. 2, 3, and 4 have 7.62 per cent, and No. 6 as much as 14.37 per cent thereof. The regular increase shows that the highest numbers must contain a large portion of endosperm.

That this is the case the microscopic examination of the different tailings has shown. No. 1 is found to consist almost entirely of the outer coatings of the grain; Nos. 2, 3, and 4 of the same mixed with a large proportion of endosperm, which is attached thereto; while in No. 6 it is difficult to discover any large amount of anything but flouring material, and the small percentage of ash shows, also, that it can not contain much bran.

In a like manner No. 4 tailings from the reductions has 13.34 per cent of gluten, which is owing to the large proportion of endosperm which it contains; and in this case, too, the fact of the presence of so much of the interior of the berry is presaged by the low percentage of ash. The remaining tailings of this class have little or no gluten, with the exception of No. 1, as they contain very little endosperm.

KINDS AND QUANTITIES OF FINAL PRODUCTS OF THE MILL.

In the foregoing table the character and composition of the products formed during the process of milling have been fully described and their purposes ascertained. The final products in the milling of wheat which reach the consumer are found as several grades of flour, and the refuse is sold chiefly for cattle-feeding purposes under the terms bran, shorts, or middlings. All of the high grade mills produce several varieties of flour from the same sample of wheat. These varieties of flour are sold under a great many different names, as will be seen in the table of analyses given further on. The highest grade of flour produced is very commonly known as Patent flour, while the lower grades are very often known as Family, Bakers', or Red Dog flours. In general it may be said that 270 pounds of wheat are required to make 200 pounds of flour. In other words about 4½ bushels per barrel. Unfortunately for our methods of computation, flour is usually sold by the barrel instead of by the 100 pounds. The barrel of flour in this country weighs 196 pounds. With a good quality of spring wheat a large milling firm in the Northwest obtains the yield given below, showing that a barrel of flour can be made from 258.35 pounds of wheat:

Materials in barrel of flour.

Product.	Pounds.	Percentage.
Patent flour	149.37	57.82
Bakers' flour	29.13	11.28
Low-grade flour	17.50	6.77
Total flour	196.00	75.87
Bran	45.56	17.64
Shorts	9.80	3.79
Screenings	4.99	1.93
Waste	2.00	0.77
Total weight of wheat	258.35	100.00

From one of the largest mills in Minnesota I have received the following statement in regard to the quantities of product formed: When an exceptionally high grade of flour is formed, the quantity produced is usually from 12 to 20 per cent of the total weight of the wheat. Of the medium or straight flours, which form the greatest part of the product, the quantity is about 50 per cent. Very low grade flours form from 2 to 10 per cent. In general about 75 per cent of the weight of the wheat is obtained as merchantable flour of some kind, of which from 60 to 70 per cent is high grade or straight flour. About 24 per cent of the weight of the wheat is obtained as feeding stuffs, and about 1 per cent of the weight disappears as waste during the process of manufacture. The miller above referred to states that in producing a certain grade of straight flour he has obtained as high as 72.2 per cent of straight flour and 8 per cent of low grade.

These figures, obtained from a Minnesota miller, are very similar to those which have been obtained in Arkansas, as reported by Teller in a bulletin of the Arkansas Agricultural Experiment Station. Two checked runs were made in a high-grade roller mill; in the one case with 7,000, and the other 3,000 pounds of uncleaned wheat, and the results obtained are shown in the following tables:

Wheat milling trial No. 1, made January 2, 1894.

[Weight uncleaned wheat, 7,000 pounds.]

Product.	Pounds.	Percentage.
Patent flour	848	12.11
Straight flour	3,964	56.63
Low-grade flour	250	3.57
Bran	1,636	23.37
Tail of mill (ship stuff)	174	2.49
Total	6,872	98.17
Screenings	78	1.11
Loss (dust, etc.)	50	.72
Final total	7,000	100.00

Wheat milling trial No. 2, made March 15, 1894.

[Weight uncleaned wheat, 3,000 pounds.]

Product.	Pounds.	Percentage.
Patent flour	529.5	17.65
Straight flour	1,510.5	50.35
Low-grade flour	69.5	2.32
Shorts	33.0	1.10
Dust room contents	24.5	0.82
Bran	723.0	24.10
Screenings	81.0	2.70
Sample cleaned wheat	1.5	0.05
Loss	27.5	0.91
Total	3,000	100.00

COMPOSITION OF FLOUR OBTAINED IN THE FRENCH MILLS.

In 1894 a commission was appointed by the minister of commerce of France to study the processes of milling in the French Republic. Prof.

Aimé Girard was the president of this commission, and interesting data are contained in its report.[1]

The principal object of the commission was to determine what percentage of fine flour could be obtained suited to making first-class bread. In addition to this a careful chemical study was made of the different grades of flour which were produced. Several large mills were placed at the disposal of the committee, where wheat of different qualities in large quantities was ground and every process of the milling carefully watched. The different grades of flour produced were sent to the bakery, where the commission supervised the baking of the bread. The conclusion of the committee was that the point of limitation in regard to the quantity of flour made from average wheat which would produce a white bread, porous, well leavened, and easily digestible, and suited to the demands of modern cookery, varies from 60 to 65 per cent of the weight of the wheat used. Beyond that point it is possible to obtain another 5 per cent of flour, which will make a fairly good bread, but showing a change in color and not having the digestible and palatable qualities of the bread as made from the first 60 per cent extraction.

The results obtained by the French commission are practically in accord with the data collected from our own millers. A good average wheat under the best conditions will yield about 60 per cent of high-grade flour, about 8 per cent of a good inferior article, and a small quantity of a very low grade, unsuited to making light-colored and porous loaves.

GRADES OF FLOUR.

The different grades of flour are based more upon their color and general appearance than upon their nutritive properties. It often happens that low-grade flours—that is, those which make a rather off-colored bread—are more nutritious than the highest grade and whitest flours, which make the whitest bread when judged by chemical data alone. A great many people prefer a delicate cream tint to the flour and bread rather than a product which is pure white. One of the largest milling firms in Minnesota writes me that the highest grade flour which it makes is used for the family trade, being what is called a patent spring wheat flour, used largely in the Northwest, and corresponding to the winter wheat patent flour used in the Southern States. The next grade produced is called high grade bakers' flour, used extensively by bakers in this country, and also exported in large quantities to Great Britain and Holland. The lowest grade of flour produced is known as Red Dog flour, which is used largely for feeding domestic animals.

Another miller writes as follows:

We are sending you 1½ pounds each of our Patent, Family, and Bakers' flour. Each of these flours is what is commonly known as a blended flour. They are the result of careful consideration and experiments by us, for the purpose of producing

---

[1] Comptes rendus, vol. 121, p. 922.

a Patent and a Family flour that will combine the strength and the quality of retaining moisture of spring wheat flour and the sweetness and tenderness of the winter wheat.

The flour is manufactured from choice, selected hard spring wheat and from several kinds of winter wheat of the finest quality obtainable from various sections of the country, and is combined in such proportions as to produce a flour which will fulfill, we believe, the requirements that we are seeking after.

The patent produces a bread that raises well, retains moisture, and is at the same time tender and sweet and eminently fitted for a family flour, to be used for the production of both bread and pastry of superior quality. The Family flour does not produce as white a loaf of bread as the Patent, but is in other respects like the Patent. The Bakers' or low-grade flour is a dark family flour, which is to-day very largely used by the people who desire a sweet, nutritious, and palatable loaf of bread at a low price, without regard to the fact that it is not as white as the bread to which they have been accustomed in better times.

I am not sure that you desired information as fully as the above, but feel that we are sending you a set of samples practically unique in their line, which will produce results, in the hands of a good baker, that are surprising.

FLOURS WITH SPECIAL NAMES.

In looking over the names of the flours which have been analyzed it will be seen that there are many which have special names. Graham flour is a term which was originally applied to the coarse, unbolted flour which was made by crushing the whole wheat. Strictly speaking the term Graham flour should convey the idea of a flour made from well-cleaned and dusted wheat, ground, but not bolted. Flours, however, are often sold as Graham flour in which the bolting process has been carried to a greater or less extent. The true Graham flour would contain practically the same substances as the wheat kernel itself, and in the same proportions.

Entire wheat flour.—This name would naturally carry the idea of a flour corresponding to the Graham flour above. It is, however, a trade-mark for the flour produced in a special manner, by grinding the whole wheat after the removal of the outer coverings. It therefore contains all of the ingredients of the wheat grain, save those which are found in the outer coverings.

Gluten flour.—This is the name of a product which is sold very extensively and which is supposed often by purchasers to contain no starch. As will be seen by the analyses further on, this is a very grave error. The gluten flour is probably a flour made from those portions of the endosperm lying nearer the exterior of the grain, and which are known to contain a larger quantity of proteid matter than the interior portions.

It is well that we should not be deceived by the trade names of the flours which are offered for sale. As is seen above, the ideas which the name of the flour conveys are not always realized in the article itself. It is quite important, if we wish to know the nature of a flour without making a chemical examination thereof, that the actual steps which have been followed in its preparation be traced and the character of the cereal employed be known. Experts may be able to tell the difference between the soft wheat and hard wheat flours, or even between blended flours, but ordinary purchasers usually rely upon the grocer or upon the name for the information in regard to the flour which they desire.

PROPERTIES AFFECTING THE COMMERCIAL VALUE OF FLOUR.

Aside from its nutritive properties wheat flour has a commercial value depending upon its color and texture, and upon the quantity of gluten which it contains. The character of the gluten also varies largely in different varieties of wheat and in wheat grown in different localities. The gluten of the hard spring wheats appears to have the best properties for baking purposes, but it can not be denied that the very best bread in the world is made from the soft winter wheat of France. The method of manipulating the loaf, of fermentation, and of baking must therefore be admitted to have quite an important bearing upon the constitution of the finished loaf. In general, however, a flour is sold almost exclusively with regard to its relative appearance with other flours and its color, as very few purchasers make a test of the quantity of gluten contained.

PREFERENCE OF BAKERS AS TO FLOUR.

Bakers prefer a flour with a high percentage of tenacious gluten, which permits of the formation of a loaf containing a maximum percentage of water. With a flour rich in gluten it is possible to get a good, palatable loaf, without any evidence of excess of water, containing as high as 40 per cent of moisture.

The baking of bread is an art which is most successfully practiced by professionals, and the American method of home bread baking is not to be too highly commended. The ideal flour for bread making is one which contains a sufficient quantity of gluten to produce a porous and spongy loaf, but not one which permits an excessive quantity of moisture to be incorporated in the loaf itself.

Flours differ not only in the quantities of gluten in them, but also in its qualities. Some varieties of wheat furnish a gluten which is more tenacious than others, and thus produce, of course, a more desirable flour. In practice, however, where the best methods of bread making are followed, it can not be said that the hard spring wheats afford a better variety of bread than the soft winter wheats. The excellent character of the French bread above referred to is an evidence of the fact that the soft winter wheats are capable, with proper manipulation, of furnishing as high a grade of bread as is desirable.

COMPOSITION OF WHEAT FLOURS.

In the prosecution of the work looking to the preparation of this bulletin 107 samples of wheat flours have been analyzed, and the data obtained are collected in the following tables. The samples of flour submitted to analysis were obtained from those exhibited at the World's

Fair, from purchases in the open market, and from samples obtained directly from manufacturers. A description of the samples examined precedes the analytical data. This description contains the laboratory number of the sample, the name of the dealer or manufacturer from whom it was obtained, and a description embodying the trade name.

CLASSIFICATION OF SAMPLES.

It is at once evident that the classification of samples which are obtained from exhibits or which are purchased in the open market is extremely difficult. The only guide which can be followed in such an instance is the description of the sample itself, and this is often misleading because the trade name or trade-mark of the sample does not always accurately describe its composition. In order, however, to compare the different samples together as accurately as possible, they have been separated into several groups of related goods, resembling each other as nearly as possible, as far as could be judged from the descriptions of the samples.

The first group comprises the high grade so-called patent flours. This group is supposed to embrace the most desirable flours, as far as appearance and baking properties are concerned, that are to be found upon the market.

The next group embraces those flours in which no particular description was given, but which were not called high-grade patent flours. It includes the flours which are sold in bulk rather than in small packages, and in general those flours which represent the common market varieties.

The third group represents the general class of flours which are sold as bakers' or family flours, as distinguished from the high-grade patent flours and the general bulk flours represented by the first and second classes.

The fourth group represents the miscellaneous flours which are sold under different names, mostly trade-marks, which have no particular significance in respect of the character of the flour. They embrace such varieties as the "Daisy," "Golden Beam," "Model Flour," "New South," etc.

The fifth group, only four in number, contains the so-called self-raising flours.

The last class, embracing only one sample, is a gluten flour.

In making this classification there were many difficulties encountered, and it is doubtless true that many of the samples as classified above might have found a more fitting position than in the classes in which they are placed. The classification does not imply any expression in respect of the character of the flour, but is simply an attempt to group the flours together in accordance with their trade names, as they are sold in the market.

For the purpose of discussing the analytical data it is highly important that the goods representing essentially the same class as sold in the market be thus grouped together, in order that a comparison of their properties may be secured.

It is seen from the above statements that the analyses thus grouped together represent the character of the flours sold in our markets rather than typical varieties made from a uniform quality of wheat by a carefully controlled process. They represent, therefore, the character of the flours actually used by our citizens, and hence have a special value in respect of practical nutrition.

For purely scientific purposes it would be desirable to study the typical flours made from special unmixed grades of wheat. This has, however, been done heretofore in this division and in other quarters. It has therefore been thought best to confine the present investigation to the more practical aspects of the problem of nutrition as conditioned by the composition of the most important cereal articles of human diet.

Description of flours purchased in the open market.

Serial No.	Dealer.	Description.
10817	John H. Magruder, 1417 New York avenue NW.	Minnesota flour; in bulk.
10818	C. C. Bryan, 1413 New York avenue NW	Bryan's Pride.
10819	G. W. Procter & Son, G and Thirteenth streets NW.	Made by W. Lea & Sons Co., Wilmington, Del.; in bulk.
10820	G. E. Kennedy & Son, 1207 F street NW	Minnesota flour; in bulk.
10821	Charles I. Kellogg, 602 Ninth street NW	Made by J. S. Brown, Virginia. The Cook's Favorite Family Flour.
10822	Elphonzo Youngs Co., 426 Ninth street NW	Minnesota flour; in bulk.
10823	Estler Bros. & Co., C and Thirteenth streets, SW.	Joy of Home, Best Minnesota Patent Process.
10824	S. S. Tucker, C and Thirteenth streets SW	Knox's Selfraising Flour.
10825	Acme Market, 409 Seventh street SW	Cream Blend Extract of Wheat, artificially and scientifically blended; concentrated merits combined.
10826	G. J. Bubb, 420 Seventh street SW	Choice Family Flour.
10827	H. K. Dikeman, 505 Seventh street SW	Fancy Patent Process, "Olive." Made from selected wheat.
10828	Carter & Hazen, Enterprise Market, F and Four-and-a-half streets SW.	Snowflake Family Flour, Minneapolis.
10829	F. A. Newman, Four-and-a-half and G streets SW.	Golden Grain, Patent Fancy Process. Minnesota.
10830	Swiss Market, Third and H streets SW	The Early Riser, Selected Family Flour.
10831	C. L. Callis, Third and H streets SW	W. H. Tenney's Best Family Flour. Manufactured by Wm. H. Tenney & Sons, Georgetown, D. C.
10832	Wm. Lanahan, Second and H streets SW	Rulo, a fine grade family flour.
10833	Francis Leonard, Delaware avenue and H street SW.	Gem of Washington, Roller Process Flour.
10834	South Washington Grocery Co., 603 First street SW.	Blue Rose, Choice Family Flour.
10835	H. E. Fairall, First and E streets SW	Virginia Lee, Finest Minnesota Patent Flour.
10836	J. F. Russell, 730 Ninth street NW	The Franklin Mills, Lockport, N. Y. Fine Flour of the Entire Wheat. Delicious, Economical.
10837	Robert White, Ninth and I streets NW	Ceres, Patent Process Flour from Choice Minnesota Wheat.

Description of flours purchased in the open market—Continued.

Serial No.	Dealer.	Description.
10838	John W. Hardell, Ninth and P streets NW	Cissel's Great French Process. G. W. Cissel & Co., Georgetown, D. C.
10839	Edward H. Trundell, Tenth and P streets NW	Celestial, Fancy Patent Roller Process.
10840	Heer Brothers, Tenth and O streets NW	E. G. Metz's Best Roller Process Flour.
10841	J. G. McQueen & Co., 1007 M street NW	Richmond Patent Family Flour.
10842	R. P. White, Twelfth and M streets NW	Minnesota "Red River" Fancy Roller Patent.
10843	Renshaw Brothers, 1301 M street NW	Very Fancy Patent, Craig & Varney, Oxford, Mich.
10844	Wm. Bannon, Fourteenth and N streets NW	Warwick's Best Patent Process from White Wheat.
10845	Cochran & Byrne, 1317 Fourteenth street NW	"Imperial York," Fancy Patent, Warranted.
10846	Frank E. Altemus, 1410 P street NW	"Our Pride," Patent Fancy Process Flour.
10847	Wm. T. Davis, P and Fifteenth streets NW	"The Daisy." G. W. Cissel & Co., Georgetown, D. C.
10848	P. O'Donoghue, 2616 P street NW	"Golden Bean" Family Flour.
10849	H. P. Beattie, 3001 P street NW	"Model Flour." H. P. Beattie.
10850	A. Hanlon, 1444 Thirty-second street NW	"Our New South." Wm. H. Tenney & Sons, The Capitol Mills, Georgetown, D. C.
10851	J. W. Bogley & Bro., 1355 Thirty-second street NW	"Peerless" Roller Process Family Flour.
10852	John A. Girvin, 2826 Pennsylvania avenue NW	"Cereal" Minnesota Patent Process Flour.
10853	E. M. P. Harris, Thirtieth and M streets NW	"Acme," Mount Washington Fine Family Flour.
10854	Wm. E. Reynolds, 3272 M street NW	"White and Gold," Our Best Fancy Guaranteed Flour.
10855	Manogue & Jones, 3150 M street NW	"Satisfaction" Family Flour.
10856	Philip H. Ward, 2100 Pennsylvania avenue NW	Snow White Family Flour.
10857	....do	"Eclipse" Patent Flour.
10858	W. R. Brown, Twentieth and Pennsylvania avenue NW	"Beauty" Minnesota Patent Process.
10859	Matthew Goddard, New York avenue and Thirteenth street NW	Hecker's Superlative Self Raising Flour, Croton Mills, 205 Cherry street, New York, N. Y.
10860	Spignul & Co., Seventh street and Mount Vernon square NW	"Souvenir Patent Process." From choice amber wheat.
10861	Wilson & Schultz, 934 Seventh street NW	"White Lily Process." G. W. Cissel, Georgetown, D. C.
10862	A. A. Winfield, 215 Thirteen-and-a-half street SW	"Superlative," Roller Process, Minnesota Patent.
14365	N. W. Burchell, 1325 F street NW	Hecker's Old Homestead Flapjack. Flour. Hecker-Jones-Jewell Milling Co., New York, N. Y.
14367	....do	Aunt Jemima's Pancake Flour. R. T. Davis Milling Co., St. Joseph, Mo.
14373	....do	Griddle Cake Flour, Quail Brand. Nebraska City Cereal Mills, Nebraska City, Nebr.
15202	John H. Magruder, 1417 New York avenue NW	Entire Wheat Flour. The Franklin Mills Co., Lockport, N. Y.
15275	....do	Farina. Hecker-Jones-Jewell Milling Co., 203 Cherry street, New York, N. Y.
15961	Purchased for the U. S. Army by Maj. Henry G. Sharpe, St. Louis, Mo.	Hard Winter Patent Flour.
15962	....do	Hard Winter Patent Flour.
15963	....do	Winter Straight Flour.
15964	....do	Winter Patent Flour.

Flours obtained from manufacturers.

Serial No.	Manufacturer.	Description.
11102	Benjamin Ames, Lakehome Mills, Mount Vernon, Ohio.	"Staff of Life."
11103	....do....	"Perfection."
12909	Warder & Bennett, Springfield, Ohio.	Champion.
12910	....do....	Golden Fleece.
12911	....do....	Bob White.
12912	....do....	Bell.
12913	....do....	Red River, Straight.
12914	L. C. Porter Milling Co., Winona, Minn.	No. 0000 Boss, 72 per cent.
12915	....do....	"Souvenir," 50 per cent.
12916	....do....	"Souvenir Bakers'," 38 per cent.
12917	....do....	First Bakers' or Clear Stock, 20 per cent.
12918	....do....	Souvenir Low Grade, 12 per cent.
12919	....do....	Low Grade, 8 per cent.
12922	G. W. Cissel, Georgetown, D. C.	First Patent.
12923	....do....	Second Patent.
12924	....do....	First Family.
12925	....do....	Second Family.
12926	....do....	Extra.
12927	....do....	Maryland and Virginia Wheat.
12929	American Cereal Co., Akron, Ohio.	Patent.
12930	....do....	Family.
12931	....do....	Bakers'.
12937	Pillsbury & Washburn, Minneapolis, Minn.	Patent.
12938	....do....	Bakers'.
12992	L. C. Porter Milling Co., Winona, Minn.	The World's Fair Best Flour, Porter's Souvenir.
12999	....do....	Second and third break flour, or clear.

Flours exhibited at the World's Columbian Exposition.

Serial No.	Manufacturer.	Description.
11880	Hungarian Flour Mills, Denver, Colo.	Hungarian Patent Flour.
11881	....do....	Hungarian Spring Wheat Flour.
11882	Thomas Alsopp, Murrumburrah, Australia.	Roller Process Flour.
11883	Brunton & Co., Granville, Sydney, Australia.	Soft Variety Winter Wheat.
11884	Cohen & Levy, Tamworth, Australia.	Wheat Flour.
11885	Cootamundra Farmers' Cooperative Roller Milling Co., Cootamundra, Australia.	Winter Wheat Flour.
11886	Edwin Gardiner, Temora, Australia.	Wheat Flour.
11887	Edwin Grover, Glen Innis, Australia.	Do.
11888	H. C. Matthews, Bathurst, Australia.	Acme Patent Roller Soft Winter Wheat Flour.
11889	McGee & Quinn, Parker, Australia.	Patent Roller Process Wheat Flour.
11890	Pawlry & McIntyre, Innull, Australia.	Soft Winter Wheat Flour.
11891	William Tremain, Bathurst, Australia.	Patent Roller Winter Wheat Flour.
11892	F. Utz, Glen Innis, Australia.	Soft Winter Wheat Flour.
11893	Young Cooperative Roller Flour Mill Co., Young, Australia.	Do.
11894	M. McLaughlin & Co., Toronto, Canada.	Manitoba Patent Flour.
11895	....do....	Bakers' Flour.
11896	Whitlae, Baird & Co., Paris, Ontario, Canada.	Meggar Flour.
11897	John Hull, Lakefield, Ontario, Canada.	Patent Flour.

Flours exhibited at the World's Columbian Exposition—Continued.

Serial No.	Manufacturer.	Description.
11898	John Hull, Lakefield, Ontario, Canada	Patent Flour.
11899	Jacob Heinmüller, Walkerton, Ontario, Canada	
11900	W. H. Stevens, Chatham, Ontario, Canada	Kent Flour.
11901	....do	Red Pine Flour.
11902	....do	Pastry Flour.
11903	....do	Elgin Flour.
11904	....do	Thomas Flour.
11905	Austin Mills, Austin, Manitoba, Canada	Bakers' Flour.
11906	....do	Daisy Flour.
11907	Western Milling Co., Regina, Northwest Territory, Canada.	Patent Flour.
11908	....do	Bakers' Flour.
11909	D. McLean, Calgary, Northwest Territory, Canada.	Do.
11910	....do	Patent Flour.
12546	J. Mostart, Bechuanaland, Africa	
12547	Marini & Magnaschi, Santa Fe, Argentine Republic.	Wheat Flour.
12548	Fernando Albinez, Tecpam, Guatemala	Flour, second-class.
12549	Enrique Bouscoyrol, Quezaltenango, Guatemala.	Flour, first-class.
12551	American Cereal Co., Akron, Ohio	A. M. C. Blended.
12552	....do	Lake Mills Blended Family.
12553	....do	Gluten Flour.
12554	....do	F. S. Self-Rising Wheat Flour.
12555	....do	Quaker Rising Wheat Flour.
12556	Miguel Onoto, Buenos Ayres, Argentine Republic.	Wheat Flour.

DESCRIPTION OF TABLES OF ANALYSES.

In the following tables are given the detailed analyses of all the samples of wheat flour which have been examined in this division in connection with the present work. The laboratory number in the first column refers to the same number in the description of the samples. It will be observed that the proteids are contained in two columns. In the first column of proteids are given the percentages of these bodies obtained by the old factor of 6.25. The percentage of nitrogen in each sample multiplied by 6.25 gives the percentage of proteids in each case. It seems quite probable, however, from the data which have been given previously as a result of the recent investigations of the proteids of wheat, that the factor 6.25 is too high, and that more correct results in regard to proteids are obtained by multiplying by the factor 5.70. The percentages of proteids calculated by this factor are given in the second column of proteids. Since the carbohydrates in each instance are determined by difference, the calculation of proteids by two factors renders necessary a double column for the carbohydrates. In the first column the carbohydrates by difference when the nitrogen is multiplied by 6.25 are found, while in the second case the carbohydrates by difference when the carbohydrates are multiplied by 5.70 are given. It is evident, without further illustration, that the second column of carbohydrates shows a slightly larger per cent than the first.

Included in the carbohydrates are all the carbohydrate bodies of the wheat flour. As has been seen before, the principal part of these carbohydrates is composed of starch, but they also include the sugars of all kinds, the dextrin, the galactin, the fiber, and the celluloses and hemicelluloses. Inasmuch as the starch and soluble sugars make up by far the greater proportion of the carbohydrates, it has not been thought necessary to separate the other members of the series.

The proportion of crude fiber in flour is quite insignificant, and for practical purposes the determination of this material is not necessary.

The moisture, which is given in the second column, was obtained by the ordinary process of analysis. In the columns headed "Moist gluten" and "Dry gluten" are found the results of the separation of the gluten from the flour by the usual process of washing with cold water, as described in Bulletin No. 45, page 10.

It is hardly necessary to call the attention of chemical readers to the fact that the data obtained in these columns are approximate. There is no method known, by means of which the gluten can be separated in a state of purity, except by the tedious processes which are employed in the separation and estimation of the proteid matters of seeds. It will be noticed that in many instances the percentage of dry gluten is greater than the total percentage of proteids, which, of course, would be quite impossible, provided the gluten could be separated in a pure state. In the methods of separation employed for practical purposes there remain always in the gluten portions of starch and fiber and other materials sufficient, in many instances, to make the total percentage greater than that of the total proteids.

The data contained in the column headed "Moist gluten" are of considerable importance from the baker's point of view. The greater the percentage of moist gluten which a flour contains, the greater the quantity of water which can be incorporated in the loaf of bread. Where bakers sell their loaves by weight the importance of this from a commercial point of view is at once apparent. The palatability and lightness of the loaf are also influenced in a marked degree by the percentage of moist gluten.

In the column headed "Percentage of ash" are given the numbers obtained by the direct ignition of the sample with the usual precautions until an ash is secured which is practically free of carbon. The figures given, therefore, represent what is known as the crude ash—that is, the ash containing any still unburned particles of carbon—and the carbon dioxid in combination with bases arising from the combustion of the organic salts present in the wheat flour. Practically nearly the whole of the ash is composed of phosphoric acid and potash, and where such small quantities enter into calculation it is not necessary for our present purpose to make a further separation of its ingredients.

Under "Ether extract" are given the data obtained by the direct extraction of the dry sample with anhydrous ether. The ether extract consists chiefly of the vegetable oils, but it may contain also other matters soluble in anhydrous ether. It is not proper, therefore, to regard the whole of the ether extract as a pure glyceride, or a mixture of glycerides. Digestion experiments which have been carried on with ether extracts obtained in the way indicated, show that the percentage which is digestible is much less than for the pure glycerides. In computing the food or calorific values of the samples, therefore, too high results are obtained by regarding the ether extract as a mixture of pure glycerides. Since, in the case of a wheat flour, the germ which contains the principal part of the oil of the wheat has been removed, the percentage of ether extract is uniformly low, rarely rising above one-half of 1 per cent. It is entirely safe to regard at least two-thirds of this quantity as composed of pure glycerides.

Heat of Combustion of Cereals.

The heat of combustion of the sample is computed for the number of calories which would be generated by one gram of the substance burned under pressure in oxygen. In the calculation of calorimetric equivalents various factors are employed.[1]

In any given case the value of any food product as a fuel is determined experimentally by burning the substance and measuring the amount of heat evolved. By the improvement of modern appliances this measurement can be very accurately made. The heat equivalents are expressed in calories, the calorie representing the amount of heat necessary to raise 1 gram of water at a temperature of about 18° C., 1° in temperature. The amount of heat developed by the different food classes varies greatly, being least for the carbohydrates and greatest for the fats. Among the carbohydrates the pentose, dextrose, and levulose sugars have the least calorific value; sucrose and maltose come next, and starch and cellulose have the highest. One gram of a starch carbohydrate, when burned under proper conditions, affords a sufficient amount of heat to raise the the temperature of 4,200 grams of water 1°. In like manner 1 gram of pure vegetable proteid matter during combustion affords a quantity of heat sufficient to raise the temperature of about 5,900 grams of water 1°, while the combustion of 1 gram of fat or oil will afford a sufficient amount of heat to raise the temperature of about 9,300 grams of water 1°. Among the proteids, peptones have the lowest calorific value and the cereal proteids the highest. Among the fats and oils, butter fat has a low, while oleomargarine has a high calorific value. If all the fats which are ingested were consumed in producing animal heat the simple determination of their heat value would be a sufficient index of their nutritive properties. It is seen without argument, however, that the production of animal heat is only one of

---

[1] See Wiley's Principles and Practice of Agricultural Analysis, Vol. III, p. 567.

the important functions of foods, and among foods of like kinds even, it is not quite certain that their heats of combustion are reliable tests of their heat values in the body. This is illustrated very strikingly in the case of butter fat and oleomargarine, as indicated above. Moreover, in a great many substances which are largely indigestible, as for instance, wood fiber in the pure state, the complex representing the carbohydrates in fodders and cellulose affords on combustion a quantity of heat quite comparable, or in excess of that given by a digestible sugar or starch. In case it is not convenient to determine by actual combustion the calorific value of a food, its approximate value can be calculated from the analytical data showing the relative percentages of carbohydrates, proteids, and oils contained therein.

The principles on which the calculation of the calories of combustion is based are stated in the following paragraphs.

CALORIES OF COMBUSTION IN OXYGEN OF CEREALS AND CEREAL PRODUCTS, CALCULATED FROM ANALYTICAL DATA.

The calculation of the heat of combustion of food products is now quite generally practiced in analytical determinations. The development of the methods of burning in compressed oxygen, as proposed by Berthelot and Vieille, has made it possible to use this process for ordinary analytical purposes, and with a fair degree of accuracy. The data obtained by combustion in oxygen become, therefore, a check upon ordinary analytical determinations, as well as an additional means of measuring the dietetic value of foods. When the data obtained on combustion are to be used in analytical methods it is necessary to compare them directly with the data calculated from chemical analysis. A large number of difficulties arises in connection with this calculation on account of the number of combustible substances present in the cereals and their products. We have three great classes of bodies in cereals, namely, carbohydrates, proteids, and oils. In addition to these, however, there are many others which are oxidizable, and which yield heat in the process, among them amid compounds of nitrogen, organic acids, lecithins, and coloring matters. These last named, it is true, exist in minute quantities, but the combustion of the whole of them is attended with a considerable evolution of heat, which must not be lost sight of in exact comparisons. In addition to this, the groups of like matters which form the chief part of cereals and cereal products are composed of several substances. In the carbohydrates are found many different classes whose heats of combustion vary largely. For instance, there is a wide difference between the heat of combustion of a gram of pentosans and a gram of starch, and midway between these lies the number representing the heat of combustion of sucrose. The different vegetable oils vary greatly in their calorific power, and these differences must be taken into consideration in the calculations. In respect of the heats of combustion of the vegetable proteids but little is known, and we have not yet isolated sufficient quantities of the different proteids to determine the heat of combustion of each one directly. This part of the subject will be investigated further. The results of the actual determinations, however, show that the average number of small calories per gram of vegetable proteids evolved in burning in oxygen is not far from 5,900. The details of the processes employed for cereals and cereal products will be considered by classes, beginning with the carbohydrate group.

CALORIES OF THE CARBOHYDRATES.

The magnitude of the calorimetric equivalents of the carbohydrates and their derivatives show in general, regular and expected variations, depending on their constitution and molecular configuration. Isomeric bodies show similar but not always identical heats of combustion. For the three groups of carbohydrates, represented by the formulas $C_6H_{12}O_6$, $C_{12}H_{22}O_{11}$, and $(C_6H_{10}O_5)_n$, respectively, the heats of combustion at constant volume for 1 gram-molecule are about 673, 1,351, and 678 calories, respectively. In derivatives of the carbohydrates the heat value decreases in general with the increase of the hydrogen and oxygen atoms with reference to the carbon atoms, but this rule is not rigidly applicable, and does not permit a sure judgment in respect of heat value based on a knowledge of chemical composition alone. The heat value of the pentoses is generally less than that of the hexoses, and of the hexoses the more condensed forms, as, for instance the disaccharids, and the polysaccharids like starch, have a higher heat value than the simpler forms like dextrose. In round numbers the heat value of the pentoses (arabinose, xylose), and of lactose (crystallized), dextrose, and fructose is 3,750; of sucrose, maltose, and lactose (anhydrous) 3,950, and of starch and cellulose 4,200 calories per gram. In computing the heat value of a mixed carbohydrate body from analytical data it is therefore necessary to know approximately the relative quantities of these typical constituents. If, for instance, in a sample of ground wheat containing 74 per cent of carbohydrates it is desired to calculate the heat value accurately, it is first necessary to distribute the total carbohydrates into groups. Suppose it to be found on analyses that the total carbohydrates are composed of the following quantities:

	Per cent.
Pentosans	4.5
Cellulose	4.5
Sugar (sucrose)	1.0
Starch	64.0

The heat value of the pentosans is about 50 calories greater than for the pentoses, and the factor for pentosans is therefore $3,750 + 50 = 3,800$. Cellulose and starch have practically the same heat value, and the factor for these in round numbers is 4,200. The sugar is chiefly sucrose, and the factor for this is 3,950. The above numbers give the necessary data for the computation given below. The following gives the computed carbohydrate calories for one gram of a cereal flour containing 74 per cent of carbohydrates:

	Gram.
Total weight of carbohydrates	0.740
Weight of pentosans, etc	.015
Weight of starch, cellulose, etc	.685
Weight of sucrose, etc	.010

Then—

$$0.045 \times 3{,}800 = 171.0 \text{ calories.}$$
$$0.685 \times 4{,}200 = 2{,}877.0 \text{ calories.}$$
$$0.010 \times 3{,}950 = 39.5 \text{ calories.}$$
$$\text{Sum} = 3{,}087.5 \text{ calories.}$$

CALORIES OF COMBUSTION OF VEGETABLE PROTEIN.

In respect of the heat of combustion of the vegetable proteid matters, it may be said that even greater variations are noticed than with the glycerides and carbohydrates; for instance, the calories obtained by the combustion of a gram of gluten, as ascertained by Berthelot, are represented by the number 5990.3. The mean number of calories per gram of the proteids in general is stated by Stohmann to be 5730.8. The calorimetric numbers for hordein, edestin, leucosin, zein, myosin, vitelin, gliadin, glutenin, and the other minor proteid bodies occurring in the cereals have not been determined. Moreover, it must be remembered that the cereals contain a certain proportion of amid nitrogenous bodies, the heat values of which are considerably less than those of the pure proteids. It is a question, therefore, of considerable difficulty to select a factor which represents the proper number for computing its fuel value from the total nitrogen present in a cereal. In the Principles and Practice of Agricultural Analysis (Vol. III, page 559), the factor 5,500 calories per gram is proposed as a suitable one for use with the proteids. This factor is probably too low for estimating the heat produced by the combustion of cereal protein in oxygen. Before the proteids are absorbed into the body and oxidized or distributed as constituents of the tissues they are converted in the digestive organs into soluble forms, to which the general term peptones has been applied. The heat of combustion of peptones is decidedly less than that of the ordinary proteids, being represented by a factor 5,300 calories per gram. The number given above, therefore, viz, 5,500 calories per gram, is about a mean to be used in calculating the calories of combustion of peptones and proteids. For the actual calculation of heats of combustion in oxygen of proteid matter of cereals to be compared with the heats of combustion obtained in the calorimeter, the factor 5,900 is proposed as the one most nearly correct, in so far as our present knowledge is concerned.

We have made efforts to secure sufficient quantities of the pure proteids present in the different cereals to determine directly their calorific power. Owing to the difficulty of preparing these proteids in the large quantities sufficient for the work we have not yet succeeded in our object. We shall, however, continue this work and either obtain the samples from others, or, if unable to do this, prepare them ourselves, in order that the special factor for each cereal may be determined experimentally. In the absence of these special determinations we have only the recourse of making use of the factor which seems to be nearest the proper one for all, namely, 5,900 calories for each gram of vegetable protein present in the cereal.

If all the nitrogen in a cereal product be calculated as proteid matter the factor to be used in calculating the calories of combustion must be less than 5,900. The reason for this is that a small part of the nitrogen present is in a nonproteid form, existing as compounds distinctly less calorifacient than proteid matters. Only an approximate factor can be proposed for this calculation. It is best to determine the nonproteid nitrogen and then use the factor 5,900 for the residual proteids. The nitrogen as amids in this case, in so far as its fuel value is concerned, is to be calculated by a different factor. Asparagin may be selected as a representative vegetable amid, and the calories corresponding to 1 gram of asparagin are represented by the number 3,400. Asparagin contains 22.7 per cent of nitrogen, and in order to convert amid nitrogen to asparagin its percentage is multiplied by 4.05. These data afford the basis of a rational computation of heat values of the nitrogenous constituents of cereals.

Example.—The sample of wheat flour before mentioned contains 2 per cent of nitrogen, of which 0.12 per cent is of an amid nature. The proteids in the sample are calculated as follows:

$$1.88 \times 5.70 = 10.71 \text{ per cent.}$$

The amid bodies, as asparagin, are found from the following equation:

$$0.12 \times 4.05 = 0.48 \text{ per cent.}$$

In 1 gram of substance the calories of combustion are calculated as follows:

$$0.1071 \text{ gram proteids} \times 5,900 = 631.9 \text{ calories.}$$
$$0.0048 \text{ gram asparagin} \times 3,400 = 16.3 \text{ calories.}$$

Total calories due to nitrogen compounds, 648.2 calories.

CALORIES OF COMBUSTION OF CEREAL OILS.

In order to secure a basis for rational work, the oils of the cereals were extracted and purified as carefully as possible by the usual methods. Three of these oils have already been subjected to combustion, while the process of the purification of the others is still going on. The oils which have been burned gave the following calories per gram: Wheat oil, 9,359; rye oil, 9,322; Indian-corn oil, 9,280. For the nearest round numbers the factor for wheat oil would be 9,350, and for rye and Indian corn 9,300.

In making calculations from analytical data, however, the ether extract does not represent a pure oil, but all the other bodies in the cereal which are soluble in ether. It is therefore deemed desirable to determine the calorifacient power of the ether extract obtained according to the methods of the official agricultural chemists. For this purpose a considerable quantity of the ether extracts of wheat, oats, barley, and rye was prepared, and the combustion of this extract was made directly. The results per gram of ether extract for the several cereals mentioned are as follows: Wheat, 9,070; oats, 8,927; barley, 9,070, and rye, 9,196. The nearest round numbers for these bodies would therefore be: Wheat, 9,100; oats, 8,950; barley, 9,100, and rye, 9,200.

In the extraction of cereals with ether it should not be forgotten that a portion of the fatty matter is not brought into solution. Especially is this true of the lecithins. In view of this fact, it is a matter of question whether it might not be advisable, with the present light on the subject, to multiply the ether extract by the round number 9,300 rather than by the number corresponding to the calorifacient power of the ether extract itself as given above. With the exception of oats and Indian corn, the difference between the two factors would be very slight, because the ether extract is a small number. With oats and Indian corn, however, the difference would amount to several calories. In the case of oils in general the calories of combustion vary greatly with the character of the glycerides. It has been shown, for instance, that a gram of oleomargarine when burned in oxygen affords about 200 more calories than a gram of butter fat. The natural oils which exist in plants vary in respect of their fuel values. Linseed oil, for instance, has a slightly higher fuel value than olive oil. In Principles and Practice of Agricultural Analysis (Vol. III, p. 569), it is recommended to use the factor 9,300 for a general case for the heat value of a gram of glycerides. This is probably not far from the correct number for the average of animal and vegetable glycerides, being possibly a little too low. Since in natural cereals we have to do only with vegetable glycerides, and in breads often with a mixture of vegetable and animal glycerides, it is difficult to determine in every case the magnitude of the factor to be employed. For the pure cereal glycerides, however, it is recommended that the factor mentioned above be used, viz, 9,300 calories per gram. In the baking of bread the fats, especially those in the crust, are subjected to a high temperature, under which they possibly undergo a preliminary oxidation. In this case, therefore, the factor given in the Principles and Practice of Agricultual Analysis, viz, 9,300 calories per gram, may be too high.

In the ether extract of cereals there are other bodies besides fat, and it would not be proper to regard the whole mass as having the same fuel value as pure fat. It is difficult to make any accurate allowance for these bodies, which are, moreover, of an organic nature, and capable of yielding considerable quantities of heat on combustion. To avoid confusion, it may be said that the factor 9,300 calories per gram can be used also with the ether extracts of flours and meals as well as with those of the baked products. In the sample of ground wheat already mentioned the ether extract is 2 per cent. The calories afforded by the oil in burning 1 gram of the flour are therefore—

$$0.020 \text{ gram} \times 9,300 = 186 \text{ calories.}$$

It is evident that it will be impracticable to make any account in our calculations of the heat of combustion arising from the oxidation of the small quantities of coloring matters, organic acids, and other bodies not included in the above data. By using the factor 9,300 for the multiplication of the ether extract instead of the factors determined by direct investigation it is evident that a sufficient allowance will be made for the inclusion not only of the bodies mentioned, but also of the lecithins remaining unextracted and for which the calorifacient value approximates that of the true glycerides. The above data, then, give the basis for calculating the whole calorific power of a whole wheat flour having the following composition:

Carbohydrates:
Starch, cellulose, etc	per cent..	68.50
Pentoses	do....	4.50
Sucrose	do....	1.00
		74.00
Proteids	do....	10.71
Amids	do....	0.48
Ether extract	do....	2.00
Ash	do....	2.00
Moisture	do....	10.81

The heat values shown separately for each of these constituents are as follows:

Calories due to starch, cellulose, etc	2,877
Calories due to pentosans	171
Calories due to sucrose	40
Calories due to proteids	632
Calories due to amids	16
Calories due to ether extract	186
Total calories in 1 gram	3,922

COMPARISON OF CALCULATED AND ASCERTAINED CALORIES.

The principles of calculation which have been developed above have been applied in the direct comparison of the calories of combustion ascertained by experiments and those calculated from analytical data. The samples of cereals examined consisted of two samples of wheat, one of rye, one of unhulled oats, and one of hulled barley. The analytical data obtained by careful analyses follow.

Chemical composition of samples of grain.

Constituents.	Wheat No. 1.	Wheat No. 2.	Rye.	Unhulled oats.	Hulled barley.
	Per cent.	Per cent.	Per cent.	Per cent.	Per cent.
Moisture	11.33	10.65	11.71	9.26	12.20
Ash	1.69	1.77	2.31	3.78	0.93
Ether extract	2.00	2.24	1.63	4.72	0.92
Proteids	12.19	14.44	11.69	9.63	10.44
Carbohydrates:					
Sucrose	0.33	0.48	0.42	0.17	0.18
Invert sugar	0.027	0.08	0.008	0.031	0.017
Galactin and dextrin	0.16	0.25	0.22	0.26	0.14
Pentosans	5.80	5.17	8.10	13.65	6.50
Fiber	2.15	2.56	2.36	12.81	0.80
Starch	64.31	62.69	61.78	45.98	68.03

The calculated calories for each of the samples given above are as follows:

Component parts.	Wheat No. 1.	Wheat No. 2.	Rye.	Unhulled oats.	Hulled barley.
	Calories.	Calories.	Calories.	Calories.	Calories.
Ether extract	186	208	152	439	86
Proteids	719	852	690	568	616
Pentosans	220	196	308	519	247
Sucrose	13	19	17	7	7
Starch and fiber	2,800	2,741	2,694	2,469	2,891
Total	3,938	4,016	3,861	4,002	3,847

The calories found by direct combustion in oxygen are as follows:

Wheat No. 1 3,922
Wheat No. 2 4,011
Rye 3,909
Oats 4,181
Barley 3,886

The direct comparison of the two numbers is seen in the following table:

Variety of grain.	Calculated.	Found.	Difference.
	Calories.	Calories.	Calories.
Wheat No. 1	3,938	3,922	+ 16
Wheat No. 2	4,016	4,011	+ 5
Rye	3,860	3,909	− 49
Oats	4,002	4,181	−179
Barley	3,846	3,886	− 40

The agreement between the calculated calories and those actually determined in the calorimeter is satisfactory in the above cases, with the exception of the sample of oats. In this case, as will be seen, the calories directly ascertained are 179 greater than those calculated from the analytical data. This fact suggests the possibility of the heat of combustion of the unseparated complex representing the unidentified carbohydrates of hulls and fodders being higher than for starch. Where such a difference exists, the suggestion at once occurs that either the analytical data or the calories obtained by combustion are in error. One of the principal values of ascertaining the calories of combustion in analytical work is indicated by such a difference. The combustion will be a check on the analysis and, vice versa, the analysis a check on the combustion. Where the differences are as great as noted in oats, the indications are for a repetition of both the analysis and the combustion. The magnitude of the difference between the calculated and ascertained calories which can be allowed as fully within the ordinary errors of analysis and combustion, can only be determined by a long series of determinations, and perhaps after the factors employed for the calculations have been slightly changed to harmonize more closely with ascertained results. At the present time we are inclined to the opinion that when the difference between the calculated calories and those ascertained on combustion does not exceed 50 or 75 calories the check is sufficiently satisfactory.

We have examined by the above process the greater part of the cereal products treated in this bulletin. The data which are given below include 28 consecutive determinations on the products mentioned, with the exception of six, where the difference between the ascertained and calculated calories was so great as to indicate an error in one or the other.

The following table contains all the data showing a comparison between the calculated and ascertained calorific power of the several substances mentioned:

Comparison of cereal products.

FLOUR.

Name of substance.	Determined calories per gram.	Calculated calories per gram.	
		$N \times 5.70$	$N \times 6.25$
Flapjack flour	3,700	3,776	3,790
Pancake flour	3,820	3,833	3,845
Griddlecake flour	3,724	3,706	3,719
Patent flour	3,870	3,880	3,894
Mean	3,779	3,799	3,812

BREAD.

Vienna	4,420	4,372	4,394
Vienna	4,381	4,339	4,359
Home made	4,558	4,483	4,503
Home made	4,436	4,450	4,465
Mean	4,449	4,411	4,430

Comparison of cereal products—Continued.

BREAKFAST AND PARTIALLY PREPARED FOODS (WHEAT PRODUCTS).

Name of substance.	Determined calories per gram.	Calculated calories per gram.	
		N × 5.70	N × 6.25
Shredded whole-wheat biscuit	4,253	4,298	4,314
Wheat germ meal	4,362	4,404	4,420
Gluten butter wafers	4,610	4,605	4,628
Whole wheat gluten	4,544	4,542	4,566
Cooked gluten	4,432	4,406	4,425
Germea	4,445	4,403	4,417
Breakfast gem	4,379	4,405	4,420
Cracked wheat	4,453	4,395	4,413
Mean	4,435	4,432	4,450

MISCELLANEOUS.

Kaffee-brod	4,146	4,203	
Granula	4,385	4,399	
Imperial granum	4,485	4,462	
F. F. V. malt food	4,470	4,465	
Granulated barley	4,365	4,353	
H-O oatmeal	4,800	4,799	
Mean	4,442	4,447	

A study of the above data reveals the fact that while the variations in individual instances are considerable, a comparison of the means shows that the factors which have been adopted must be very nearly correct, inasmuch as the mean calculated calories differ very little from those determined by actual combustion. In calculating the calories for wheat products both the factors 5.70 and 6.25, for converting nitrogen into proteid matter, have been used. Inasmuch as the calorific power of the protein is slightly greater than that of the carbohydrates, the total calories, as calculated by the factor 6.25, are slightly greater than those calculated by the factor 5.70. In the case of breads and other baked products the differences are not so great as we had anticipated, on account of the difficulty of completely extracting the fat and oil from a bread. The individual differences, as in the case of a flour, are somewhat marked, but the means agree very closely.

While this paper was writing, in point of fact on August 2, 1897, we received Bulletin No. 33 of the Wyoming Station (June, 1897), in which Professor Slosson has called attention to work similar to ours which he has done at that station. The factors used by Professor Slosson differ slightly from those which we have adopted, his factor for fat and oil being 9,500, for protein 5,700, and for carbohydrates 4,200. In 19 samples of wheat products the calculated calories from analytical data by our factors are 4,472, and by Slosson's factors 4,447. In six samples of miscellaneous cereal products, calculated by our factors, the number is 4,833 and by his 4,810.

It is seen by the above that the mean results are not very greatly different from the two sets of factors, Slosson gaining in his higher factor for fat a portion of what he loses in his lower factor for protein, as compared with our own numbers.

We beg to call attention to the fact that in the light of the data here presented, we can with reason claim that the determination of the calorific power by combustion under pressure in oxygen is destined to be a valuable aid to the analyst in serving as a check upon the analytical data. We are further warranted in believing that whenever the calculated calories and the analytical data in hulled cereals and cereal products differ by as much as 100 from those obtained by combustion, the chemist will do well to repeat both the analysis and the combustion in order to discover the source of error. The calorimeter in this way becomes a valuable adjunct to the chemist in his work from a purely analytical point of view.

ANALYSES OF WHEAT FLOURS.

In the following tables are found the analytical data secured by the analysis of the samples of flours. The calculated calories of the combustion are obtained from the data based on the factor $N \times 5.70$ for the total proteids present. Since the correction incident to the separate determination of the amid nitrogen would be extremely small and of no practical value it is not given in the subsequent tables. In the following analytical tables are given the calories calculated from the analyses and those determined by direct combustion. The principles on which the calculations have been made are those already described. In the case of flours very few combustions were made, by reason of the fact that nearly all the flours were analyzed during the years intervening from 1892 to 1895. Inasmuch as the Department was not supplied with a bomb calorimeter until 1897, the greater part of the flour samples had been disposed of, and therefore no comparisons could be made except in the few instances indicated in the table. With the cereal products, namely, bread, breakfast foods, cakes, biscuits, etc., a nearly complete comparison has been made. All the numbers obtained have been entered, whether the agreement has been close or not. In many instances there is quite a wide divergence between the data obtained by calculation and by direct combustion. Ordinarily this difference would have led to the repetition of both the analytical and combustion work, but in order not to delay any longer the publication of the bulletin this redetermination has been omitted. By comparing the averages in each case it will be seen that a very satisfactory agreement has been secured, showing that the essential principles of calculation which have been developed are applicable, and that hereafter they will undergo only slight modifications, based upon a more extended experience.

CLASS I.—*Composition of patent wheat flours.*

Laboratory No.	Moisture.	Proteids, N×6.25.	Proteids, N×5.70.	Moist gluten.	Dry gluten.	Ether extract.	Ash.	Carbohydrates, N×6.25.	Carbohydrates, N×5.70.	Crude fiber.	Calculated calories of combustion.	Ascertained calories.
	Per ct.	Per ct.	Per ct.	Per ct.	Per ct.	Per ct.	Per ct.	Per ct.	Per ct.	Per ct.		
10823	13.02	8.84	8.06	23.09	9.20	0.97	0.37	76.80	77.58	0.15	3,825.1	....
10826	13.20	9.80	8.94	21.52	8.70	0.86	0.39	75.09	76.55	0.22	3,822.5	....
10827	13.28	11.51	10.50	20.72	8.39	0.96	0.45	73.80	74.81	0.19	3,850.8	....
10828	13.11	9.72	8.86	19.95	7.75	1.06	0.45	75.66	76.52	0.19	3,835.1	....
10829	12.88	9.19	8.38	19.43	7.88	0.87	0.36	76.70	77.51	0.15	3,830.7	....
10831	13.57	9.84	8.97	23.21	9.38	1.00	0.42	75.08	75.95	0.16	3,820.5	....
10834	14.06	9.46	8.63	23.04	9.41	0.81	0.33	75.34	76.17	0.16	3,783.7	....
10835	13.13	10.07	9.18	20.01	10.03	0.72	0.33	75.75	76.64	0.12	3,827.5	....
10837	12.97	11.26	10.27	29.52	11.40	1.14	0.43	74.20	75.19	0.13	3,870.0	....
10839	12.83	9.19	8.38	22.25	9.05	0.94	0.40	76.64	77.45	0.10	3,834.8	....
10841	13.68	10.15	9.26	23.43	9.51	0.95	0.37	74.85	75.74	0.14	3,815.8	....
10842	12.97	11.03	10.06	28.30	11.17	1.08	0.37	74.55	75.52	0.15	3,865.8	....
10843	13.60	9.37	8.55	24.73	9.15	0.95	0.50	75.49	76.31	0.14	3,797.9	....
10844	12.75	10.77	9.82	27.49	10.41	0.87	0.49	75.12	76.07	0.26	3,855.2	....
10845	13.33	11.03	10.06	23.32	10.66	0.72	0.45	74.47	75.44	0.16	3,829.0	....
10846	13.95	10.33	9.42	24.50	10.51	0.76	0.40	74.56	75.47	0.20	3,796.2	....
10852	13.19	11.03	10.06	27.72	10.48	1.13	0.49	74.16	75.13	0.15	3,854.1	....
10857	12.82	10.68	9.74	20.74	10.93	0.92	0.47	75.11	76.05	0.19	3,854.3	....
10858	12.13	10.42	9.50	24.02	9.48	0.91	0.48	76.06	76.98	0.14	3,878.3	....
10862	13.93	9.45	8.62	22.32	9.08	0.80	0.40	75.42	76.25	0.12	3,785.5	....
11880	13.27	9.45	8.62	23.40	8.84	1.03	0.39	75.86	76.69	0.10	3,825.4	....
11881	13.24	9.36	8.54	20.74	7.84	0.96	0.46	75.98	76.80	0.17	3,818.7	....
11888	12.26	9.28	8.46	24.00	9.01	1.13	0.48	76.85	77.67	0.22	3,866.4	....
11889	11.00	8.58	7.82	21.93	8.21	1.48	0.47	77.57	78.33	0.22	3,888.9	....
11891	12.30	6.83	6.23	17.92	6.38	1.11	0.30	79.28	79.88	0.15	3,825.8	....
11894	12.63	12.95	11.81	36.54	14.03	1.21	0.41	72.80	73.94	0.30	3,914.9	....
11897	13.61	8.23	7.51	20.13	7.59	1.10	0.38	76.68	77.40	0.15	3,797.2	....
11898	13.02	9.98	9.10	22.62	8.36	1.21	0.41	74.78	75.66	0.07	3,730.2	....
11907	12.53	13.83	12.61	40.73	16.74	0.79	0.51	72.34	73.50	0.25	3,907.0	....
11910	12.49	14.53	13.25	40.05	14.90	1.86	0.46	70.66	71.94	0.17	3,976.2	....
12540	15.30	11.03	10.06	28.95	9.23	0.32	0.89	72.46	73.43	0.82	3,707.4	....
12922	11.62	9.03	8.78	24.07	9.34	0.82	0.38	77.55	78.40	0.07	3,887.1	....
12923	11.48	10.22	9.32	28.99	10.35	1.14	0.44	76.72	77.62	0.15	3,910.0	....
12926	10.74	12.44	11.35	38.12	13.85	1.54	0.50	74.69	75.78	0.30	3,905.7	....
12929	10.64	10.79	9.84	32.43	10.99	1.14	0.44	76.99	77.94	0.20	3,900.1	....
12937	11.40	12.56	11.45	23.54	9.14	1.86	0.42	73.76	74.87	0.20	3,993.0	....
12902	9.39	12.75	11.63	30.70	11.47	1.06	0.41	76.39	77.51	0.47	4,040.1	....
15961	12.09	14.94	13.62	....	....	0.79	0.59	71.59	72.91	0.38	3,930.3	3,971
15962	13.07	10.88	9.92	....	....	0.82	0.53	74.70	75.66	0.42	3,839.3	3,869
15964	12.75	10.60	9.63	....	....	0.87	0.48	75.30	76.27	0.43	3,852.4	3,862
Average.	12.77	10.55	9.62	25.97	9.99	1.02	0.44	74.76	76.14	0.21	3,858.0	3,901

[1] The average for last three samples to be compared with ascertained calories is 3,877.

ANALYSES OF FLOUR.

CLASS II.—*Composition of common market wheat flours.*

Laboratory No.	Moisture.	Proteids, N×6.25.	Proteids, N×5.70.	Moist gluten.	Dry gluten.	Ether extract.	Ash.	Carbohydrates, N×6.25.	Carbohydrates, N×5.70.	Crude fiber.	Calculated calories of combustion.
	Per ct.	Per ct.	Per ct.	Per ct.	Per ct.	Per ct.	Per ct.	Per ct.	Per ct.	Per ct.	
10817	13.31	10.94	9.98	24.57	9.85	1.02	0.40	74.83	75.29	0.12	3,845.0
10819	13.36	10.07	0.18	23.05	9.48	1.06	0.42	75.09	75.98	0.22	3,831.3
10820	13.06	11.12	10.14	22.48	8.94	1.01	0.50	74.26	75.26	0.30	3,855.9
10822	13.71	8.84	8.06	18.40	7.31	0.86	0.35	76.24	77.02	0.25	3,790.3
10833	13.57	11.51	10.50	29.00	11.99	0.99	0.49	73.44	74.45	0.19	3,838.5
11882	12.13	6.65	6.06	15.64	5.88	0.97	0.43	79.82	80.41	0.22	3,824.0
11883	12.10	8.67	7.91	21.61	7.78	1.00	0.46	77.68	78.44	0.22	3,862.5
11884	12.32	6.92	6.31	18.46	7.15	0.82	0.46	79.48	80.09	0.25	3,812.4
11885	12.15	8.05	7.34	21.59	7.52	1.09	0.45	78.26	78.97	0.17	3,851.2
11886	11.70	7.18	6.55	17.31	6.61	0.95	0.42	79.75	80.38	0.35	3,850.8
11887	12.71	9.98	9.10	29.43	11.56	1.08	0.73	75.50	76.98	0.40	3,845.3
11890	12.30	9.45	8.02	25.22	9.40	1.27	0.38	76.60	77.43	0.22	3,878.7
11892	12.38	8.40	7.66	23.41	9.07	1.34	0.49	77.39	78.13	0.25	3,858.1
11893	11.54	7.88	7.19	20.25	7.71	1.41	0.50	78.67	79.36	0.27	3,888.5
12547	13.93	12.08	11.02	13.20	4.77	0.34	0.46	73.19	74.25	0.25	3,803.3
12556	13.37	11.55	10.58	27.30	9.20	0.63	0.39	74.06	75.08	0.27	3,833.3
12918	9.28	15.94	14.54	44.81	17.42	3.27	1.02	69.89	71.29		4,156.1
12919	9.92	15.40	14.04	29.54	11.64	3.84	1.01	68.93	70.29	0.82	4,137.7
12931	10.46	12.75	11.63	40.30	11.70	1.05	0.78	74.36	75.48	0.32	4,009.7
Average	12.28	10.18	9.28	24.55	9.21	1.30	0.61	75.63	76.53	0.28	3,882.5

CLASS III.—*Composition of bakers' and family flour.*

Laboratory No.	Moisture.	Proteids, N×6.25.	Proteids, N×5.70.	Moist gluten.	Dry gluten.	Ether extract.	Ash.	Carbohydrates, N×6.25.	Carbohydrates, N×5.70.	Crude fiber.	Calculated calories of combustion.
	Per ct.	Per ct.	Per ct.	Per ct.	Per ct.	Per ct.	Per ct.	Per ct.	Per ct.	Per ct.	
10821	13.19	9.98	9.10	24.36	9.79	1.10	0.41	75.32	76.20	0.22	3,839.6
10830	12.56	9.98	9.10	27.31	11.08	0.82	0.37	76.27	77.15	0.10	3,855.3
10832	13.61	10.15	9.26	25.14	10.34	0.87	0.45	74.92	75.81	0.19	3,811.2
11895	12.87	13.83	12.61	36.42	14.85	1.45	0.49	71.36	72.58	0.25	3,927.2
11902	12.45	10.33	9.42	28.65	11.29	1.06	0.60	75.47	76.38	0.12	3,862.3
11905	12.65	11.38	10.38	36.27	14.48	1.44	0.48	74.05	75.05	0.17	3,898.5
11908	12.40	14.88	13.57	45.84	16.99	1.16	0.51	71.05	72.36	0.25	3,947.6
11906	12.60	14.70	13.41	40.49	15.23	1.50	0.60	70.60	71.89	0.32	3,950.1
12916	10.14	14.97	13.65	48.18	16.55	1.06	0.70	72.14	73.46	0.30	4,072.9
12917	10.21	14.33	13.07	45.08	16.18	1.97	0.86	72.03	73.89	0.27	4,057.7
12924	11.68	10.22	9.32	32.49	11.61	1.11	0.49	76.50	77.40	0.15	3,903.9
12925	13.09	11.83	10.79	36.67	13.57	1.60	0.71	72.77	73.81	0.22	3,885.4
12930	9.41	11.00	10.03	32.33	11.70	1.21	0.50	77.88	78.85	0.15	4,016.0
12938	10.73	14.38	13.11	26.63	9.39	0.88	0.68	73.28	74.55	0.27	3,986.4
Average	11.60	12.28	11.20	34.70	13.07	1.30	0.57	73.67	74.98	0.22	3,929.6

CLASS IV.—*Composition of miscellaneous wheat flours.*

Laboratory No.	Moisture.	Proteids, N×6.25.	Proteids, N×5.70.	Moist gluten.	Dry gluten.	Ether extract.	Ash.	Carbohydrates, N×6.25.	Carbohydrates, N×5.70.	Crude fiber.	Calculated calories of combustion.	Ascertained calories.
	Per ct.	Per ct.	Per ct.	Per ct.	Per ct.	Per ct.	Per ct.	Per ct.	Per ct.	Per ct.		
10818	13.36	12.43	11.34	26.38	10.12	1.35	0.44	72.42	73.51	0.14	3,882.0	....
10825	13.13	10.15	9.26	24.38	9.62	0.84	0.37	75.51	76.40	0.21	3,833.3	....
10836	12.70	13.39	12.21	29.47	11.40	1.61	1.03	71.27	72.45	0.63	3,913.0	....
10838	13.42	8.32	7.59	20.26	8.40	0.74	0.35	77.17	77.90	0.09	3,788.5	....
10840	13.75	8.03	8.14	21.40	8.44	0.90	0.40	76.02	76.81	0.16	3,790.0	....
10847	13.25	10.07	9.18	22.07	8.95	1.07	0.48	75.13	76.02	0.19	3,833.9	....
10848	13.55	9.28	8.46	22.52	8.50	1.08	0.50	75.59	76.41	0.15	3,808.8	....
10849	13.42	11.29	10.30	27.90	11.32	1.12	0.45	73.72	74.71	0.19	3,902.8	....
10850	13.55	10.33	9.42	24.09	9.52	0.96	0.47	74.69	75.60	0.13	3,820.2	....
10851	13.30	9.98	9.10	25.07	9.91	0.97	0.46	75.20	76.08	0.14	3,822.4	....
10853	13.33	10.85	9.90	27.74	11.30	1.12	0.52	74.18	75.18	0.17	3,843.7	....
10854	13.07	10.68	9.74	26.52	10.44	0.98	0.48	74.79	75.73	0.13	3,840.4	....
10855	13.36	10.50	9.66	26.48	10.07	0.86	0.54	74.05	75.58	0.17	3,824.2	....
10856	13.02	10.42	9.50	28.98	10.87	1.04	0.56	74.96	75.88	0.18	3,844.2	....
10860	11.96	9.54	8.70	21.03	7.91	0.83	0.43	77.24	78.08	0.13	3,860.9	....
10861	13.02	9.37	8.55	23.35	9.30	0.69	0.40	76.52	77.34	0.11	3,816.9	....
11102	12.44	11.38	10.38	27.87	10.73	1.85	0.62	73.71	74.71	0.27	3,922.3	....
11103	11.99	9.72	8.86	25.75	10.00	0.97	0.67	76.65	77.51	0.13	3,868.3	....
11896	13.53	8.40	7.66	29.05	7.53	1.05	0.35	76.67	77.41	0.25	3,800.9	....
11900	13.08	8.93	8.14	23.47	8.77	1.02	0.32	76.65	77.44	0.20	3,827.6	....
11901	12.76	8.93	8.14	25.01	9.70	1.09	0.40	76.82	77.61	0.17	3,841.2	....
11903	12.08	9.45	8.62	26.35	10.34	1.16	0.44	76.87	77.70	0.22	3,879.8	....
11904	12.55	8.40	7.66	21.73	8.73	1.04	0.32	77.69	78.43	0.17	3,842.8	....
11906	12.60	12.43	11.34	39.91	15.53	1.20	0.41	73.36	74.45	0.15	3,907.0	....
12548	15.71	10.68	9.74	27.00	8.41	0.28	0.79	72.54	73.48	0.30	3,686.8	....
12552	12.67	12.60	11.40	37.24	13.53	0.88	0.55	73.30	74.41	0.25	3,885.0	....
12900	13.30	8.75	7.98	21.88	8.21	0.93	0.37	76.56	77.33	....	3,805.2	....
12910	12.63	9.81	8.95	26.21	9.92	1.14	0.44	75.08	76.84	....	3,861.4	....
12911	11.30	10.07	9.18	29.90	11.12	1.14	0.49	77.00	77.89	....	3,919.1	....
12912	11.50	11.47	10.46	35.88	12.15	1.40	0.70	74.09	75.94	....	3,936.8	....
12913	11.72	9.44	8.61	28.67	10.09	1.06	0.52	77.20	78.00	....	3,886.3	....
12914	11.90	11.32	10.32	35.22	13.23	1.33	0.52	74.93	75.93	0.27	3,921.7	....
12915	11.48	11.72	10.60	34.61	13.04	1.23	0.48	75.00	76.12	....	3,942.2	....
14367	10.27	9.75	8.89	....	....	1.18	0.18	78.62	79.48	0.44	3,972.4	3,780.0
15262	12.08	13.75	12.54	....	....	1.93	0.90	71.34	72.55	0.74	3,966.5	3,990.0
15275	11.54	10.81	9.86	....	....	0.78	0.30	76.48	77.30	0.47	3,904.6	3,918.0
15963	12.96	13.32	12.15	....	....	1.06	0.57	72.09	73.26	0.45	3,892.3	3,930.0
Average.	12.73	10.45	9.52	26.80	10.22	1.08	0.49	75.23	76.15	0.25	[1]3,846.3	3,904.5

[1] The average for last four samples to be compared with ascertained calories is 3,934.

CLASS V.—*Composition of self-raising wheat flours.*

Laboratory No.	Moisture.	Proteids, N×6.25.	Proteids, N×5.70.	Moist gluten.	Dry gluten.	Ether extract.	Ash.	Carbohydrates, N×6.25.	Carbohydrates, N×5.70.	Crude fiber.	Calculated calories of combustion.	Ascertained calories
	Per ct.	Per ct.	Per ct.	Per ct.	Per ct.	Per ct.	Per ct.	Per ct.	Per ct.	Per ct.		
10824	12.14	9.72	8.86	20.68	8.18	0.75	4.30	73.99	73.95	0.16	3,698.4	....
10859	12.91	9.19	8.38	27.12	9.93	0.57	3.65	73.68	74.49	0.11	3,676.0	....
12554	11.90	10.85	9.90	30.22	9.96	0.70	4.00	72.55	73.50	0.12	3,736.2	....
12555	12.12	10.65	9.71	29.84	10.53	0.64	3.95	72.64	73.58	0.10	3,722.8	....
14365	9.78	9.81	8.95	......	......	0.77	4.88	74.76	75.62	0.39	3,775.7	3,700
14373	9.83	8.25	7.52	......	......	0.79	5.92	75.21	75.94	0.37	3,706.6	3,724
Average.	11.45	9.75	8.89	26.97	9.65	0.70	4.45	73.66	74.51	0.21	¹3,719.3	3,712

¹ The average for last two samples to be compared with ascertained calories is 3,741.2.

CLASS VI.—*Composition of gluten wheat flours.*

Laboratory No.	Moisture.	Proteids, N×6.25.	Proteids, N×5.70.	Moist gluten.	Dry gluten.	Ether extract.	Ash.	Carbohydrates, N×6.25.	Carbohydrates, N×5.70.	Crude fiber.	Calculated calories of combustion.
	Per ct.	Per ct.	Per ct.	Per ct.	Per ct.	Per ct.	Per ct.	Per ct.	Per ct.	Per ct.	
12553	12.90	13.30	12.13	39.68	14.84	1.05	0.55	72.11	73.28	0.32	3,891.1

DISCUSSION OF RESULTS—CLASS I.

The samples whose analyses are given under Class I may be regarded as representing the best high-grade patent wheat flours on our markets. As has been previously noted, we can not be certain that the classification here made is entirely correct. It is more than probable that some samples of low-grade flours are included in the table on account of the names which they bear. On the contrary, it is equally probable that some of the highest grade flours are found in the other tables. The reader must again be cautioned in regard to this classification, that it is not rigid, and that it is no expression of commendation of a sample to have it placed in one or another of the classes under consideration. In the classification the only guide at our disposal was the name and description of the sample, and this has been used as judiciously as possible in grouping the samples into the various classes.

Moisture.

In the samples of Class I there is an extremely uniform percentage of moisture. The variations from the mean, which is 12.77, are usually very small. The extreme plus variation is found in sample No. 12549, with a content of moisture of 15.30 per cent, the variation being 2.52 per cent in this case. The minimum percentage of water is found in sample No. 12992, containing 9.39 per cent, a variation from the mean of 3.38 per cent.

The data show that the flours of this grade are placed upon our markets under very uniform conditions in respect of moisture. This arises either from the fact that the quantity of moisture in the grains from which the flours are made is remarkably constant, or that the flours when prepared exhibit equal hygroscopic properties which tend to regulate the quantity of moisture therein contained. The only marked variations from the mean percentage of moisture are found in the two samples mentioned above and in No. 10834. Leaving out of consideration these three samples, the remarkable uniformity of moisture is made more strikingly apparent.

Proteids.

Uniformity of composition as regards moisture, which is mentioned in the preceding paragraph, is no longer shown when we consider the percentage of proteids in the different samples. In the following remarks the second column of proteids, viz, those obtained by $N \times 5.70$, is referred to. The mean percentage of proteids in the high-grade flours is 9.62. The variations, however, are more marked than in the case of moisture, although this variation is more apparent than real. The actual maximum and minimum departures from the standard are found in sample No. 11910, with a plus variation of 3.63 per cent, and in sample No. 11891, with a minus variation of 3.39 per cent. In comparing the two samples it is seen that No. 11891 has less than half as much proteid matter as No. 11910.

As has been shown in previous bulletins of this division, the influence of climate and soil upon the content of proteid matter in wheat is extremely marked, and inasmuch as samples of wheat flour bought in the open market can not always be traced to any particular locality, it is not surprising that this striking variation in proteid matter should be found. Again, it must be considered that the quantity of proteid matter in a high-grade wheat flour is uniformly less than in the whole wheat grain, since in the separation of the germ and of the bran, or of the next to the outer coating, the particles of the grain which are less rich in starch and more rich in proteid matter are removed. A few other samples show quite wide variations from the mean, notably No. 11889 and 11897 with a deficit of proteid matter, and No. 11907 with an excess. Leaving out the five samples mentioned above as showing extreme variations, the other samples show quite a uniform composition in respect of proteid matter. A simple determination of nitrogen, as has already been indicated, is not sufficient to determine the value of the sample in respect to this constituent.

The wheat kernel, as has been stated before in this bulletin, contains two proteid matters which, in the presence of water, unite to form the gluten. It is this glutinous portion of the proteid matter present— constituting, in fact, nearly the whole of it—to which wheat flour owes its high character as a bread making material. Gluten also varies in its qualities, so that the determination of the moist and dry gluten, while it gives approximately the glutinous characteristics of the flour, does not always portray them exactly. The quality of the gluten which gives it its high value is found in its ability to entangle and hold particles of gas. During the process of fermentation which takes place in the raising of bread, particles of carbon dioxid are set free by the decomposition of the sugar of the flour and its conversion into carbon dioxid and alcohol. After the fermentation has gone far enough and the bread is placed in the oven, the particles of carbon dioxid which are entangled in the gluten expand during the early part of the baking, and the alcohol which is present in a liquid state is volatilized and acts, while in this condition, in the same manner as the carbon dioxid itself. The result is that on baking a loaf which has been properly fermented we secure a mass of material which is spongy and porous, and this condition has been made possible by the presence of the gluten, which expands in minute hollow spheroids, carrying with them the starchy particles of the loaf. Before the temperature has reached a sufficient degree to set the gluten the expansion is complete, having taken place principally during the fermentation state and partially during the early parts of the baking.

Other cereal grains contain either no gluten at all or a much less quantity, and of a much poorer quality than the wheat. It is for this reason that wheat is, among all the cereals, the most highly prized for bread-making purposes. There is no reason, however, for believing that the gluten is any more nutritious than any other form of the proteid matters occurring in cereals, which are, nevertheless, incapable of showing the phenomenon just described as taking place during panification.

Dry gluten.

By reason of the indefinite character of the determination of dry gluten, it is not surprising to find wide variations in the different samples. Beginning with a mean of 9.99 per cent, which is greater than the total proteid matter of the flour, we find constant variations from this mean in the different samples. The maximum variation is found in sample No. 11907, with a content of dry gluten of 16.74 per cent, showing a variation from the mean of 6.75 per cent. The other extreme is shown in sample No. 11891, where the dry gluten amounts to only 6.38 per cent, a variation from the mean of 3.61 per cent. In general, it is seen that there is a common agreement in the flours between the percentages of dry gluten and of total proteid matter. In other words, those samples which have a remarkably high content of total proteid matter also show a high content of dry gluten. This is illustrated by Nos. 11907, 11910, and 11894. Each of these samples has a high content of dry gluten and a high content of total proteid matter, and the samples having the highest content of dry gluten, it is seen, have the highest content of total proteid matter.

Moist gluten.

In moist gluten the variations are still more marked. The mean content of moist gluten in the samples is 25.97 per cent. The maximum content is found in sample No. 11907, namely, 40.73 per cent. The minimum content is found in sample No. 11891, namely, 17.92 per cent. The general rule is also shown here; namely, that those flours with a high content of total proteid matter and a high content of dry gluten also show, as a rule, a high content of moist gluten, and the reverse. This is well illustrated on the one hand by Nos. 11907 and 11910, and on the other by Nos. 11891 and 10829. As has been stated before, the content of moist gluten is a factor of great importance to bakers, as it is possible to produce a loaf from flour of this quality which contains a higher percentage of water than would be found in bread from a flour which has a low percentage of moist gluten. In domestic bread making this is a matter of no financial importance, but where loaves are bought by weight it is easily seen that much less nutriment is secured in the purchase of a loaf with 40 per cent of water than is obtained in the purchase of one of the same weight with 30 per cent of water. Aside from this, however, a flour which yields a high content of moist gluten lends itself more readily to the fabrication of a loaf of greater porosity and sponginess; so that, aside from the higher content of water in such a loaf, there are many advantages in using a flour with a high content of moist gluten.

Ether extract.

The average quantity of matter soluble in anhydrous ether present in a flour of the first class is 1.02 per cent. The maximum content of ether extract in any sample is found in No. 12926, where it rises to 1.54 per cent. The minimum is found in sample No. 12549, where it sinks to 0.32 per cent. The relative quantity of ether extract which is obtained from a flour depends almost solely upon the degree of perfection with which the grain is freed from its germ. Where a portion of the germs is left in the product the ether extract will be high. Where the germs are almost completely removed the ether extract will be low. These statements are strictly applicable where samples of wheat contain practically the same quantity of fat or oil. A glance at the table of ether extracts will therefore reveal with a good deal of accuracy the degree of germ extraction which is reached in the milling. The fat is a valuable food, but it must not be supposed that the whole of the ether extract is composed of fat. Resins, chlorophyl, and coloring matter soluble in ether are found also in connection with the fat or oil in ether extract. The food value of the ether extract is not, therefore, as a rule, to be based upon the total percentage, but upon a certain proportion thereof. It is probably safe to say that 75 per cent, at least, of the ether extract is composed of pure glycerides, and possibly a larger proportion.

CARBOHYDRATES OF FLOUR.

Content of ash.

The content of ash, as is the case with the content of ether extract, is quite a reliable index of the character of the milling to which the wheat has been subjected. In proportion as the external coverings of the wheat grain are removed will the content of ash fall. The mean percentage of crude ash in the samples is 0.44 per cent. The remarkable uniformity of the data shows that the milling processes are practically the same in all cases except in respect to the thoroughness with which the external coats of the wheat grains are removed. The maximum percentage of crude ash in the samples is found in No. 12549, viz, 0.89 per cent. The minimum percentage is found in samples No. 10834 and No. 10835, each of which has 0.33 per cent. The mineral matters of the ash are composed chiefly of potash and phosphoric acid, as is seen in the data representing the analyses of the ash and of flours given on page 1212.

Carbohydrates.

The discussion of the percentage of carbohydrates will be based on the data obtained in the column headed "Carbohydrates, N × 5.70." The mean percentage of carbohydrates in the flours examined is 76.14. The variations from this mean are very slight, considering its magnitude. The maximum percentage of carbohydrates is found in sample No. 11891, viz, 79.88 per cent; the minimum percentage of carbohydrates is found in sample No. 11910, viz, 71.94 per cent. The variations from the mean in these two instances are, respectively, 2.74 per cent and 4.20 per cent.

As has been previously explained, the carbohydrates of this column present the whole of the carbohydrates of the wheat flour. The most important of them, from the baker's and the nutritive standpoint, are the starch and sugar; the sugar by reason of its undergoing fermentation in the process of raising the bread, and the starch on account of its large quantity and food value. The quantities of crude fiber, pentosans, dextrin, and other carbohydrates in wheat flour are quite insignificant, probably amounting to less than 0.5 per cent in all. These bodies, therefore, have little importance from a practical or dietetic point of view. The mean percentage of fiber in the flours of Class I is about 0.2 per cent.

The carbohydrates of patent flours include the following bodies in the proportions mentioned:

	Per cent.
Sucrose	0.10
Dextrin, galactin, and soluble starch	0.20
Pentosans and reducing sugars	Trace.
Crude fiber	0.20
Starch (proteid factor, 5.70)	75.60

DISCUSSION OF RESULTS—CLASS II.

The chemical composition of the common market wheat flours is not very greatly different from that of the high-grade patent flours already mentioned. It is seen that the common flours have slightly less moisture, almost exactly the same quantity of proteids, less gluten, higher ether extract, higher ash, and higher crude fiber. This shows that in the milling process by which these flours are made there is not so perfect a degermination as in the other instance, nor is there such a perfect separation of the branny materials, as is indicated by the higher content both of ash and of crude fiber. From a dietetic point of view, however, there is scarcely any difference between the two typical flours. The carbohydrates of the common market flours are approximately composed of bodies in the proportions noted in the following table:

	Per cent.
Sucrose	0.25
Dextrin, galactin, and soluble starch	0.20
Crude fiber	0.30
Pentosans and reducing sugars	0.01
Starch (proteid factor 5.70)	75.80

DISCUSSION OF RESULTS—CLASS III.

The mean data showing the composition of bakers' and family flours vary only slightly from the mean composition of the two classes already studied. The remarkable uniformity of moisture will be noted. The content of ash in the family flours is higher than that in the high-grade patent flours, but slightly lower than in the flours of Class II. The most marked variation in the samples is found in the content of gluten, both the moist and the dry gluten in the bakers' and family flours being considerably in excess of the same constituents in Classes I and II. In fact, the glutens in this class of flours are nearly as abundant as in the single sample of the so-called gluten flour comprising Class VI. It is evident that flour which is made especially for bakers' use, therefore, belongs to that class known as "strong" flour, containing a high content of gluten, and affording a material which will make a bread holding a large excess of water.

The variations in Class III in important constituents are well marked. The minimum percentage of proteids is 9.1, found in samples Nos. 10821 and 10830. The maximum percentage is found in sample No. 11908, where it rises to 13.57. In many instances it will be observed that the dry gluten is greater in quantity than the whole of the proteid matter. The reason for this has been previously given. The ash varies from 0.37 per cent in sample No. 10830 to 0.86 in sample No. 12917. In respect to the carbohydrates and other constituents, the same general remarks may be made as were applied in Class I. The least quantity of carbohydrates, viz, 72.36 per cent, is found in sample No. 11908, and the highest, viz, 78.85 per cent, in sample No. 12930.

The carbohydrates of this class of flours are composed approximately of the following constituents in the proportions named:

	Per cent.
Sucrose	0.10
Dextrin and galactin	0.15
Crude fiber	0.25
Pentosans and reducing sugars	Trace.
Starch (proteid factor 5.70)	75.65

DISCUSSION OF RESULTS—CLASS IV.

The miscellaneous wheat flours, as has already been explained, have been grouped together from those where the descriptions were insufficient to place them in any of the other classes. They therefore represent the general run of ordinary flours found upon the market. In the data giving the mean composition of these flours we find again a remarkable agreement with those of the other classes. The figures for dry and moist gluten are very close to those of Class I, as are those also for the proteids. The mean data for the other constituents show a general agreement with the preceding classes, especially Classes I and II. Considerable variations of composition are noted in individual cases. The smallest percentage of proteids, namely, 7.59, is found in sample No. 10838, and the highest, viz, 12.21, in No. 10836. The highest content of ash is in sample No. 10836. This sample, however, is marked "Flour of the entire wheat," and hence is supposed to contain all parts of the wheat grain except the outer, branny layer. The large increase in the ash in this sample is, therefore, due to the incorporation of a large portion of the bran in the flour. This is a sample which would be more properly compared with Graham flours than with ordinary wheat flours. The smallest quantity of ash, viz, 0.32 per cent, is found in sample No. 11900.

DESCRIPTION OF RESULTS—CLASSES V AND VI.

The number of samples embraced in these two classes is not large enough to warrant an extended discussion. In the self-raising flours the natural increase to be looked for would be in the ash, and this shows that about $3\frac{1}{2}$ per cent of mineral matter had been added in the form of baking powders; in other words, $3\frac{1}{2}$ pounds of the baking powder are found in each 100 pounds of the mixture. This addition of mineral matter naturally produces a corresponding decrease in the other ingredients, measured in per cents. The single sample of so-called gluten wheat flour is seen by the data to be made of a wheat not exceptionally rich in proteids. Many examples of a wheat with a higher percentage of gluten are found in the preceding classes.

TYPICAL AMERICAN FLOURS.

From a careful study of the foregoing data it is possible to arrive at a correct idea of the composition of typical American flours of the classes indicated above.

HIGH-GRADE PATENT FLOUR.

A high-grade American patent flour has, approximately, the following composition:

	Per cent.		Per cent.
Moisture	12.75	Ether extract	1.00
Proteids (N × 6.25)	10.50	Ash	0.50
Proteids (N × 5.70)	9.50	Carbohydrates (N × 6.25)	75.25
Moist gluten	26.00	Carbohydrates (N × 5.70)	76.25
Dry gluten	10.00	Crude fiber	0.20

COMMON MARKET WHEAT FLOUR.

It is evident that the flours commonly placed upon the market in bulk in any given locality will vary in composition according to the composition of the wheat from which they are made and the kind of milling process by which they are produced. If the flours in any given locality are formed from the wheats of the neighborhood, they would evidently partake of the character of those varieties of wheat. It is probable that, as a whole, the flours which are exposed for sale in a market like that of Washington will be representative of the flours of the whole country, as very little of the local supply comes from the wheat grown in the vicinity. The data obtained, therefore, from the analyses of a large number of samples bought in the open market may be relied upon as giving a fair indication of what a typical common market bulk flour is. The composition of such a typical flour, as indicated by the data, is approximately as follows:

	Per cent.		Per cent.
Moisture	12.25	Ether extract	1.30
Proteids (N × 6.25)	10.20	Ash	0.60
Proteids (N × 5.70)	9.30	Carbohydrates (N × 6.25)	75.65
Moist gluten	24.50	Carbohydrates (N × 5.70)	76.55
Dry gluten	9.25	Crude fiber	0.30

BAKERS' FLOURS.

The typical American flour which is sold under the name of bakers' flour and which, as a rule, is regarded as somewhat inferior to the high-grade patent flours, has a composition which, as determined by the foregoing analyses, is approximately represented by the following numbers:

	Per cent.		Per cent.
Moisture	11.75	Ether extract	1.30
Proteids (N × 6.25)	12.30	Ash	0.60
Proteids (N × 5.70)	11.20	Carbohydrates (N × 6.25)	74.05
Moist gluten	34.70	Carbohydrates (N × 5.70)	75.15
Dry gluten	13.10	Crude fiber	0.20

Again we are struck here with the practically identical composition of the bakers' flours with the high-grade patent flours. The chief differences are found in the fact that the bakers' flours are drier, containing about 1 per cent less moisture. They have, too, a distinctly higher percentage of proteids as compared with the high-grade flours, due to the fact, doubtless, that large quantities of the outer part of the kernels enter into the composition of these flours. The quantities of gluten are more than correspondingly increased, which indicates that the glutinous part of the proteids tends to accumulate in flours of this character, and this is due to the nature of the milling process and to the separation of the various parts of the wheat kernel. The quantity of ether extract is also higher than in the high-grade flours, showing a less perfect degermination of the grain during the milling process. The ash is also slightly higher than in the high-grade flours, while the carbohydrates are somewhat lower, due to the higher percentage of proteids.

In a general comparison of bakers' flours with high-grade patent flours it is seen that the nutritive ratio is much narrower in the bakers' flour and the percentage of proteids higher. Judged by the common theories of nutrition, therefore, the bakers' flour would make a bread better suited to the laboring man, while the high-grade patent flours would form a bread with a greater tendency to produce fat and animal heat.

MISCELLANEOUS FLOURS.

In Class IV wheat flours have been collected of the miscellaneous samples which, by reason of their names or descriptions, were not capable of classification with the three preceding grades of flours. These flours largely represent the product of small mills, and are derived from the most diversified sources. As would be expected, they show among themselves a considerable degree of variation, although the mean composition does not differ very greatly from that of the previously described grades. The typical flour of this miscellaneous class, judged by the data which have been obtained, will have the following approximate composition:

	Per cent.		Per cent.
Moisture	12.75	Ether extract	1.05
Proteids ($N \times 6.25$)	10.30	Ash	0.50
Proteids ($N \times 5.70$)	9.35	Carbohydrates ($N \times 6.25$)	75.30
Moist gluten	26.80	Carbohydrates ($N \times 5.70$)	76.25
Dry gluten	10.20	Crude fiber	0.25

The important feature of such a typical flour is its almost exact identity, from a commercial point of view, with the high-grade patent flours. The averages of the two classes are so nearly alike that they could be interchanged with each other with no appreciable modification of chemical composition. This fact emphasizes in a most marked degree a point which has been brought out in the previous discussions; viz, that the commercial value of flour depends almost exclusively upon the nature of the milling process and upon the color and general appearance of the flour, and has little or nothing to do with nutritive properties.

SELF-RAISING FLOURS.

The small importance, from a commercial point of view, of self-raising flour gives little encouragement for the endeavor to establish a typical standard for this class of nutrients. It is evident, without discussion, that the self-raising properties of a flour are due to the incorporation therewith of some of the ordinary chemical leavening agents which will be described further on. In other words, by mixing with the flour an ordinary baking powder, or the essential leavening constituents thereof, the so-called self-raising flour is produced. This flour, it is evidently intended, should be used immediately for bread making without being subjected to any previous fermentation.

Only a few samples of self-raising flours have been examined. A typical self-raising flour, representing nearly the mean of the samples examined, has the following composition:

	Per cent.		Per cent.
Moisture	11.30	Ether extract	.70
Proteids ($N \times 6.25$)	10.10	Ash	4.00
Proteids ($N \times 5.70$)	9.20	Carbohydrates ($N \times 6.25$)	72.90
Moist gluten	27.00	Carbohydrates ($N \times 5.70$)	73.80
Dry gluten	9.65	Crude fiber	0.20

As was to be expected, the chief variation of a self-raising flour from a typical flour of the other grades described is found in the percentage of ash which it contains. This percentage of ash arises from the mineral residue of the leavening reagents added for the purpose of securing the raising of the loaf when the flour is mixed for bread making. Since the normal ash constituent of a flour is about 0.5 per cent, it is seen that there are added to the flour for leavening purposes about $3\frac{1}{2}$ per cent of mineral matters. The manifest unfitness of flours of this kind for general baking purposes will prevent a very wide commercial use of such articles. If chemical leavening agents are to be used it is undoubtedly the better plan to mix them with the flour at the time of baking rather than to buy them in an already mixed condition.

COMPOSITION OF TYPICAL FRENCH FLOURS.

The composition of typical French flours derived from samples of wheat of known origin has been determined by analyses made by Girard,[1] in which some novel methods of investigation were used.

Four samples of typical wheat were used for the examination, the composition of which is shown in the following table in percentages:

Constituents.		Wheat from—			
		Bordeaux.	Altkirch.	Flanders.	St. Laud.
Moisture	per cent	14.97	14.50	15.12	14.94
Mean weight of the kernel	grams	0.051	0.038	0.041	0.050
Composition of the kernel:					
Coatings	per cent	12.52	13.90	15.61	14.12
Germ	do	1.50	1.41	1.35	1.16
Rest of the kernel	do	85.98	84.69	83.04	84.72

[1] Comptes rendus, vol. 124, April 26 and May 3, 1897.

COMPOSITION OF FRENCH FLOURS.

The study of the subject by Girard was based chiefly on the point of view of the miller, and in the preparation of the material he had constructed a small mill on the roller-process plan, which would give practically the same results in a small way as are obtained in the large mills on the large scale. This mill operated so satisfactorily that the total loss of the material between the entire wheat and the finished products was not more than one half of 1 per cent. By his mill he separated the samples into two portions; viz, of flour consisting of 70 per cent of the weight of the entire grain and the different residues constituting the other 30 per cent. The separation of the water soluble content of the flour was accomplished by treating in ice-cold water, he having found that at the ordinary room temperatures the natural enzymes of the flour produce a solution of starch during the several hours' contact which is necessary to secure a complete solution of the water soluble matters. For this reason it is impossible to obtain any satisfactory results in working with water at ordinary room temperatures. The action of the enzymes, however, was found to be entirely suspended at a temperature near zero, and acting on this knowledge, Girard was able to secure the complete water soluble contents of a flour without the complication of the activity of the enzymes rendering a portion of the starch soluble.

The action of ice-cold water on flour subjected to constant stirring is complete in about four hours, and this has been the time adopted for securing the water soluble content. The aqueous solution, after filtration, is treated with four times its volume of 95 per cent alcohol, by which the nitrogenous matters which have entered into solution are precipitated, together with a considerable quantity of galactin, which by many investigators has been mistaken for dextrin. Girard has never been able to detect the least trace of dextrin in the aqueous solution of a flour made under the conditions mentioned above. The starch is obtained mechanically by separation on silk bolting cloth of the requisite degree of fineness. The fatty matters are obtained by using benzene as the solvent at a temperature sufficiently high to secure complete solution. The flours obtained from the four samples mentioned above were subjected to analysis by the method just outlined, and they were found to have the following composition:

Constituents.	Flour made from wheat from—			
	Bordeaux.	Altkirch.	Flanders.	St. Laud.
	Per cent.	Per cent.	Per cent.	Per cent.
Moisture	15.42	14.92	15.58	14.74
Materials soluble in water:				
Dextrose, or reducing sugars	0.21	0.16	0.20	0.09
Sucrose	0.86	1.20	1.70	0.98
Nitrogenous matters	1.10	1.02	1.02	1.28
Galactin	0.52	0.59	0.78	0.99
Mineral matters	0.36	0.32	0.30	0.22
Not determined	0.07	0.32	0.30	0.22
Total	3.12	3.29	4.00	3.56

Constituents	Flour made from wheat from—			
	Bordeaux.	Altkirch.	Flanders.	St. Laud.
	Per cent.	Per cent.	Per cent.	Per cent.
Materials insoluble in water:				
Gluten	7.45	8.04	8.32	8.14
Starch	71.22	70.93	69.88	71.22
Fat	1.07	0.84	1.12	0.95
Mineral matter	0.20	0.29	0.40	0.40
Cells and débris	0.23	0.25	0.22	0.23
Total	80.17	80.35	79.94	80.94
General total	98.71	98.56	99.52	99.24
Unknown and lost	1.29	1.44	0.48	0.76
Acidity expressed as sulphuric acid	0.009	0.006	0.009	0.011
Ratio of glutenin to gliadin:				
Glutenin	25	25	25	25
Gliadin	87	70	62	72

It is evident from an inspection of the data obtained by Girard that a considerable quantity of the germ is incorporated in the flour, as indicated by the high percentage of sucrose.

The 30 per cent of residue obtained from the entire wheat by the operation of the small mill in like manner was subjected to analysis, with the following results:

Constituents.	Residues from flour made of wheat from—			
	Bordeaux.	Altkirch.	Flanders.	St. Laud.
	Per cent.	Per cent.	Per cent.	Per cent.
Moisture	15.12	14.56	14.89	14.33
Materials soluble in water:				
Nitrogenous	2.72	2.80	2.48	2.92
Carbohydrates	5.74	6.58	6.57	5.91
Mineral matters	2.04	1.82	1.50	1.72
Total	10.50	11.20	10.55	10.55
Materials insoluble in water:				
Gluten	4.78	4.31	4.36	4.67
Starch	28.35	26.36	26.40	29.79
Nitrogenous and ligneous matters	5.05	6.49	6.52	4.88
Fat	3.55	3.65	2.68	3.16
Celluloses and pentosans	29.87	30.26	31.38	29.06
Mineral matters	2.12	1.82	1.86	1.81
Total	73.72	72.89	73.20	73.37
General total	99.34	98.65	98.64	98.25
Unknown and lost	0.66	1.35	1.36	1.75
	100.00	100.00	100.00	100.00

The composition of the total wheat calculated from the two sets of analyses is shown in the following table:

Constituents.	Composition of entire wheats from—			
	Bordeaux.	Altkirch.	Flanders.	St. Laud.
	Grams.	*Grams.*	*Grams.*	*Grams.*
Mean weight of kernel	0.051	0.038	0.041	0.050
Composition of the kernel:	*Per cent.*	*Per cent.*	*Per cent.*	*Per cent.*
Coatings	12.52	13.90	15.61	14.12
Germ	1.50	1.41	1.35	1.16
Rest of kernel	85.98	84.69	83.04	84.72
Moisture	14.97	14.50	15.12	14.94
Nitrogenous matters:				
Gluten	6.64	6.92	7.13	7.10
Soluble diastases, etc	1.59	1.54	1.37	1.74
Ligneous	1.51	1.95	1.95	1.46
Starch	58.35	57.55	56.84	58.78
Fat	1.81	1.68	1.58	1.61
Soluble carbohydrates:				
Sugars	0.75	0.95	1.33	0.75
Galactin	0.36	0.41	0.55	0.69
Others (from the envelope)	1.79	1.97	1.97	1.77
Celluloses and pentosans	9.12	9.08	9.56	8.88
Mineral matters	1.49	1.51	1.50	1.54
Unknown and lost	1.62	1.94	1.30	0.74
Total	100.00	100.00	100.00	100.00

In general it may be said of the analyses mentioned above that the mechanical separation of the starch, as has been shown by experiments in this laboratory, is apt to give a product mixed to a certain degree with finely divided celluloses and pentosans. In respect of the other constituents it may be said that the percentages obtained agree quite well with the results of the general analyses which have been conducted in this division, except that the French flours seem to have a larger percentage of sucrose than those of American origin.

VISCOSITY OF DOUGH.

The viscosity of a dough made from wheat flour is a valuable indication of the character of the gluten therein. Many forms of apparatus have been devised to measure this viscosity in terms of the speed with which a cylinder of given weight penetrates the mass, or the depth to which it sinks.

THE USE OF FARINOMETERS.

Several methods have been employed for determining the viscosity of flour. One of the most satisfactory is the use of the farinometer.

KEDZIE'S FARINOMETER.

The Michigan farinometer was devised by the chemist of the experiment station of the Michigan Agricultural College for grading the quality of flour made from winter wheat raised in that State. It is patterned somewhat upon the plan of Jago's viscometer. The instrument is shown in parts in fig. 1. The instrument in use is exhibited in fig. 2.

Parts shown in fig. 1 are as follows:

No. 1 is the stand or support of the posts.

No. 2 is the cap of No. 1, and discloses the half-inch opening (half closed by the slide) through which the dough is forced by the pressure of the rod, No. 4. The slide by which this opening is opened and closed is plainly shown; also the socket for holding No. 3.

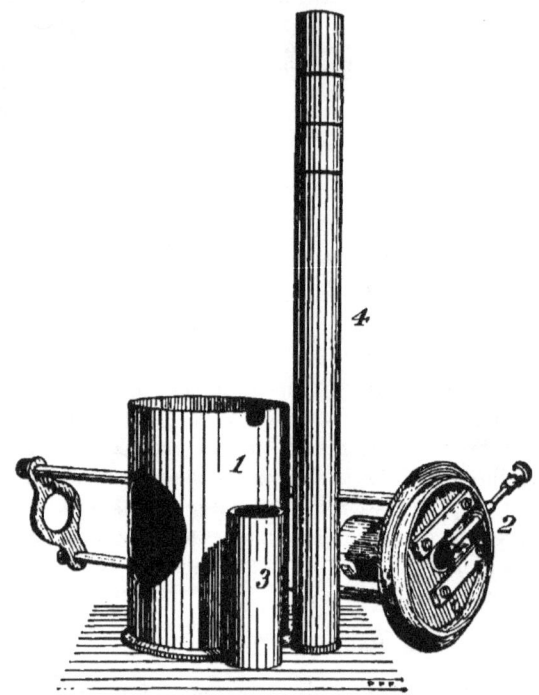

FIG. 1.—Kedzie's farinometer showing the parts.

No. 3 is a brass tube 3 inches high and 1 inch internal diameter, with a small knob to fit into the notched opening in the side of the socket seen in No. 2, to hold No. 3 firmly in place.

No. 4 is a steel rod $\frac{15}{16}$ inch in diameter and 13 inches long, with a thin brass cap 1 inch in diameter, beveled slightly so that the front edge fills the barrel of No. 3 without friction, and is yet dough-tight. Near the top the rod is marked into inch spaces.

The farinometer was made by the American Brass Novelty Works, of Grand Haven, Mich.

In using the farinometer two points are considered:

1. The water-absorbing power of a flour, or the percentage of water it will take up to form a dough of a certain consistency.

2. The viscosity of such dough, or its resistance to change of form under a uniform force; e. g., the length of time in seconds required to force a cylinder of dough 1 inch high through a hole one-half inch in diameter under the pressure of a vertical steel rod 13 inches long and weighing 2½ pounds avoirdupois. From these data combined I hope to find a compound factor which will express the strength of a flour. If, in addition to this, a scale of colors can be secured to represent the tints of colors for winter-wheat flours, the means for grading such flours would seem to be at hand. It is for these results that the chemical department at the Michigan station is working. It hopes to present a bulletin on grading flours in the near future.

KNAIS'S FARINOMETER.[1]

Knais has constructed a new apparatus for the valuation of flour, which consists of an alcohol lamp and a vessel filled with oil. A cylindrical tube is soldered on the cover of the latter, into which a smaller cylinder, which serves to contain the dough, may be slipped. In the oil bath is placed a piece of alloy consisting of 0.75 lead and 0.25 tin, and on this stands a metallic tube having a pointed end and connected at the top with a bell. The alloy melts at 289°, at which point the pointed tube penetrates the alloy and sets the bell in motion. Into the smaller cylinder are placed 20 grams of dough consisting of 2 parts flour and 1 part water. The oil bath is then heated until the bell rings, when the flame is extinguished and the empty space in the cylinder measured. This space is proportionate to the rising of the dough.[2]

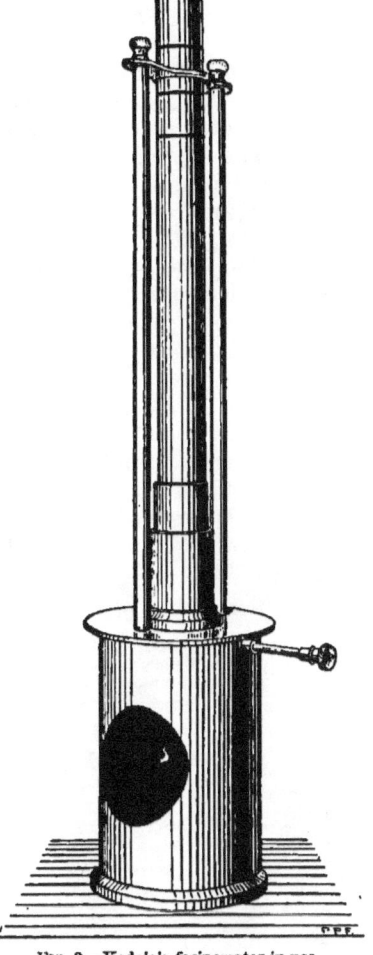

FIG. 2.—Kedzie's farinometer in use.

---

[1] Zeitsch. f. Nahrungsmittel Untersuch. in Hygiene, 1892–1896, 217.
[2] Rev. intern. des falsif. 1892, p. 160.

Note of abstractor.—This apparatus is not new, as J. Moeller in 1889 described it in Realencyklopädie für die gesammte Pharmacie under the article Mehl, Bd. VI, page 606, stating that it is identical with Bolland's aleurometer.

GLUTEN TESTER.

The character of the gluten separated from a wheat flour is tested by Foster as indicated below.

The gluten tester shown in the accompanying illustrations (figs. 3 and 4) is made of brass, and consists of two cylinders of like diameter, and 8 inches long, in which the gluten is placed, and a piston of a certain weight is placed on top of the gluten. The water in the gluten, as it becomes heated, is converted into steam, expands the gluten, and forces up the piston. Gluten of the greatest elasticity will force the piston highest, making it possible to obtain a record in inches of expansion of glutens from like quantities of different flours. One Troy ounce of flour, 480 grains, is taken as a basis with this instrument.

Since an even and easily controlled temperature is necessary in the operation, the cylinders are heated in an electric oven.

The oven is 5 feet long, 26 inches wide, 3 feet 6 inches high, is built of sheet steel, two thicknesses 2 inches apart and filled between with mineral wool to aid in retaining the heat, which is furnished by an electric current. The heat can be changed from top to bottom of oven, as desired. The windows make it possible to see just what is going on inside without opening the oven and losing heat. The temperature is determined by a thermometer inserted through the side.

The following data were obtained by using the above-described apparatus:

Estimations of gluten quality of separations in roller milling.

[Flour and gluten grades are standards, the colors of which are registered by colored glasses—Lovibond's tintometer. Column 3 indicates the expansion in inches of gluten as baked in gluten tester. Column 4 indicates percentage of wet gluten to flour.]

Products.	Grade of flour.	Grade of gluten.	Expansion of gluten.	Gluten.
			Inches.	*Per cent.*
Break:				
No. 1	85	90	4½	50.00
No. 2	86	92	6	53.00
No. 3	86	92	6	53.00
No. 4	70	75	6½	67.50
No. 5	50	65	5½	68.75
No. 6	45	50	4	69.00
Middlings:				
No. 1	100	100	4½	42.71
No. 2	98	96	3½	40.21
No. 3	96	96	2½	40.00
No. 4	95	96	5½	44.38
No. 5	96	98	4½	42.02
No. 6	85	90	6½	46.67
No. 7	90	88	4½	42.08
No. 8	88	88	3½	43.13
Germ:				
No. 1	98	96	3½	40.21
No. 2	65	56	2	37.50

GLUTEN TESTER.

1273

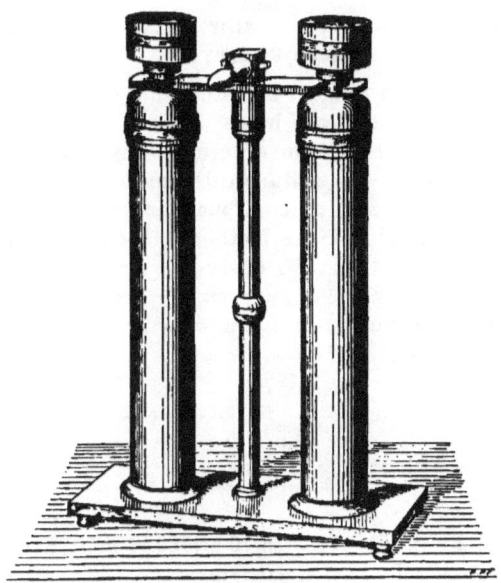

FIG. 3.—Gluten tester in use.

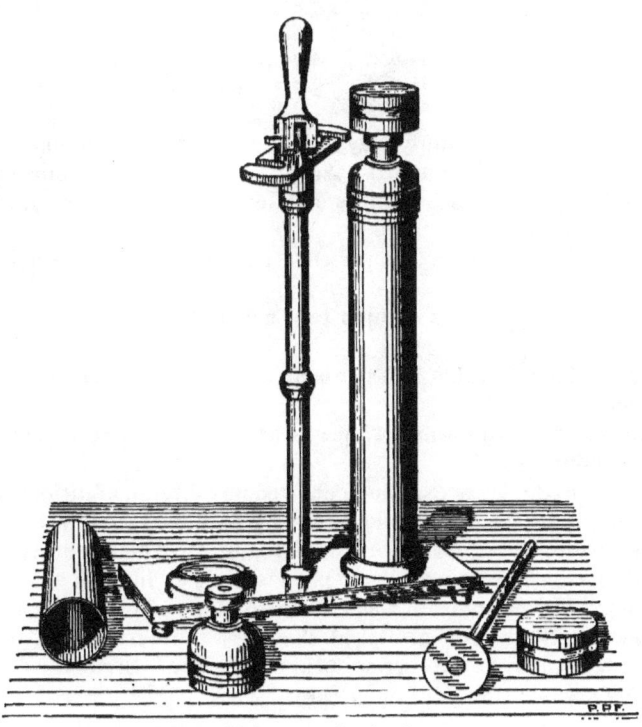

FIG. 4.—Gluten tester showing the parts.

AN EXAMINATION OF FLOURS BY A NEW METHOD OF DETERMINING THEIR QUALITY.[1]

While examining a large number of Hungarian flours Vidrodi found that the ash and the quality stood in a certain relation to each other. So far, the quality of a flour has been determined by comparing it either dry on a small black plate with a standard flour or by preparing a thin dough and comparing this with a dough made in exactly the same manner from the standard flour. These methods depend naturally on the experience of the eye, and no two observers are apt to agree. By applying the above relation the quality can be determined with much greater precision. The following average percentages of ash were found in flours of different quality:

	Per cent.		Per cent.
No. 0	0.31	No. 5	0.66
1	0.36	6	0.98
2	0.41	7	1.53
3	0.47	8	2.24
4	0.58		

The ash determination is made with 10 grams of flour, and the following limits are recommended for wheat flours:

	Per cent.		Per cent.
No. 0	0.20–0.34	No. 5	0.61–0.70
1	0.35–0.39	6	0.71–1.16
2	0.40–0.43	7	1.17–1.80
3	0.44–0.52	8	1.81–3.15
4	0.53–0.60		

These figures naturally apply only to Hungarian flours, and may have to be changed for other countries. Adulteration with rye flour has a very marked effect on the fineness as determined by this method, reducing it materially.

A No. 0 rye flour contains 0.44 per cent ash and corresponds to a No. 3 wheat flour.

A No. 1 rye flour contains 0.68 per cent ash and corresponds to a No. 5 wheat flour.

A No. 2 rye flour contains 1.15 per cent ash and corresponds to a No. 6 wheat flour.

A No. 2B rye flour contains 1.47 per cent ash and corresponds to a No. 7 wheat flour.

Not one of the 335 flours examined showed any foreign additions, and all were perfect in taste and odor. Many cases were found, though, where they were wrongly marked with regard to their quality, and unfortunately this is often done on purpose. It is in such a case an adulteration. The flours were also examined microscopically for flours of other grains, the starch grains of the cereals differing very materially in form from those of other seeds or substances. Stone dust from the millstones was not found in any case.

---

[1] Victor Vidrodi, Ztschr. angew. Chem., 1893, p. 691.

An attempt was made to grade the flours examined in this laboratory by the above method, but if the retail prices are any indication of the grade the method is not reliable.

PARTICLES OF DÉBRIS IN THE FLOUR.

By the modern processes of milling it is possible to obtain flours which make a pure white or creamy bread, porous, and possessing all the qualities which are most prized in the perfect loaf. Even the best methods of milling, however, are not able to prevent a portion of the débris—that is, the envelopes of the grain or fragments of the germ— from entering the flour. The object of modern milling is to secure as large a yield as possible of a flour which will make the characteristic loaf mentioned. The exact quantity of such a flour which can be obtained depends, of course, upon the quality of the wheat. It is probable that not more than 60 per cent of a first-class flour can be obtained on an average from different kinds of wheat which enter the mill. Any additional quantity of flour will begin to show itself in the depreciated quality of the loaf, either in a change of color or in a change for the worse in some of the physical properties which give the loaf its value. The detection and estimation of the amount of débris in a high-grade flour is a matter which is evidently attended with considerable difficulties, and can only be accomplished with the aid of the microscope. A method for determining the number of débris particles in a cubic millimeter of a flour has been worked out by Girard.[1] For the purpose of making a microscopic observation of the débris a glass plate containing a number of small cells was constructed in such a way as to be easily placed in the field of vision of the microscope. The section of these cells was 1 mm. square, and their depth one-tenth millimeter. When covered with a thin cover glass, therefore, each one would hold one-tenth of a cubic millimeter. These cells were filled for observation with the liquid holding in suspension the débris of the wheat prepared in the manner to be described. The volume of this débris held in suspension was so regulated that each cubic millimeter of it represented a cubic millimeter of the original flour. By counting the number of particles of the débris in each cell, therefore, the number in a cubic millimeter of the flour was known, from which the number in one gram is easily computed.

PREPARATION FOR THE MICROSCOPE.

In the preparation of the flour for microscopical examination a mixture of equal parts of glycerol and sirupy glucose is employed. The density and viscosity of this mixture are such that the débris of the flour rests indefinitely suspended therein when once thoroughly mixed. The separation of the débris from the starch and the gluten is based upon the theory that the particles of the débris are larger than the granules of starch, or at least are of such an irregular shape that they

---

[1] Comptes rendus, vol. 121, p. 858.

will not pass through a silk cloth the meshes of which are of such a size as to allow the starch granules to pass through. The separation of the débris particles is then accomplished, first, by separating the moist gluten in the usual way by mixing with water, allowing it to stand for some time, and then washing in a stream of cold water until all the starch and débris are removed from the moist gluten. The wash water is collected, and when the starch and débris have settled they are brought upon a silk sieve, French No. 220. All the débris can be collected upon this sieve, while the starch granules pass through. The silk sieve and the débris are carefully dried by pressing between sheets of filter paper, and the débris transferred to a small graduate, where the particles are covered, according to their number, with one or more cubic centimeters of the viscous liquid above described. By means of a glass rod the mixture of the débris with the viscous liquid is thoroughly made.

RESULTS UNDER THE LENS.

A drop of the magma is finally deposited upon the little glass cells described above, covered with a cover glass, and subjected to microscopical examination. The number of particles in each little square is counted until ten different cells have been enumerated. The total number, each cell holding one tenth cubic millimeter, represents the number of granules in a cubic millimeter of the mixture, and the proportions of the materials should be so adjusted as to make this correspond to 1 cubic millimeter of the flour. This is accomplished by operating at first upon 10 grams of the flour in the separation of the gluten from the starch and débris as at first mentioned, and noting the volume of the viscous liquid in which the particles are finally suspended. The whole number of fragments of débris contained in 1 gram of fine flour varies with the percentage of the extraction. When 60 per cent of the flour is extracted from the wheat the number of débris particles in a gram was found to be 12,900; when 70 per cent of flour was obtained from the wheat the number of particles of débris rose to 16,200 per gram, and when 88 per cent was obtained from the wheat the number of particles of débris rose to 61,600.

In another set of experiments, made in 1895, the number of particles found were as follows: First, for roller mills: For 66 per cent extraction, 10,700; for 70 per cent extraction, 32,300; for 80 per cent extraction, 44,100. For flour ground by millstones: For 70 per cent extraction, 18,700 to 22,300.

MICROSCOPIC EXAMINATION OF CELLULOSE PARTICLES IN FLOURS.[1]

As long ago as 1890 E. Vinessa noticed that cellulose cells could be colored with anilin dyes, while parenchymatic cells remain uncolored or were merely tinged by those dyes, which in practice are used for coloring cotton. The process described below rests upon the above observations.

---

[1] E. Vinessa in Ztschr. für Nahrungsmittel Untersuchung, February 24, 1895, p. 53.

Two grams of the well-mixed sample of flour are rubbed to a fine paste in a dish with 5 c. c. of hydrochloric acid, and 100 c. c. of water are added with constant stirring. The pestle is cleaned by means of a washing flask, and the whole mass boiled for ten minutes. After cooling, the contents of the flask are placed in a high cylinder and the undissolved matters are allowed to subside. If time is to be saved separation may be made in a centrifugal machine. The clear liquid is carefully poured off and the residue exactly neutralized or made slightly alkaline and a weak acid reaction restored with acetic acid. After this the cylinder is filled with a thin, lukewarm solution of solid green containing about one-half of 1 per cent of coloring matter. The solid residue is again separated by subsidence or by the centrifugal machine and washed onto a filter. On the filter it is washed with a dilute warm solution, about 1 per cent, of delta-purpurin, and afterwards with distilled water. Finally, the residue is rubbed to a fine powder in an agate mortar when it is examined under the microscope, all the thickened or woody cells being found colored green while the envelopes of the starch cells appear red. Since it is chiefly the first-named cells which are used for adulteration, they can be thus easily quantitatively estimated for each kind of flour. The cover glasses are divided into squares of 5 mm. The number of cells in one of these squares is counted and the number of cells peculiar to each kind of flour determined. The cover glasses can be prepared by anyone by covering them with a film of paraffin, marking them with a sharp needle, and etching with hydrofluoric acid.

MILLING OF INDIAN CORN.

The flour made from Indian corn is known in this country usually as corn meal. There are many different methods of preparing it. The simplest, and one of the most prevalent until within a few years, consisted in grinding the kernels between stones and using the whole meal, coarsely sifted, thus produced. Immense quantities of Indian corn meal prepared in this way are still used throughout all parts of the country, especially in the Southern States. It is evident that an Indian-corn meal prepared in this way would have nearly the same composition as the kernels from which it is prepared. A finer grade of Indian-corn flour is produced by grinding as above indicated and bolting to remove a large portion of the bran.

The flour thus produced differs only from that first described in having a smaller content of fiber and mineral matters, due to the removal of all or a portion of the bran by bolting. On account of the high percentage of oil in the germ of Indian corn, and by reason of its hygroscopic character, the flour thus prepared is apt to become rancid or moldy. To prevent this change and also to secure a more palatable grade of flour, the modern improved processes of grinding and preparing Indian corn have been introduced. Following is the description of the process of preparing the flour from Indian corn as practiced by one of the largest mills in this country.

The Indian corn is passed through a machine called a degerminator, which breaks the corn and removes the germ, but does not separate it. The separation is made by means of bolting cloths and currents of air. After the germ and hull are removed, the corn is ground between iron rolls properly corrugated. The meal is again submitted to the process of bolting and purifications by currents of air and the refined product is the granular meal. The offal consists of the hull, germ, floury particles, and some of the flinty portion of the corn which is lost by the process not being sufficiently perfect to remove it and include it in the granular meal. The offal thus removed constitutes from 30 to 35 per cent of the weight of the corn, depending upon the conditions of the grain. Artificial heat is used in the manufacture of corn meal, which insures better results, and the meal will keep longer. This granular meal is not in favor in the Southern States. They prefer a soft meal made in the old way.

Aside from the method of manufacture there are two distinct grades of Indian-corn meal found in the markets of the country, and these are distinguished by their color. There are two leading varieties of Indian corn in the United States distinguished by color, viz, the white and the yellow. The white corn makes a flour of a color and texture which in some instances is said to be quite like those of flour made from wheat. On the other hand, the yellow corn makes a flour of a rich yellow color, which is highly prized in some quarters on account of imparting its color to the bread made therefrom. When prepared in the same way there is probably but little difference in the nutritive value and palatableness of these two varieties.

In Europe, as has been mentioned before, Indian corn is not considered fit for the manufacture of bread for the use of man. This prejudice seems quite baseless when we consider the very extensive use of this material for bread-making in this country and the high nutritive properties which it possesses. With a diet of Indian-corn bread and pork the workmen of this country are capable of enduring the greatest fatigue and performing the greatest amount of physical labor. The high nutritive value of Indian-corn bread was well illustrated in a marked degree in the military service during the civil war between the States. Both experience and chemical analysis show that there is little, if any, difference between the nutritive properties of bread made from wheat and the whole Indian corn deprived only of the coarsest parts of the bran.

MICROSCOPIC CHARACTER OF INDIAN-CORN MEAL.

Deros[1] gives the following as the microscopic characteristics of Indian-corn meal. Evidently his study of samples was confined to those made from yellow varieties.

---

[1] Le micrographe preparateur, March, 1895, p. 44.

Maize flour is of a yellowish color and rough to the touch. The starch is in grains of a tolerably uniform volume. The minimum diameter appears to be about 6 micromillimeters, while the largest may reach as much as 17 micromillimeters. The greater part have diameters of from 13 to 15 micromillimeters. The starch granules are polyhedric in shape when they come from the external zone. They are of rounded shape, on the contrary, in the floury zone. The upper face appears to be somewhat spherical. The hilum is punctiform and sometimes stellated. The concentric layers are well marked and the fracture is most frequently from the exterior toward the interior. Heated in water at $62.5°$ the starch granules swell up and become deformed, except a few—especially the smaller ones—which resist the action of water at that temperature.

In maize, as in oats, the starch granules are polyhedric, but the resemblance extends no further, the maize granules being larger and never becoming agglomerated and forming compound particles. Their action also on polarized light is characteristic. The starch granules of maize depolarize the light and present a black cross very marked and very distinct when the field is obscure. This cross persists for a long time when the field is illuminated little by little, and it is distinguished much more easily and with an illumination much more pronounced than that which suffices to extinguish this phenomenon in other common starches. Nevertheless this cross is not long visible when the field is fully illuminated. With the selenite plates, by preference working on a neutral field, the grains of starch of the maize are seen to be colored red, with a green cross, or reciprocally. This coloration is very brilliant.

If the starch granules are treated with caustic potash, there is found in the midst of the débris a number of amorphous cellules of the amylaceous tissue irregularly arranged, in which may sometimes be distinguished a final residue of the protoplasmic matter which surrounds the starch granules.

The glutinous cells of maize resemble those of rye. They are disposed in a single row, quadrangular, a little rounded on the angles and much thicker on the exterior side than on the others. The glutinous cells of ordinary varieties of maize, like those of rye, are colored blue by ether, but the starch cells of maize are easily distinguished from those of the rye by their action on polarized light.

COMPOSITION OF FINE INDIAN-CORN FLOUR.

The composition of the ordinary Indian corn meal produced by grinding the whole grain and removing only the coarser bran is, as has already been said, practically that of the whole grain itself. Analyses of the refined Indian corn flours show that they differ chiefly from the whole grain in having a smaller content of fat, fiber, and proteids and a correspondingly higher content of carbohydrates. The low content of proteids is due to the fact that the germ and the finer envelopes are rich in protein matter and are removed in the process of milling. The low content of oil is due, of course, to the fact that the germ has been extracted. The content of fiber, while low compared with the whole grain, is high compared with a high-grade wheat flour.

A description of the samples analyzed and their composition follows:

Composition and description of Indian-corn flours.

[Purchased for United States Army by Maj. H. G. Sharpe, St. Louis, Mo.]

Serial No.	Moisture.	Proteids, N × 6.25.	Ether extract.	Ash.	Crude fiber.	Carbohydrates, N × 6.25.	Calculated calories of combustion.	Ascertained calories.	Description.
	Per ct.	Per ct.	Per ct.	Per ct.	Per ct.	Per ct.			
15958	12.66	6.94	1.21	0.52	0.63	78.67	3,827.3	3,840	"Bent."
15959	12.05	8.50	1.76	0.83	1.17	76.86	3,895.1	3,898	"Topeka."
15960	13.01	5.94	1.02	0.47	0.80	79.56	3,787.9	3,912	"Decatur."
Average	12.57	7.13	1.33	0.61	0.87	78.36	3,836.8	3,883.3	

PRODUCTION OF RYE MEAL.

The principles of the preparation of rye meal are essentially those which are observed in preparing meal or flour from wheat and maize. As has before been intimated, rye meal is not a very important source of bread making among the native citizens of the United States. It is used, however, to a considerable extent, and rye bread is easily obtained in all large cities. In Germany rye is one of the principal sources of the bread of the people, and the preparation of rye meal and the fabrication of bread therefrom have therefore been carried in that country to the highest degree of perfection. Many attempts have been made to remove the outer covering of the rye by means of chemicals, especially sulphuric acid and soda lye, but in practice these processes have had no success. The removal of the outer coating of the rye by mechanical methods before the regular grinding takes place has, however, to a certain extent been successfully accomplished by rubbing the grains in a bowl-shaped vessel with pestles of steel covered with sharp quartz sand. By this process the envelope of the grain is completely or partly removed, according to the duration of the process, with the exception of that portion which is found in the linear depression. The rye, after the outer covering is removed in this way, is subjected to the ordinary milling and sifting operations. By this process about 12 or 13 per cent of the total weight is obtained by the first grinding with the quartz sand, 75 per cent as flour, and 12 per cent as bran. By this process a rye meal is obtained which gives a white and palatable bread, whereas, if the grain be ground directly without the removal of the brittle outer covering, this latter is also reduced to a fine meal, and in the sifting process is left mixed with the flour.

Many other mechanical devices for removing the outer envelope of the grains are found in operation in Germany, but in general rye bread which is made with the meal as usually obtained without the precautions mentioned is rather dark and to some extent unpalatable to those who are not used to eating it.

ERGOT IN RYE FLOUR.

The presence of ergot in rye flour may produce serious disturbances of the health of the consumer. The well-known effect of ergot in producing abortion is only one of the forms of its toxic action. Only the careless miller, however, would admit rye mixed with ergot into his factory.

The easiest method of detecting ergot in rye flour is by means of the microscope.

The flour which is thought to contain ergot is macerated for twelve hours in 5 grams of water. The tissue of ergot is composed of cylindrical cells with their walls closely joined. They contain an oleaginous matter, but no starch. The exterior coating is of a blackish color, inclining to violet. Transverse sections of the cell show a polygonal area due to the pressure of the cells together as in a honeycomb. A section of a number of these cells looks like a fine network. There is little difficulty in distinguishing these cells, and to a certain extent they retain their distinctive shape after baking.

When bread containing ergot is eaten a species of intoxication ensues, with dizziness in mild cases and convulsions where large quantities of ergot are involved. The continued consumption of such bread tends to produce gangrene.

COMPOSITION OF RYE FLOUR.

Rye flour would evidently have the same composition as the cereal from which it was made, as modified by the abstraction of certain ingredients such as the germ and a portion of the bran during the milling process. Only one sample of rye flour has been found in the local market, and this was a preparation sold under the name of granulated rye. It is manufactured by the Health Food Company, 61 Fifth avenue, New York City, and is described by the manufacturers as follows: "Made from the best rye, hulled by the wet process, and reduced to a granulated meal without the injurious heating of mill grinding." It was purchased from G. G. Cornwell & Son, 1412 Pennsylvania avenue, Washington, D. C., and the package cost 25 cents. The analytical data obtained on its examination were as follows:

Composition of rye flour, serial No. 15329.

	Per cent.		Per cent.
Moisture	11.41	Ash	1.55
Proteids	13.56	Crude fiber	1.86
Ether extract	1.97	Carbohydrates other than fiber	71.51

BARLEY FLOUR.

As has before been intimated, barley is not used to any great extent in this country as a cereal food for man. Only one sample of barley flour has been found in the local market during this investigation. As malt extracts and in malted products barley has a limited use as a food. Of all the cereals it has the highest enzymic power, and where it is desirable that the conditions be supplied for a rapid conversion of starch into maltose and dextrin the presence of barley is highly important. It must be remembered, however, that this maximum enzymic power is not exercised until after the barley has been sprouted, and it is evident, therefore, that the use of the unsprouted barley in the form of ordinary flour would not secure in the highest degree the activity of the enzymic ferments. The single sample of barley flour which has been purchased in the open market was manufactured by the Health Food Company, No. 61 Fifth avenue, New York City, and the package cost 25 cents. The analytical data obtained on its examination are as follows:

Composition of barley flour, serial No. 14372.

	Per cent.		Per cent.
Moisture	10.92	Crude fiber	0.67
Proteids	7.50	Ash	0.86
Ether extract	0.89	Carbohydrates other than fiber	79.83

The extremely low percentage of proteids in the sample is to be remarked, probably being due to the method of preparation of the flour from the original grain, whereby portions of the grain rich in proteid matter have been removed. It will not be possible, from the examination of a single sample, to make any statement in regard to what the composition of a typical barley flour should be. When we compare the data obtained from this analysis, however, with the average composition of barley as determined by the samples collected at the World's Columbian Exposition, we see the great variations shown in its composition in respect of ash, ether extract, and proteids. It is evident that in the process of milling the germ, which contains the chief part of the oil, has been largely removed, as well as the outer envelope, containing the chief portion of the ash. The more starchy parts of the grain have been preserved, and consequently the relative percentage of starch in the meal is very much higher than in the grain itself.

BUCKWHEAT FLOUR.

This flour is used very extensively in the United States, chiefly for making cakes. The cake is prepared from batter which is mixed with yeast over night, or until the proper fermentation takes place. The leavening is also sometimes accomplished by means of baking powder. It is baked on a piece of smooth, hot iron, previously greased to prevent sticking. The batter is poured over the iron in such quantity as to produce a cake which is about a quarter of an inch or a little less in thickness when finished. The baking is done very quickly. As soon as the cake is brown from contact with the hot iron it is turned by the cook with skillful movement, so that both sides are baked brown. It is evident in this process that the starch can be but very little changed, except such change as a high temperature, probably reaching not much above the boiling point of water in the interior, can produce in a few moments. The cakes are eaten hot with some kind of sirup. In the hotels the cakes are usually served with maple sirup, which may be either genuine or a compound containing no maple at all, but a sirup flavored with the extract of hickory bark, which gives the maple flavor to the whole mass. Other forms of sirup, such as melted sugar, molasses from sugar cane or sorghum, honey, or a compound consisting of glucose flavored with a little sugar-house sirup, are employed.

The buckwheat cake is highly valued, not only as a food, but as a delicacy. One of the largest manufacturers of buckwheat flour in the United States is the Larrowe Milling Company, of Cohocton, N. Y. The proprietors of this establishment have kindly furnished a description of the methods of preparing the flour. During the process of milling the buckwheat grains pass to a receiving separator, which removes all the coarse particles, stones, straws, etc., by means of a series of sieves. At the same time any dust which they contain is blown out by a current of air. The sifted grains pass next to the scouring machines, in which they are thoroughly scoured, cleaned, and polished. From these machines the grains pass to a separator containing magnets, by means of which any pieces of metal in the form of nails, screws, pieces of wire, etc., are removed.

The grains next pass through a steam dryer for removing the greater portion of the water employed for the scouring. As soon as they are dry they are again treated to a blast of air, which removes any dirt, dust, or light particles which may have been detached during the process of drying. The grains next pass to the shelling rolls, where the greater part of the outer hulls is removed. This process is accomplished by means of an apparatus which is called a sieve scalper. After the separation of the outer hulls the residue of the material passes to a drying chamber, where the moisture is reduced to about 10 per cent, thus insuring the keeping qualities of the flour. After drying the grains are ready for the rolls. After entering the rolls the process is practically the same as that which is employed in milling wheat, consisting of a series of breaks and reductions, with the attendant bolting and grading, and this process is prolonged until the flour is practically removed from the feed or middlings. The sifting cloths used in the bolting of buckwheat flour are somewhat coarser than those for wheat, and this allows some of the dark particles of the inner hulls to pass into the flour, which gives it a dark color on baking. It is quite possible to make a buckwheat flour as white as that from wheat, but in this country the public taste requires a darker product, so that the white flour does not readily sell. The requisite degree of darkness is secured by using bolting cloths which will allow enough of the inner hulls (middlings) to pass into the flour. Two grades of flour are generally produced—a whiter one, in which finer cloths are used, and a darker flour made by using coarser bolting cloths, allowing larger quantities of middlings to pass through. The outer hulls, which are first removed, are used for fuel, although from their composition it is seen that they contain a large quantity of carbohydrates and might be very profitably used in connection with some highly nitrogenous food, such as cottonseed meal or buckwheat middlings for feeding cattle. The middlings are used principally as cattle food, and especially by dairymen. Following is an analysis of the several products obtained by the milling, from samples furnished by the Larrowe Milling Company mentioned above:

Composition of buckwheat products from Larrowe Milling Company, Cohocton, N. Y.

Serial No.	Sample.	Moisture.	Proteids.	Ether extract.	Ash.	Crude fiber.	Carbohydrates by difference.	Calculated calories of combustion.
		Per ct.	Per ct.	Per ct.	Per ct.	Per ct.	Per ct.	
16139	Buckwheat hulls	7.06	3.31	0.47	2.19	2.96	84.01	3,892
16140	Buckwheat feed or middlings	10.20	31.31	8.30	4.97	5.84	39.38	4,527
16141	Buckweat flour (white)	11.89	8.75	1.58	1.85	0.52	75.41	3,854
16142	Buckwheat flour, more middlings than 16141	11.19	9.81	2.33	1.53	0.73	74.41	3,954

DISCUSSION OF BUCKWHEAT PRODUCTS.

One of the most remarkable facts revealed by the above data is seen in the relative composition of the outer hulls and the inner hulls, known as the buckwheat feed or middlings. It would naturally be expected that the outer hulls, being the coarser particles, would contain the larger quantity of ash and fiber, but the analytical data show that this is not the case. There is perhaps no other cereal hull or envelope which contains so large a quantity of carbohydrates as is seen in the buckwheat hulls, viz, 84 per cent of the whole weight. This product is, of course, correspondingly poor in proteid matter and fats. The inner coatings of the grain, constituting the middlings, contain a large excess of proteid matter, viz, a little over 31 per cent. The middlings also contain the germ of the seed, as is shown by the high content of fat, viz, over 8 per cent. They also contain a large excess of fiber, which shows that the inner hulls are tougher and firmer in texture than the outer ones. The quantity of ash is also, strange to say, very much larger in the inner than in the outer hulls. The carbohydrates are correspondingly low. A study of the data for these two products shows that they could be mixed together in a finely ground state and make a very evenly balanced cattle food. The analytical data show a very close agreement between the white and the dark buckwheat flours, but the relative composition is not the same in every case, as would be expected. For instance, the white flour is found to contain more ash than the dark flour, which would not be expected from a comparison of the preceding data. It must be remembered, however, that the data represent only a single analysis, and this would probably not be found true if a large number of analyses were made. In other respects the differences between the dark and white flours are such as would be obtained by mixing 5 or 10 per cent of the middlings with 95 or 90 per cent of white flour. It is probable that in respect of adulteration there is a larger amount of it practiced in the case of buckwheat than with any other cereal product. Only a careful microscopical study of the samples, however, can reveal the extent and character of the adulteration. The price of buckwheat being relatively higher than that of rye and other cereals from which a flour corresponding to that of buckwheat can be made, renders it profitable to adulterate buckwheat with other cereal flours. This adulteration is probably no detriment from a nutritive point of view, but as in the case of all other, even harmless, adulterations, it deserves condemnation on economical and ethical grounds.

FLOUR AND MEAL SUBSTITUTES.

In this country, where the cereals are so abundant and so cheap, there is little inducement to seek for substitutes for them in the process of bread making. Many substitutes, however, have been and are still used in different parts of the world for cereals in the preparation of bread. In localities where starch is made from wheat an attempt has been made to use the glutinous residue for the fabrication of a flour containing very little carbohydrate matter. Only such a flour should bear the name of a gluten flour or gluten meal. The glutinous residue or by-product of the manufacture of starch from wheat is dried and ground and added to ordinary flour in different proportions for the purpose of increasing the percentage of nitrogenous matter and diminishing that of the carbohydrates. The bread made from such a mixture, it is easily seen, is not a normal one, but has been recommended largely by physicians for persons suffering from diabetes. The material secured by grinding the glutinous residue is very commonly known as aleuronat flour. Other materials which are used for mixing with wheat or rye flour are the meal of Indian corn, dari corn, oats, barley, and sorghum seed.

SUBSTITUTES OTHER THAN CEREALS.

According to l'Echo Agricole, Nov. 18, 1897, there are many frauds practiced in France by mixing the flour of maize and the flour of rice with wheat flour. It is said that the merchants of Bordeaux mix 10 per cent of maize flour and 5 per cent of flour of rice with the wheat flour.

The foregoing materials all belong to the cereal class, and therefore a bread made from these mixtures is a true cereal bread. When we pass to another character of substitutes, however, this statement can not be applied, for numerous attempts have been made and are making for the substitution of pea and bean meal, peanut meal, castor-bean meal, and protein-rich materials which possess a pleasant taste and can be used without exciting suspicion as substitutes for wheat and flour. In some cases, also, the condensed whey obtained from cheese factories has been employed as a substitute for the cereal. The whey is evaporated to a thick sirup and mixed directly with the flour. A bread made from such a mixture was found to have the following composition:

	Per cent.		Per cent.
Moisture	39.20	Ash	1.93
Proteids	8.14	Crude fiber	0.30
Ether extract	0.70	Carbohydrates other than fiber	49.73

In the above case the carbohydrates consist largely of the milk sugar which is present in the whey. A whey bread is said to possess a pleasant, sweet taste, which is not at all disagreeable.

USE OF MAIZE MEAL FOR WHEAT AND RYE FLOUR.

It is a curious fact, especially so to the large part of the population of this country who so readily eat bread made of Indian meal, to know that this substance is considered in Germany unfit for bread-making. Nevertheless, attempts have been made in that country to substitute Indian meal for a portion of the rye meal employed in the ordinary process of panification. In general, it is said that not more than 25 per cent of maize meal should be used for this purpose; otherwise the bread will become unpleasant and have a dry taste. On the other hand, a bread which does not contain more than 25 per cent of maize meal is said to have a pleasant taste, to be sufficiently moist, and upon mastication to excite no unpleasant sensation in the mouth, provided, however, that the maize meal is of good quality.

In this country, also, in many localities there is a practice of mixing maize meal with wheaten flour with no fraudulent intent, but in general a corn bread made of maize meal alone is preferred, and it has not been found, as in Germany, that it excites any unpleasant sensation in the mouth during the process of mastication. The Germans recommend a maize meal prepared by Sheppard's process, which is as follows: The maize is first broken into large pieces and dried with steam at a temperature of from 105° to 110° C. The hot material then passes into a mill composed of two stones, which revolve very rapidly in opposite directions. The swollen portions of the meal, which have been reduced to a kind of a gum by the high temperature, are separated in this process from the covering or bran of the kernels. A swollen mass of starchy material leaves the mill in the form of small noodles, which are completely freed of any particles of bran by sifting. In this manner a material is obtained which is quite free from crude fiber and

MAIZE MEAL AS AN ADULTERANT. 1287

fat. The starchy masses are subsequently dried and ground to a fine meal. The composition of a maize meal prepared by the above process is as follows:

	Per cent.		Per cent.
Moisture	9.70	Crude fiber	0.35
Proteids	12.68	Dextrin, gum, etc	19.51
Ether extract	1.19	Starch	51.97
Ash	0.60		

The composition of four samples of bread made of pure white rye meal and mixtures of this with Sheppard's maize meal are shown in the following table in percentages.

I is a bread made of pure white rye meal.

II contains three-fourths rye meal and one-fourth yellow maize meal.

III and IV are composed of three-fourths rye meal and one-fourth white maize meal made by Sheppard's process as indicated above.

Composition of rye and maize mixture.

Constituents.	I.	II.	III.	IV.
Moisture	40.54	40.32	40.99	40.00
Proteids	7.43	7.44	7.44	7.37
Ether extract	0.94	0.82	0.88	1.02
Ash	0.87	0.77	0.84	1.13
Crude fiber	0.69	0.48	0.53	0.78
Dextrin, gum, etc	7.80	9.54	8.89	6.95
Starch	41.73	40.34	40.43	42.15

In regard to the use of Indian-corn meal for mixing with wheaten flour in this country, a prominent army officer of large experience in the Commissary Department, under date of March 20, 1897, gives the following information:

The Indian-corn flour used in adulterating wheat flour is especially prepared at at least two mills in this section of the country, one in Cincinnati and the other in Kansas, and such Indian-corn flour is not put upon the market at all. It is made and solely prepared for use in adulterating wheat flours. To an unpracticed eye the corn flour made at the Cincinnati mill, without any mixture, could be passed off as a spring-wheat flour. It has the same feel, and the same appearance to the inexpert; of course, it lacks taste and color when critically examined, but it is of such a nature that it is difficult to detect it in mixtures, even though in very large proportions.

DETECTION OF CORN MEAL IN FLOUR.

The directions which are given in works on food adulteration for the detection of the presence of Indian-corn flour in the wheaten flour, aside from a microscopic examination, are of little value. It has been stated that pure wheat flour is colored yellow when treated with ammonium hydroxid, whereas Indian corn flour which has been treated in the same way assumes a pale-brown color. In certain samples of winter-wheat flour it has been found that ammonium hydroxid produces hardly any color at all, at most only a very indistinct yellow with a greenish tinge. In flours made from spring wheats the color tests with ammonium hydroxid are more marked. With Indian-corn flour the ammonium hydroxid produces also a yellow color with a greenish tinge. The colorations produced by this reagent are of such an indistinct character that no reliable indications can be given by its use, especially in a mixture.

A method of detecting an admixture of maize meal in wheat flour is described in Northwestern Miller of March 19, 1897. This process has not been tried by us, but is highly commended by the journal above cited.

The only apparatus needed is a small piece of No. 14 bolting cloth and a wide-mouthed jar; a fruit jar will do very well. Take a small sample of the suspected flour, such as can readily be held in the hand, and dough it up. Then fasten the bolting cloth with a string or rubber band over the mouth of the jar, thus making a sieve, and gently knead the dough under a trickling stream of running water, holding it over the sieve. The starch will run off with the water into the jar, and when nothing more can be kneaded away there will remain in the hand a residue of gluten and fiber, which should be dried; and then, in the case of pure wheat flour, this residue will be of an even yellowish color, but with an admixture of only a small per cent of corn flour the residue will be streaky, and when dried out the unevenness is so marked that no one can fail to see it. The corn-flour residue is a chalky white, and the wheat-flour gluten a dark yellow color. When the glutens are washed out, they may be left to dry out naturally, or the drying may be done in a moderately warm oven or over a heater. For convenience in handling, it is well to put them on small pieces of cardboard. Instead of kneading the dough in the hand, it may be put directly on the sieve and worked with the handle of a teaspoon. By the method herein described an admixture of as low as 5 per cent of corn flour can be readily detected, and we have detected admixtures of only 1 per cent of corn flour.

We have examined many samples of corn flour, and find that when sifted with a No. 16 sieve very little of the corn flour goes through, while winter-wheat flour usually sifts through; hence we have tested suspected flour by first sifting it and then making two doughs, one of the siftings and one of the sieve tailings. When treated as above described, the difference in the case of mixed flours is marked. The gluten of the finer flour shows scarcely a trace of corn flour, while the gluten of the coarser part shows a large proportion of the corn-flour residue.

The feeling of the corn flour is a very good rough guide. It feels entirely different from wheat flour or middlings, and is more like some grades of fine sugar. An expert can tell the presence of a small per cent of corn flour in wheat flour by merely feeling it, but the washing-out test we have described is a certain indication that anyone can readily apply.

Inasmuch as wheat flour contains no zein, and the protein of maize meal consists chiefly of this substance, attempts have been made in this laboratory to establish the presence of maize meal in wheat flour by separating and identifying the zein. The method is promising, but no practical process depending on it has yet been worked out. Any process of this kind would be useless if maize starch instead of maize meal were the adulterant.

USE OF POTATOES FOR CEREALS.

The use of potatoes in bread making is very extensively practiced in Europe, and is not unknown in this country. The result of mixing potatoes with flour in bread making is an increase of the carbohydrates and a decrease of the proteid matter in the loaf. There is no objection to the use of potatoes in bread making from a hygienic point of view, provided the amount of admixture is not sufficient to make too wide a nutritive ratio. The natural proportions of proteid matter and carbohydrates in cereals are evidently best adapted to the nourishment of man, and any wide departure from that ratio, either in the one case in increasing the amount of gluten, as in gluten breads, or in the other by diminishing the amount thereof, as in the use of potatoes, should be avoided. In this country the use of potatoes in bread making is largely practiced in private families, where the bread is prepared for home use. In many parts of the country it is quite a constant custom to mix a portion of potatoes with the flour, as it is thereby supposed that a better bread can be secured. This idea, however, is probably erroneous. The chief object of mixing the potatoes with the bread is to prevent a too rapid drying of the loaf. The drying of the loaf, however, can be very effectively prevented by proper baking, inclosing the moist interior with a practically impervious crust. From a financial point of view the admixture of potatoes with wheat flour in bread making is remunerative only when the price of the potato starch, as compared with that of the same amount of material in cereals, is less. While this character of adulteration, as has been said, is not prejudicial to health, it should not be practiced by bakers and others who sell loaves without informing the purchasers of the character and extent of the admixture. It would probably be very difficult to detect the presence of added potatoes in bread, provided the mixture of the dough was thoroughly accomplished and the baking was attended with a sufficiently high temperature to disintegrate the starch granules. Moreover, before mixing, the potatoes are boiled and reduced to a fine paste, whereby the structure of the starch granules is so disorganized as to make their detection by ordinary microscopic tests difficult and almost impossible. Bread showing an abnormally low percentage of proteid matter might be suspected of being mixed with potatoes, but it would be difficult, as indicated, to secure a convincing proof of this fact in the absence of the testimony of the baker himself.

REPORTS AS TO MINERALS AND WOOD AS SUBSTITUTES.

The use of chalk, terra alba, and other substances of like character in flour is, as far as my knowledge extends, never practiced in the United States. Instances are on record of such adulterations in foreign flours, but as a rule the price of cereals in this country is so low as to make it of little object to practice this form of adulteration. Of course any admixture of these mineral substances could be detected in the ash of a flour. In a flour showing an excessively high content of ash it must always be supposed that some mineral substances are added. In the self-raising flours we know what these substances are. If, however, the analysis should reveal the presence of a large quantity of ash not due to the ingredients usually employed in the preparation of leavening agents, it might be worth while to examine further in regard to the character of the added material. It is evident, however, that the percentage of such material which would render its use as an adulterant profitable would be so great as at once to be revealed upon a simple ignition. In the examination of hundreds of flours in the laboratory of this division no instance of such an adulteration has ever been noted.

In the same category may be placed the reports of admixing ground dry wood with flour and meal. Such an adulteration is reported in the Industrial American of May 15, 1892, copied from a newspaper of large circulation. It is stated that white beech wood, after the removal of the bark, is reduced to shavings, which are afterwards dried and ground, and the powder thus secured employed for adulterating flour. Such reports are probably without foundation, but unfortunately are believed by a large number of credulous people.

Since the foregoing was written an article has been published in the American Grocer of June 15, 1898, calling unfavorable attention to an advertisement of "Mineraline," consisting of ground soapstone as an adulterant of flour.

The use of other materials as substitutes for cereal meals in bread making will be noticed on page 1332 et seq.

RELATIVE NUTRITIVE PROPERTIES OF WHEAT AND MAIZE.

There is a widespread opinion that the products of Indian corn are less digestible and less nutritious than those from wheat. This opinion, it appears, has no justification, either from the chemical composition of the two bodies, nor from recorded digestive and nutritive experiments. A study of the analytical data of the whole grain shows that in so far as actual nutrients are concerned the maize is fully as nutritious as wheat. The ash content of maize and its products is probably not quite so high as that of wheat, and there is, therefore, a slight deficiency of the mineral foods employed in the nourishment of the body. Inasmuch, however, as the cereals contain an excess of mineral matters above the needs of the body, this slight deficiency is of no consequence. In respect of its content of fat, Indian corn and its products easily take precedence of all the other cereals, with the exception of hulled oats. In round numbers, it contains twice as much fat or oil as wheat, three times as much as rye, twice as much as barley, and two-thirds as much as hulled oats. In regard to digestible carbohydrates, that is, starch, sugar, dextrin, and digestible fiber, it possesses a higher content than hulled oats, almost the same as wheat, and slightly less than rye or barley. Comparing the content of nitrogenous matters with that of other cereals, it is found that the first place must be awarded to oats, especially if they have been hulled. Indian corn, however, has nearly the same quantity of proteid matter as the other leading cereals, oats excepted.

EXPERIMENTS IN FEEDING CORN AND WHEAT.

In regard to the digestibility of Indian corn and wheat, it must be admitted that a larger amount of experience has accumulated with Indian corn than with wheat. The low price of wheat in the last few years has, however, directed a considerable amount of attention to the use of that cereal instead of Indian corn in the feeding of animals. The data which have been obtained in this country, secured from comparative feeding experiments, are not always uniform. In some instances it has been thought that, pound for pound, wheat gave a slightly better result in feeding animals than Indian corn, while in others the preference is given by the experimenter to Indian corn. In experiments made in the South Dakota station (Bulletin 38) pigs were fed with different cereals, among others with ground Indian corn and ground wheat. The comparative results obtained were as follows:

Summarized results of experiments with pigs.

Kind of cereal.	Weight of lot at beginning.	Average daily gain per pig.	Total grain consumed by lot.	Grain eaten per pound of gain.	Average gain.		Price realized per bushel of grain.	Shrinkage in dressing.
					Per 100 pounds of grain.	Per bushel of grain.		
	Pounds.	*Pounds.*	*Pounds.*	*Pounds.*	*Pounds.*	*Pounds.*	*Cents.*	*Per cent.*
Lot 3, ground corn	192	1.40	1,159	4.58	21.83	12.22	60.00	14.0
Lot 4, ground wheat	205	1.32	1,144	4.81	20.79	12.49	58.39	16.5

In the data obtained in this experiment the Indian corn, pound for pound, was found to give the better results in every respect.

COMPARATIVE ASSIMILATION OF WHEAT AND CORN.

The comparative digestibility of wheat and Indian corn has been studied in the Minnesota station (Bulletin No. 36). The data obtained, with the exception of the digestibility of the ash, are as follows:

Digestion coefficients of wheat and other grains.

Constituents.	Cracked wheat.	Cracked corn.
Dry matter	82	90
Proteids	80	90
Ether extract	70	78
Crude fiber	60	48
Nitrogen-free extract	83	94

From these data it is seen that the wheat was slightly less digestible than the Indian corn. From a study of the data at the Minnesota station it is stated that when corn and wheat are both selling at 50 cents per bushel, the 50 cents will purchase the same amount of digestible dry matter in both instances. In the case of wheat, however, the purchaser will obtain 2½ pounds more digestible protein, and in the case of Indian corn 2½ pounds more digestible carbohydrates. The quantity of heat generated by the food in each case is almost exactly the same. The result of these experiments, therefore, is to establish with certainty that the digestible coefficient of Indian corn is not inferior, but, if there be any difference, superior to that of wheat. Data of the kind mentioned above, based on carefully controlled feeding experiments, checked at every point by chemical analyses, are evidently of far greater value than those which are reported by the Kansas State board of agriculture for the quarter ending September 30, 1894, where circulars were sent to prominent growers of stock and reports of their observations on the comparative value of wheat and Indian corn were tabulated. As a result of the preponderance of testimony given by these circulars, it was concluded that wheat was superior to Indian corn, pound for pound, as a food for animals. These reports, however, were based merely upon observation, and were not controlled in any way by weighing or chemical analysis. The conclusion, therefore, is not valuable as evidence when contrasted with that of the feeding experiments at the Minnesota station above mentioned.

Comparative Production of Pork from Wheat and Maize.

In experiments made at the Ohio State University, collected in Experiment Station Record, vol. 6, page 466, it was found that a bushel of wheat produced 13.7 pounds of pork, while a bushel of corn made 12.3 pounds. When the difference of weight between a bushel of wheat and a bushel of corn is considered, the actual gain, it is seen, is almost the same for both. Calculated on the market price of wheat and Indian corn, it cost $4.01 to produce 100 pounds' increase with wheat, and $2.85 to produce the same increase with Indian corn.

Carefully weighing all the reliable evidence at hand, the conclusion is inevitable that from the point of view of chemical composition, of digestibility, and of nutritive value Indian corn with its products, pound for pound, is fully equivalent to wheat. In the case of food for man, which this bulletin particularly has to consider, there must be taken into account the additional element of palatability. It is evident that in the case of two given foods of almost the same chemical composition, and of equal digestibility, the more palatable will be the more valuable food for man. In regard to palatability, as has already been mentioned, there is the widest difference of opinion. European writers on dietetics uniformly condemn Indian corn and its products as being unfit for food for man. On the other hand, the ample experience of our own country shows that it is an extremely palatable food, as well as nutritious, and a large part of our population prefer it, from a gustatory point of view, to wheat. It must be admitted, therefore, that in respect of palatability usage is an important factor, and it is evident that other nations, when accustomed to the use of Indian corn and its products as food for man, would find it equally as palatable as it is found to be in the United States.

COMPARATIVE NUTRITIVE VALUE OF THE CARBOHYDRATES.

In respect to the comparative nutritive value of the hemicelluloses, celluloses, sugars, and starches, investigators have not secured agreeing results. The greater number of authors place the nutritive value of digestible pentosans and celluloses after that of starch and sugar.

It has been shown, however, that very little of the digested pentosans appear in the urine, and it is therefore evident that nearly all the digested hemicelluloses suffer oxidation in the animal organism. When carbohydrates are oxidized to carbon dioxid and water their nutritive value is nearly the same. It is different, however, if a portion of them is converted into methane, in which case the oxidation is only partially complete. There is little ground, however, for the common assumption that methane is derived exclusively from celluloses and pentosans. It is more likely to come from the starches or sugars, which are more readily attacked by the ferments producing marsh gas. It is probable, therefore, that as much or more starch than pentosans or celluloses escapes complete oxidation. It is true pentosans do not undergo alcoholic fermentations, but it is not true that they are not fermentable, for they may undergo a lactic or butyric fermentation in which marsh gas is one of the products. The digestible pentosans and celluloses, therefore, must be regarded as having a food value nearly or quite equal to that of starch.

THE ACTION OF SULPHUROUS ACID ON FLOUR.

If sulphur be burned for purposes of fumigation or for the destruction of insects in a mill, the flour subjected to the fumes may undergo some slight changes. This action has not been verified by any experiment in this laboratory, and the following statements are published without indorsement.

Several flour magazines had been very thoroughly fumigated for the extermination of *Ephestia kuehniella*. The magazines were empty, excepting one containing a few sacks of flour. When, some time afterwards, this flour was taken out for use, it was found impossible to obtain a good dough from the same.

NO LOSS OF NUTRITIVE PROPERTIES.

The following experiment will explain the changes that had taken place, and also prove that none of the nutritive properties had been lost, the flour still being serviceable for making bread.

The flour was of a good medium quality, in chemical and physical composition, containing in 100 parts—

	Per cent.
Moisture	13.00
Gluten (moist)	28.00
Ether extract	1.83
Ash	1.13

There were no sulphates in the ash.

---

[1] M. Ballard, Jour. de pharm. et de chimie, V series, Tome XXII, Sept., 1890, p. 241

EFFECT ON FERMENTATION.

A paste made of this flour and kept at a gentle heat was in full fermentation after twenty-four hours, at the end of that time giving rise to a good odor of leaven.

At first sight the flour presented no anomaly either to the eye, touch, taste, or smell, but on closer examination it was found that, though no change had taken place in the quantity of moisture and fatty matter present, the gluten had entirely lost its cohesive properties. On attempting to collect it by the ordinary methods it nearly all escaped with the wash water.

Flour taken from the center of the sack with a sampler showed this same peculiarity to a less degree, most energetic kneading failing to remedy the defect.

A paste made from the flour in the same manner as above showed but traces of fermentation at the end of thirty hours. The presence of sulphurous products can not be doubted, as on raising the cover from the dough that had been standing for this length of time there was a slight odor of hydrogen sulphid. On placing a bright silver coin in the center of one of the sacks it became black at the end of eight hours, but in a similar control experiment performed on one of the original sacks a coin remained bright. The weight of the ashes had not changed, but a trace of sulphate was found and the acidity of the flour had increased by 0.037 gram in 100.

Hence the effects of the sulphuration are plain. It is well known that sulphurous and sulphuric acid may be partially reduced to sulphur under the influence of ferments. This fact was a hint to study the effect of the various sulphur compounds in gluten.

From good flour containing 30 per cent of gluten, pastes with variable but very minute quantities of hydrogen sulphid acid, sulphurous acid, sulphuric acid, and sulphides of potassium, sodium, and ammonium were made, and in all cases it was found impossible to extract all the gluten.

On the other hand, good moist gluten soaked in water containing the above sulphur compounds disaggregates rapidly, and it is thus shown that the impossibility of collecting the gluten in the sulphured flour was due to the presence of these compounds.

MODIFICATION OF GLUTEN.

The following observations prove that the gluten is only modified, preserving its nutritive properties.

(1) If on the one hand there are substances, as the above named, which prevent the agglutination, there are others favoring the same. The sulphured flour gave 28 per cent of gluten when made to a dough with these three salts,[1] that is, as much as the flour gave before sulphuring.

---

[1] Sodium chlorid, alum, and copper sulphate. Mémoire sur les farines (Journ. pharm. et chim., 1882.)

(2) On kneading 25 grams of sulphured flour with 10 grams of moist gluten obtained from an ordinary flour, and adding enough water, a very flexible dough was obtained. From this dough 17 grams of gluten were obtained, proving that the 7 grams present in the flour had become agglutinated to the 10 grams of gluten added.

Hence it may be presumed that by adding gluten and salt to sulphured flour, and by forcing fermentation with a strong leaven, proper panifaction can be obtained. Experiments have confirmed this.

EXPERIMENTS IN BREAD MAKING WITH SULPHURED FLOUR.

A first batch, of one-third sulphured and two-thirds foreign flour, made under ordinary conditions of baking gave an excellent bread containing 31.5 per cent moisture after sweating.

A second batch, with equal parts of sulphured flour and fresh flour, increasing the leaven and salt in the proportion of 10 per cent, made a very good bread holding 1 per cent more water than the preceding.

A third batch of two-thirds sulphured and one-third fresh flour, increasing salt and leaven by another 10 per cent, is more difficult still in working, but makes a bread of good appearance. On taking it out of the oven there is a slight odor of hydrogen sulphid, disappearing after sweating. The bread contains 1.3 per cent more water than that of the first batch.

Finally, a fourth batch made of sulphured flour alone, again increasing leaven and salt by 10 to 12 per cent, requires tedious and long working, and after fermentation the bread is more soggy and flat. The salt taste is not too pronounced. The odor of hydrogen sulphid is very appreciable, but after sweating entirely disappears. The bread contains 2.4 per cent more water than the first lot.

It may be added that biscuit (crackers) prepared without salt or leaven show all the characteristics of a good product and there is nothing that might lead to the supposition that physically or chemically the gluten had been disaggregated by the sulphuring.

METHOD OF TESTING FLOURS PRACTICED BY THE VIENNA BOARD OF HEALTH.[1]

The board of health of Vienna has proposed that Professor Vogl's method of testing flours be adopted so as to expedite the judgment of suspicious samples.

This method requires a reagent composed of 70 per cent alcohol containing 5 per cent hydrochloric acid. A number of test tubes is all the apparatus required. Two grams of the flour are mixed with 10 c. c. of the reagent, well shaken, and allowed to settle. The color of both the precipitate and the supernatant liquid is then observed.

Pure rye or wheat flour remains white and the liquid is colorless. Inferior flours show a slight yellowish tinge. Pure barley or oat flour imparts a pure yellow, somewhat of a straw color, to the liquid. The flour of cockle seed as well as that of the *Lolium temulentum* give it an orange color. An addition of 5 per cent of cockle seed to either wheat, barley, or rye flour is shown by a distinct orange color of the liquid. Cowpea as well as bean flour color it a beautiful purplish red; ergot, blood red. From 5 to 10 per cent of cowpea flour imparts a beautiful rose-red color which a higher percentage changes to a violet, while 5 per cent of ergot will color it an intense pink. An addition of oat, barley, or maize flour to wheat or rye flour is indicated by a pure pale yellow color of the liquid. Naturally the result of this preliminary investigation must be definitely proved by a subsequent examination at the laboratory, but the use of this preliminary method will materially decrease the laboratory work and expedite the exclusion of unsound and adulterated flours.

This test tried with samples in this laboratory gave the following results:

Wheat and barley kernels ground to a fine flour gave a colorless supernatant liquid when shaken with the reagent.

Rye and oat flour gave a rather deep yellow coloration. Maize flour (yellow) gave a light green coloration which faded after twenty-four hours.

A slight increase in the strength of the acid caused a marked increase in the strength of the color. These tests appear to have but little practical value.

MAKING AND BAKING OF BREAD.

Under the term bread are included all the products secured by baking the flour of cereals, whether mixed or unmixed with condiments or leavening agents. The term also includes like products in which the flour of cereals forms a notable or predominating part of the whole. For the purposes of this bulletin the term bread does not include that large class of products made from cereals in which sugars of different kinds are incorporated for giving them a sweet taste or for other purposes. From a scientific point of view there is no reason why the latter class of bodies should not be included in the term bread if that term be reserved for the baked products of the cereals. In more popular language, however, bodies of the class last described are known as cakes or puddings.

In addition to the bodies above named, products of other starchy bodies than cereals are baked into loaves and known as bread. Among these the most important, perhaps, are the starches of various descriptions, whether coming from potatoes or the family of the arrowroot. Bread is also made in limited quantities from the banana and other tropical fruits. Attempts have been made to use the cakes left after the pressure of oil from oil seeds for the manufacture of bread. In these cases, however, the whole loaf is not made, as a rule, from the meal derived from the oil cakes, but this meal is used only as an adulterant. The use of these various bodies is practically unknown in this country, except in an experimental way, and therefore, in order to prevent this bulletin from covering too large a field of inquiry, these bodies are excluded from discussion. There are to be considered here, therefore, under the term bread, only those products which, in the common language of the country, can properly be designated by the term bread.

VARIETIES OF BREAD.

All the breads in common use may be classed under two great heads, viz, leavened and unleavened. By far the greater quantity of bread consumed belongs to the former class, unleavened bread being used only during certain religious festivals or in the form of biscuits or in certain varieties of Indian-corn bread, such as hoecake and johnnycake.

In general, leavened breads are intended for consumption within at least a few days after they are prepared. Exposed to the air, the loaves of leavened bread gradually lose moisture, and the soft, spongy texture which gives them so much of their value from a gustatory point of view is lost. For hygienic reasons it is advisable not to eat leavened bread immediately after baking, but only after twenty-four hours, and when it is cold. Certain varieties of leavened bread, however, in this country are always eaten hot, especially for breakfast. This is especially true of the rolls made with chemical leavening agents, such as the baking powders of commerce. Hot rolls made by yeast fermentation are also very common as a breakfast diet. In this country it is not customary to keep leavened bread longer than a few days. On the contrary, the unleavened bread, such as the biscuits of commerce, can be kept much longer without losing any of their palatable or nutritious properties. This form of bread is especially adapted for migratory bodies of men, such as hunters, lumbermen, and soldiers. Its value as a ration, especially of soldiers and hunters, is vastly increased on account of its compactness. A species of biscuit commonly known as hard-tack was one of the chief forms of bread used by the soldiers during the civil war, and its high nutritious properties are well known. The leavened bread consumed in the United States, unlike that in most other countries, is chiefly baked in the household. The American people, except to a limited extent in the larger cities, are in the habit of making their own bread. As a result of this there is little uniformity in the character and composition of the bread consumed. One need only go from family to family in different parts of the country and eat the bread as it is prepared for daily consumption to be convinced of the accuracy of this statement.

The leavened breads may be divided into certain distinct classes in respect of the leavening agents employed. Thus we have class 1, where yeast is used as a leavening agent; class 2, where the natural ferments of the flour or meal are employed, as in the manufacture of salt-rising bread; class 3, where the leavening is secured by the chemical reactions taking place within the loaf; and class 4, where carbon dioxid is mechanically incorporated in the dough. The character of these different leavening agents will be briefly described later on.

The unleavened bread is found also in several typical forms. The first class includes the biscuits of commerce sometimes called crackers, intended for use soon after baking; second, biscuits intended for long storage, such as the hard-tack above mentioned; third, wafers and other delicate forms of unleavened bread for special uses; fourth, the unleavened loaves which are made most frequently from Indian-corn meal; and fifth, the miscellaneous collection of unleavened loaves or cakes made in various ways and for different purposes. In nearly all forms of unleavened bread made from wheat flour, the dough is thoroughly beaten in order to make it lighter in color and more crisp and hard after baking. In the unleavened bread made from Indian-corn meal, various forms of cooking are practiced. Bread may be baked in a pan in the ordinary way; it may be spread upon a board and held before a hot fire; it may be imbedded in hot ashes or baked in an oven with hot coals underneath, and also hot ashes and coals on the lid. All these different forms of preparing unleavened bread are practiced in different parts of the country. For religious festivals the unleavened bread is prepared in a special manner, and is used only for a special purpose. The full details of these special methods of the preparation of bread can be found in works devoted exclusively to bread making.

PROCESSES OF LEAVENING.

The principal part of the bread consumed by man is leavened. The leavening process consists in the incorporation with the dough of some material or organism by means of which gases can be developed. These gases become entangled in the dough and are held principally by the nitrogenous constituents thereof. In expanding, either through natural pressure or under the influence of heat, these gases produce a porous and spongy condition of the dough, which on baking becomes fixed in the bread. The leavening processes employed in bread making may belong to one of three different classes. In the first place, it may be due to the activity of germs. This is the method which is usually employed. It is not the purpose of this bulletin to go into a minute description of the action of yeast in the leavening of bread. In general it may be said that the flour is mixed with water or milk and a sufficient quantity of yeast to distribute throughout all particles of the kneaded dough the necessary germs for the production of the fermentation. The parts of the meal which are especially attacked by the fermentative germs are the sugars. Under the influence of a convenient temperature, say about blood heat or more, the yeast germs rapidly develop, attack the sugar and decompose it into carbon dioxide and alcohol. A lactic fermentation also takes place. The particles of carbon dioxide which are formed become entangled in the dough, and, expanding, produce a considerable degree of porosity, which in common language is known as the raising of the dough. The final action of the fermentation is found in the production of acetic or lactic acids, so that a considerable degree of acidity occurs, especially if the raising process be continued for a long time.

CHARACTER OF THE YEAST FERMENTATION.

The panary fermentation due to yeast has been recently subjected to a careful investigation by Leon Boutroux.[1] The two principal theories which have been proposed in explanation of panary fermentation are the theory of the normal alcoholic fermentation due to yeast and the theory of fermentation due to bacteria.

Panary fermentation consists essentially of a normal alcoholic fermentation of the sugar preexisting in the flour to which may perhaps be added the sugar formed by the saccharification of a trace of insoluble carbohydrate. In the one case it has been shown that yeast is the essential agent of fermentation which causes the dough to rise. In the other case it is probable that under particular conditions otherwise favorable to the rising of the dough it may happen that the soluble part of the flour alone is strongly modified during panary fermentation, the gluten and the starch being affected but very slightly. The microbes other than those of the yeast which are found in the leaven or in the dough, can only be useless and objectionable.

EXPERIMENTS WITH YEAST.

The following is a series of control experiments which Boutroux made to determine this:

Three small flasks were charged, first, with the gluten from 10 grams of flour, and, second, with 5 c. c. of water holding in solution 0.4 gram of glucose. This is approximately the composition of a dough from which the starch has been separated. The gluten was raw and unsterilized. A yeast germ A was introduced into one of these flasks in a considerable quantity. In the second flask was introduced a quantity of a germ less active, and which is called B. The third flask, which served as a check, received no yeast. The three flasks were placed in an oven and heated to 32°. At the end of six and one-half hours the flask containing the germ A had perceptibly fermented, while the others gave no sign of life. The following day there was a liberation of gas from the three flasks, but the appearance of that containing the germ A was very different from the other two. The gluten in this had risen in vertical columns, which were separated at the base from the flask. In the other two flasks there was no solid gluten remaining. In these latter the gluten formed a skin sticking to the surface. Under the microscope the first showed only the yeast germ, the second showed

---

[1] Ann. de chim. et de phys. (6), 25, 145-201.

no bacilli and very little yeast, and the third showed only the bacilli in abundance.

After three days the flasks were opened. The odor of the contents of that containing the yeast germ A indicated an alcoholic fermentation. The flask containing the check experiment had an odor of butyric acid and taste resembling vinegar. The acidity of the liquid in the flask containing the yeast germ titrated against barium hydrate, using phenolphtalein as an indicator, was equivalent to 4.86 c. c. decinormal acid per 10 c. c. of liquid. The acidity in the check experiment was 11.34 c. c.

DISCUSSION OF DATA.

We see from this experiment that the yeast, in addition to causing the dough to rise by the liberation of gas, also prevented the dough from souring and taking on a butyric odor. A yeast germ sufficiently active and added in sufficient quantity hinders the development of the bacilli. These latter only become abundant after the termination of the alcoholic fermentation. It is for this reason that the bakers add yeast to renew the leaven.

By successive cultures the predominance, which the yeast germ has lost in the old leaven, is restored and acid fermentation is prevented.

The following experiment contributes still more to the evidence in regard to the respective rôles of the various micro-organisms. From flour and salt water were made three similar doughs with the exception that to the first was added the yeast germ A; to the second a little of the liquid from the check flask of the preceding experiment, that is, the liquid containing bacteria and fermented gluten; and to the third nothing was added. These three doughs were placed in the oven at 33°. The following day they had risen in the proportions shown in the table:

The dough with the yeast germ	3.1
The dough containing the bacteria from the gluten	1.2
For the third sample (nothing added)	1.6

A thin skin separated the gluten from each of these samples. The dough containing the yeast germ gave an almost normal gluten both in quality and quantity. The quantity amounted to 0.8 of that normally present in the flour. The dough treated with bacteria from the gluten did not yield any gluten on washing with water. The dough to which nothing was added yielded a gluten, which was very sticky, amounting to about one-third of the normal quantity.

CONCLUSIONS FROM EXPERIMENTS.

One may see, then, the following results:

1. The bacteria which dissolved the gluten in the preceding experiment were far from causing the bread to rise, in fact, prevented it from doing so, as shown by the fact that the sample which had risen least was that treated with bacteria.

2. The yeast germ protected the gluten, on the contrary, from the attacks of the bacteria which it contained, as is evident from the fact that this sample contained more gluten at the termination of the experiment than those which were not treated.

These two experiments show that bacteria play an objectionable rôle. They alter the gluten and acidulate the dough; and further the greater the activity of the yeast germ the less are the effects due to the bacteria.

It has been shown that bread acidulated with tartaric acid—that is, bread where the gluten is dissolved—does not produce a light loaf, while the neutral dough—that is, containing no added acid—gains in lightness. The preservation of the gluten by the yeast germ is hence an important matter. In a dough where the gluten is not altered during the fermentation, pockets for the bubbles of gas are formed which in the baking become almost impermeable. Thus the gas is retained and each bubble in dilating augments the volume of the cell which contains it, while if the gluten loses its cohesion the gas in dilating passes the cell walls which inclose it and accumulates in large caverns separated from one another. As will be seen (page 1302), however, it appears from the investigations of others that certain bacteria are probably active in making bread porous.

SPONTANEOUS FERMENTATION.

The fermentation of the dough may also be secured by the enzymes naturally present in the flour. This process of bread making is known as the salt-rising method. A convenient quantity of wheat meal and corn meal is mixed with a little salt and hot milk and set in a warm place. In the course of a few hours fermentation ensues and the whole mass becomes porous. In this condition it is mixed with the wheaten flour to form a dough, which, when set aside in a warm place, undergoes a fermentation which in many respects is similar to that produced by yeast.

METHOD FOR MAKING SALT-RISING BREAD.

The most active natural enzymes of wheat are found near the outer branny layers of the grain, and are consequently chiefly removed during the process of milling. For this reason it is somewhat difficult to secure a prompt and satisfactory fermentation with the purest wheat flours. In general, the following method of procedure will be found satisfactory.

A quarter of a pint of fresh whole milk is slowly heated to near the boiling point, but not allowed to boil. This process will sterilize the milk and prevent the development of a too rapid lactic fermentation in the subsequent processes. The heated milk is added to a quantity of maize meal sufficient to make with the milk a stiff batter, and the whole is thoroughly mixed. The vessel containing the batter is wrapped with paper and then with a heavy flannel cloth, and kept in a warm place at a uniform temperature of about blood heat for several hours, until fermentation is fully established and the batter assumes a definite sour odor. At this point a teaspoonful of salt is stirred into a pint of blood-warm water, and into this a sufficient quantity of high grade wheat flour is stirred to make a moderately stiff batter. This is thoroughly mixed with the sour mass obtained by the previous fermentation and the mixture exposed for from three-fourths to one hour to a blood heat as before. If the fermentation has been well conducted the mass will now be in a sufficiently active state to secure a proper porosity of the loaf. The salt-rising thus prepared is mixed with a wheat-flour dough made with warm water in sufficient quantities to make from four to six loaves, the whole mass well kneaded, molded into loaves, and put aside at a temperature of blood heat until the fermentation has proceeded far enough to make the loaf light and spongy. The loaf is then baked in the ordinary way.

Salt-rising loaves, when carefully made, are extremely palatable, free of objectionable acidity, and grateful, especially to the taste of those accustomed to their use. In the beginning of the baking process the alcohol which has been formed is volatilized, and in the gaseous state adds to the porosity of the loaf until the temperature reaches its maximum. The fermentation of the sugars in a flour or meal may be also secured by bacteria as well as by yeasts.[1]

A *bacillus levans* has been separated from fermenting masses of dough and secured in a pure state by successive cultures. It belongs to the group of the *bacillus coli communis* which is found in the alimentary canal, from which it is difficult to distinguish it in form. This bacillus is always found in flours and meals of every description, and produces a lively evolution of gases, viz., carbon dioxid, hydrogen, and nitrogen. It also is capable of producing almost as great a degree of acidity as is found in the ordinary fermentations with yeast. The presence of yeast prevents, to a certain extent, the development of this bacillus. In general, it may be said that there are a great many enzymes, bacilli, yeasts, and molds which are capable of working upon the fermentable portions of a dough with the production of gaseous products. All of these germs, therefore, may be used in the leavening of bread. Properly, however, the yeasts are the chief ones which are employed for this purpose. For a description of the methods of preparing yeasts and their use in producing leavened bread, standard works on bread-making may be consulted.

AERATION BY MEANS OF ALREADY-FORMED CARBON DIOXID.

In some quarters there exists a prejudice, doubtless without foundation, against the use of bread which has been leavened by the process of fermentation. There is no evidence whatever of a convincing nature which goes to show that the natural or induced fermentations which

---

[1] Chemiker Zeitung, 1894, vol. 18, p. 276; vol. 19, p. 775.

take place in the leavening of bread result in the production of any substance whatever injurious to health. On the contrary, it is not at all improbable that the effects of the fermentation, aside from the porosity produced, are beneficial rather than otherwise to the processes of digestion and assimilation. Moreover, the small quantity of nutrients destroyed during fermentation, probably not more than 1 per cent of the weight of the flour, is of little consequence from an economic standpoint.

Nevertheless, attempts have been made to incorporate carbon dioxid into the dough from supplies prepared beforehand, and thus obviate the necessity of the fermentation process. A process for making bread in this manner was patented many years ago, and has been used in the original or modified forms to a limited extent for the past forty years. This method, however, has never come into general use, although when properly applied the bread made by this process is light and porous, and the loaves themselves are absolutely free from any acidity or other condition due to the activity of the fermentative germs. The principle of the process consists in introducing into the dough carbon dioxid, previously prepared, and most conveniently dissolved in cold water. Where proper apparatus for mixing can be secured, the incorporation of the carbon dioxid may be made under pressure in inclosed vessels in which the water, flour, and carbon dioxid under pressure are introduced and mixed by mechanical means. The modern appliances, by means of which carbon dioxid can be secured in the liquid state, will doubtless greatly increase the efficiency of this method of bread making. The details of the method may be found in works especially devoted to panification, and a description is also found in Part V of this bulletin. The process has been chiefly used in England, where it was originally invented, and as far as I know has never been introduced on a commercial scale in this country.

CHEMICAL AERATING AGENTS.

In the third place, the aeration of bread may be secured by the evolution of carbon dioxid by chemical reactions taking place within the dough itself. This method of aeration is secured by the application of some of the leavening mixtures commonly known as baking powders, which are made and sold in such large quantities in this country. From a sanitary and gustatory standpoint this method of aeration is probably the least to be recommended of those that are in use. It has the merit, however, of quickness, which to many Americans is one of prime importance. The ability to secure a well-leavened roll from the flour in the course of a few minutes is often regarded as of more importance than the other characteristics of bread. Baking powders or leavening mixtures permit the cook to secure this result in a comparatively short period of time. Within thirty minutes of the time the flour leaves the barrel the finished rolls can be placed upon the breakfast table. The almost universal source of the carbon dioxid of all these leavening bodies is found in the sodium bicarbonate. The ease with which this compound gives up its carbon dioxid, the large percentage thereof which it contains, and the comparative innocuousness of the residue give to it its high value for this purpose. Many chemical reagents are used for setting free the carbon dioxid from the bicarbonate of soda. Among the simplest of these may be mentioned the lactic acid which is present in sour milk. By mixing together sodium bicarbonate, sour milk, and flour, the housewife secures a cheap and active leavening agent, which has obtained, especially in this country, a very wide use. One of the objections to the direct use of the sodium bicarbonate in this way is in the fact that any undecomposed particles of this alkaline salt tend to stain the flour or dough a yellow color, and to give to it an unpleasant taste. Rolls which are made in this way, therefore, when done, instead of being of a pure white or cream color, as desired, often show yellow spots, which render them objectionable from an æsthetic point of view and also give to them a disagreeable flavor. It is not possible in any given case that the housewife can judge accurately of the quantity of sour milk required to decompose a given portion of the sodium bicarbonate. To remedy this fault, leavening agents are usually prepared according to balanced chemical formulæ in such a manner as to give a complete reaction during the process of panification, whereby the total available carbon dioxid is secured in a gaseous form and residues are secured which have no longer sufficient alkaline properties to stain the bread or give it an unpleasant taste.

The subject of baking powders has been exhaustively treated in Part V of this bulletin. This publication, however, is out of print. A brief statement of some of the properties of these aerating agents may prove useful.

CLASSIFICATION OF BAKING POWDERS.

Baking powders may be conveniently classified according to the nature of the acid constituent they contain. Three principal kinds may be recognized as follows:

(1) Tartrate powders, in which the acid constituent is tartaric acid in some form.

(2) Phosphate powders, in which the acid constituent is phosphoric acid.

(3) Alum powders, in which the acid constituent is furnished by the sulphuric acid contained in some form of alum salt.

All powders sold at present will come under some one of these heads, although there are many powders which are mixtures of at least two different classes.

TARTRATE POWDERS.

The form in which tartaric acid is usually furnished in this class is bitartrate of potassium, or "cream of tartar." Sometimes free tartaric acid is used, but not often. Bitartrate, or acid tartrate of potassium, is made from crude argol obtained from grape juice. It contains 1 atom of replaceable hydrogen, which gives it the acidity that acts upon the carbonate. The reaction takes place according to the following equation:

$$\underset{\substack{188 \\ \text{Potassium} \\ \text{bitartrate.}}}{KHC_4H_4O_6} + \underset{\substack{84 \\ \text{Sodium} \\ \text{bicarbonate.}}}{NaHCO_3} = \underset{\substack{210 \\ \text{Potassium-sodium} \\ \text{tartrate.}}}{KNaC_4H_4O_6} + \underset{\substack{44 \\ \text{Carbon} \\ \text{dioxid.}}}{CO_2} + \underset{\substack{18 \\ \text{Water.}}}{H_2O}$$

It will be seen that the products of the reaction are carbonic acid or carbon dioxid and double tartrate of potassium and sodium, the latter constituting the residue which remains in the bread. This salt is generally known as Rochelle salt, and is the compound formed when the component parts of Seidlitz powders are mixed and moistened. A Seidlitz powder yields 210 grains of this salt, but the crystallized salt contains 4 molecules of water, and thus the actual amount of crystallized Rochelle salt formed in the baking-powder reaction is greater than the combined weight of the two salts used. That is to say, if 188 grains of bitartrate and 84 grains of bicarbonate are used in a baking there will be a residue in the dough equal to 282 grains of Rochelle salt. The directions that accompany these powders generally give two teaspoonfuls as the proper amount to use to the quart of flour; probably more is generally used. This would be at least 200 grains; deducting 20 per cent for the starch filling, we have 160 grains of the mixed bitartrate and bicarbonate, and this would form 165 grains of crystallized Rochelle salt in the loaf of bread made from the quart of flour, or 45 grains less than is contained in a Seidlitz powder. The popular idea is that the chemicals used in a baking powder mostly disappear in baking, and that the residue left is very slight. Probably not many persons understand that when they use tartrate powders, which are considered to be the best class, or at least one of the best classes of such powders, they consume in a loaf of bread made from it three-fourths of the equivalent of one Seidlitz powder.

Yet the character of this residue is probably the least objectionable of any of those left by baking powders. Rochelle salt is one of the mildest of the alkaline salts. The dose as a purgative is from one-half to 1 ounce. "Given in small and repeated doses it does not purge, but is absorbed and renders the urine alkaline." (United States Dispensatory).

Free tartaric acid, used instead of the potassium bitartrate, would give less residue. In this case the reaction would be as follows:

$$\underset{\substack{150 \\ \text{Tartaric} \\ \text{acid.}}}{H_2C_4H_4O_6} + \underset{\substack{168 \\ \text{Sodium} \\ \text{bicarbonate.}}}{2NaHCO_3} = \underset{\substack{230 \\ \text{Sodium} \\ \text{tartrate.}}}{Na_2C_4H_4O_6.2H_2O} + \underset{\substack{88 \\ \text{Carbon} \\ \text{dioxid.}}}{2CO_2}$$

Here 150 grains of tartaric acid, with 168 grains of bicarbonate of sodium, give 230 grains of residue, or 88 grains less than the combined weight of the two ingredients. As to the character of this residue little has been published in regard to the physiological properties of sodium tartrate, but probably it is essentially similar to the double tartrate. The United States Dispensatory says of it (p. 1762):

> This salt, in crystals, has been recommended as an agreeable purgative, almost without taste, and acting with power equal to that of the sulphate of magnesium in the dose of 10 drams [600 grains].

It is not clear why this combination should be used so seldom by baking-powder manufacturers. The free tartaric acid is more expensive than the bitartrate, but less of it is required in proportion to the amount of bicarbonate used. The former is more soluble, and this would probably be a practical objection to its use, as it is an object in baking powders that the gas should be liberated slowly. It would perhaps be more difficult also to prevent action of the free acid upon the alkali, so that the powder would be more likely to deteriorate in keeping. Only one sample among those examined was found to have been made with the free acid.

One obstacle formerly encountered in the manufacture of bitartrate powders was the difficulty of obtaining the bitartrate pure. It contained from 5 to 15 per cent of calcium tartrate, incident to the method of manufacture. This brought a large quantity of inert material into the powder and lowered its efficiency. Potassium bitartrate can now be had 99 per cent pure, quoted and guaranteed as such in the markets; so that there is no excuse for manufacturers to use the impure salt, which can properly be considered adulterated.

PHOSPHATE POWDERS.

The salt commonly used to furnish the phosphoric acid in this class is acid phosphate of lime, sometimes called superphosphate. The pure salt is monocalcium phosphate, $CaH_4(PO_4)_2$. It is made by the action of sulphuric acid upon phosphate rock, the result being an impure monocalcium phosphate with calcium sulphate. This mixture is sold as superphosphate for a fertilizer. The salt is of course more or less purified for use in baking powders, but the calcium sulphate is very difficult to get rid of entirely, and most phosphate powders contain considerable amounts of this impurity. The reaction which occurs when a phosphate powder is dissolved—that is, the action of sodium bicarbonate upon monocalcium phosphate—is not well established, and perhaps varies somewhat with conditions. The following equation probably represents it fairly well:

$$\underset{\text{Monocalcium phosphate.}}{\underset{234}{CaH_4(PO_4)_2}} + \underset{\text{Sodium bicarbonate.}}{\underset{168}{2NaHCO_3}} = \underset{\text{Monohydrogen calcium phosphate.}}{\underset{136}{CaHPO_4}} + \underset{\text{Disodium phosphate.}}{\underset{142}{Na_2HPO_4}} + \underset{\text{Carbon dioxid.}}{\underset{88}{2CO_2}} + \underset{\text{Water.}}{\underset{36}{2H_2O}}$$

Two hundred and thirty-four grains of monocalcium phosphate combined with 168 grains of sodium bicarbonate give 136 grains of monohydrogen calcium phosphate and 142 grams of disodium phosphate.

But crystallized sodium phosphate contains 12 molecules of water, and and has a molecular weight of 358. So the total amount of residue from 402 grains of the powder would be 494 grains, of which 136 grains is calcium phosphate and the rest sodium phosphate. So we see that here also the quantity of chemicals introduced into the dough is fully equal to the amount of the baking powder used, including filling. As to the nature of this residue in phosphate powders, it would seem to be about as unobjectionable as in the tartrates. Sodium phosphate is "mildly purgative in doses of from 1 to 2 ounces" (480–960 grains), according to the United States Dispensatory. Calcium phosphates have the general physiological effect which is ascribed to all forms of phosphoric acid, but which does not seem to be well understood.

Phosphates are administered therapeutically in some cases of defective nutrition, and especially in scrofula, rickets, phthisis, etc. On account of their being an essential constituent of animal tissues there would seem to be some ground for their preference over other forms of powders. The makers of phosphate powders claim that the use of such powders restores the phosphoric acid present in the whole grain of wheat, which is largely removed in the bran by milling processes. This claim would have more weight if there were not ample sources of phosphoric acid in other forms of food, and if the quantity introduced by a baking powder were not much greater than is required to make up the loss in the bran and greater than is required by the system, unless in those cases where its therapeutic use is indicated, as in some of the conditions of malnutrition given above.

Acid sodium phosphate is said to have been used in former years as a constituent of baking powders, but appears to have been entirely superseded by the calcium salt.

ALUM POWDERS.

In this class the carbon dioxid is set free from the bicarbonate by the substitution of sulphuric acid, which combines with the sodium. The sulphuric acid is furnished by some one of the general class of salts known as alums, which are composed of a double sulphate of aluminium and an alkali metal. The alum is precipitated as hydroxid, while that portion of the sulphuric acid which was combined with it goes to displace the carbon dioxid in the bicarbonate. The alkali sulphate of the double salt remains unchanged.

The alum of commerce is either *potash alum*, $K_2Al_2(SO_4)_4.24H_2O$, or *ammonia alum*, $(NH_4)_2Al_2(SO_4)_4.24H_2O$, the one or the other predominating according to the relative cheapness of the alkali salt it contains. At the present time nothing but ammonia alum is met with, but at previous periods potash alum was the salt sold exclusively as "alum." The two salts are alike in general appearance and can not be distinguished by cursory examination.

Potash alum may be made directly from some minerals, such as the "alum stone" mined in Italy, which contain all the constituents combined. Ammonia alum, however, as well as most potash alum, is made by the combination of the constituents obtained from different sources. The aluminum sulphate is obtained by the action of sulphuric acid upon criolite, bauxite, or pure clays, and the ammonium sulphate from the residue of gas works. Solutions of the two salts in proper proportions are mixed and the double salt obtained by evaporation and crystallization.

Crystallized potash or ammonia alum contains twenty-four molecules of water, nearly one-half of its weight. Part of this water is lost at as low a heat as 60°, and it is driven off entirely, though slowly, at 100°. "Burnt alum" is simply alum deprived of its water of crystallization. It is somewhat hygroscopic, but dissolves more slowly in water than the crystallized salt.

I have been unable to ascertain in what condition the alum is used for compounding baking powders. Burnt alum would seem to be the form best adapted for this purpose on account of its slow solubility. Professor Cornwall says this is the form[1] used, but does not tell how he obtained the information; and he states further that "crystallized alums may be used in connection with burnt alum to secure at first a more rapid escape of carbonic-acid gas." It is probable that the amount of drying given the alum used differs with different manufacturers, but it is not likely that the water of crystallization is entirely driven off.

The following equation shows the reaction taking place in a baking powder made with burnt ammonia alum:

$$\underset{\text{Aluminum and ammonium sulphate.}}{\overset{475}{(NH_4)_2Al_2(SO_4)_4}} + \underset{\text{Sodium bicarbonate.}}{\overset{504}{6NaHCO_3}} = \underset{\text{Aluminum hydroxid.}}{\overset{157}{Al_2(OH)_6}} +$$

$$\underset{\text{Sodium sulphate.}}{\overset{426}{3Na_2SO}} + \underset{\text{Ammonium sulphate.}}{\overset{132}{(NH_4)_2SO_4}} + \underset{\text{Carbon dioxid.}}{\overset{264}{6CO_2}}$$

If potash alum were used, the reaction would be precisely the same, with the substitution of potassium for ammonium wherever it occurs in the equation, potassium sulphate being formed instead of ammonium sulphate.

A study of the equation will show that 475 grains of burnt alum with 504 grains of bicarbonate will produce 264 grains of carbon dioxid and leave a residue consisting of 426 grains of sodium sulphate, 132 grains of ammonium sulphate, and 157 grains of aluminum hydroxid, the last named being a precipitate insoluble in water. Sodium sulphate crystallizes with ten molecules of water, so that the total weight of residue from the 979 grains of mixed chemicals would be 1,255 grains. If a hydrated alum is used in the powder, the proportion of residue to powder would of course be less, and the proportion of gas evolved would also be less. The character of the residue is seen to be more com-

---

[1] Report of the Dairy Commissioner of New Jersey, 1888, p. 70.

plex than is the case with any of the classes previously discussed and deserves special attention. The sodium sulphate is similar to other alkali salts in its physiological action. Ammonium sulphate is not used therapeutically, but probably has an action similar to that of other ammonia salts, such as the chlorid. Professor Cornwall,[1] in his report, speaks as follows concerning this point:

> It is possible, however, that too little attention has been paid to the presence of ammonium salts in the residues from ammonia alum powders. * * * We do know, however, that ammonia salts, in general, are much more irritating and stimulating in their action than the corresponding soda salts, or even than the potash salts. For instance, Stillé and Maisch, speaking of ammonium bromide, state that it has a more acrid taste and is more irritating than potassium bromide. Its unpleasant taste and irritating qualities render it less convenient for administration than the bromide of potassium.
>
> We all know how mild a substance is chloride of sodium (common table salt); but of ammonium chloride Stillé and Maisch write: "The direct effects of doses of 5 to 20 grains of this salt, repeated at intervals of several hours, are a sense of oppression, warmth, and uneasiness in the stomach and some fullness in the head. If it is used for many days together in full doses, it disturbs the digestion, coats the tongue, and impairs the appetite." We have already seen how active a drug carbonate of ammonia is, and while, in the absence of proof, it would be rash to assert that sulphate of ammonia in five-grain doses is certainly injurious, yet there is abundant ground for further investigating its effect before asserting that it is milder in its effects than Rochelle salt. It may be that this question of the presence of ammonium salts in any considerable quantities in the residues of baking powders deserves more attention than it has hitherto received.

It would seem from the above that there would be considerable difference between the physiological effects of potash and ammonia alums themselves. Yet the medical authorities make no such distinction. Ammonia alum is officinal in the British Pharmacopœia, and while the United States Pharmacopœia specifies potash alum, the particular form met with in trade is entirely determined by the comparative cheapness of manufacture.

The question of the relative harmfulness of these different salts in the residues of baking powders is really one for the physiologist or hygienist to decide, not the chemist. Physiological experiments alone can decide them positively.

The consideration of the residue of aluminum hydroxid is taken up on page 1311.

POWDERS CONTAINING MORE THAN ONE ACID INGREDIENT.

As might be expected, some powders are met with which have been made up with various proportions of different acid ingredients, and which belong therefore to more than one of the above-mentioned classes. Professor Cornwall speaks as follows concerning some of these mixed powders:

> The makers of alum baking powders sometimes add tartaric acid or bitartrate to their powders, either with or without the addition of acid phosphate of lime. This is doubtless done with the best intentions, either to secure a more rapid escape of

---

[1] Op. cit., p. 77.

carbonic acid gas at the outset or otherwise to improve the powder. We have found such additions in the case of several of our samples, but the presence of tartaric acid or tartrates in alum powders is very objectionable. If added in sufficient quantity to otherwise pure alum powders, they prevent the precipitation of the insoluble hydrate of aluminum entirely when the powder is boiled with water, and they may render much of the alumina soluble in water even after the bread is baked. Without doubt it would then be readily soluble in the digestive organs, producing there the effects due to alum or any other soluble aluminum compound. With one of our samples we found that the simple water solution seemed to contain as much alumina as a nitric-acid solution. In neither of these solutions could any of the alumina be thrown down by a slight excess of ammonia water, although it was readily precipitated from the solution first rendered alkaline with caustic soda, then slightly acidified with acetic acid and boiled with excess of phosphate of soda.

ALUM AND PHOSPHATE POWDERS.

A case in which the character of the powder appears to be improved by such mixing, however, is furnished by the alum and phosphate powders. This combination seems to be a favorite one with manufacturers. In fact there are now comparatively few "straight" alum powders in the market, most of the cheaper grades being made of mixtures in various proportions of the alum with acid calcium phosphate. The reaction it is intended to obtain is probably the following:

$$\underset{\text{Ammonia alum.}}{\underset{475}{(NH_4)_2 Al_2(SO_4)_4}} + \underset{\substack{\text{Acid calcium} \\ \text{phosphate.}}}{\underset{234}{CaH_4(PO_4)_2}} + \underset{\substack{\text{Sodium} \\ \text{bicarbonate.}}}{\underset{336}{4NaHCO_3}} = \underset{\substack{\text{Aluminum} \\ \text{phosphate.}}}{\underset{245}{2Al(PO_4)}} +$$

$$\underset{\substack{\text{Calcium} \\ \text{sulphate.}}}{\underset{136}{CaSO_4}} + \underset{\substack{\text{Aluminum and} \\ \text{ammonium sulphate.}}}{\underset{132}{(NH_4)_2SO_4}} + \underset{\substack{\text{Sodium} \\ \text{Sulphate.}}}{\underset{284}{2Na_2SO_4}} + \underset{\substack{\text{Carbon} \\ \text{dioxid.}}}{\underset{176}{4CO_2}} + \underset{\text{Water.}}{\underset{72}{4H_2O}}$$

If this equation be compared with the one representing the reaction in a powder made with alum alone, on page 1308, it will be seen that in the former the aluminum goes into the residue as phosphate instead of hydroxid, and the insoluble calcium sulphate takes the place of one molecule of sodium sulphate. Otherwise the reactions are similar. This reaction will only take place, of course, when the different ingredients are mixed in just the proper proportions to produce it. A number of variations may be produced by changing the relative proportions of the different ingredients.

RESIDUES OF BAKING POWDERS.

The question of the harmfulness of the residues left after the chemical decomposition taking place during the process of baking with chemical leavening agents is one which has been extensively discussed. In the preceding paragraphs some references have been made to the quantity and nature of the residue. This general principle may be stated as broadly covering the physiological and dietetic aspects of the question. Mineral substances are essentially elements in the nourishment of animal bodies. In natural foods, as a rule, the mineral elements are so distributed as to supply in an entirely satisfactory manner the requirements for the nutrition and growth of the body. With water and in all kinds of solid and liquid foods more or less of those substances essential to nutrition are ingested. The nature of the residues from leavening agents has been fully set forth in the preceding paragraphs. A question arises if the increase in the percentage of mineral matter due to these residues is sufficiently great to derange the function of digestion. This is a question on which there is room for a wide difference of opinion. It seems to be pretty well established that slight excesses of many mineral substances, such as common salt, potassium tartrate, potassium and sodium phosphate, etc., exert no injurious effects upon the digestive system.

CHARACTER OF ALUM RESIDUE.

The residues from alum baking powders are open to a more serious objection inasmuch as alum itself, while not strictly poisonous in the ordinary sense of that term, is highly injurious when ingested in any large quantities. If the temperature of baking were sufficient to render the residues containing alum wholly insoluble so that they would not be acted upon subsequently by the gastric and intestinal juices there would probably be no valid grounds for objecting to the use of alum as a leavening agent. The manufacturers of alum baking powder claim that the aluminum hydroxid which is left in the residue is insoluble in the digestive juices and therefore does not produce the effect which is attributed to the soluble forms of aluminum. From a strictly chemical point of view this position is not tenable, for while aluminum hydroxid is insoluble in water, even in the gelatinous state in which it is first precipitated, it is readily soluble in dilute acids until it has been heated to a high temperature and lost all of its water of hydration. It is clear that this condition is never reached in the ordinary baking of bread, for the temperature of the interior of the loaf rarely rises above that of boiling water. If the alumina remain as a phosphate in the loaf it is in a condition which is more soluble than in the form of hydroxid. In many cases investigations of the action of the digestive juices on aluminum hydroxids and phosphates have been undertaken at the instigation of rival baking powder companies, and while the high character of the gentlemen engaged in such a study precludes the possibility of any misstatement of facts, yet the commercial bias of such an investigation does much to render it partisan. Chemical and physiological investigations, which have for their chief object the promotion of the sale of one compound and the repression of the sale of another, lose at the outset much of that claim upon the public which such investigations made from a purely scientific point of view should have.

COMPARATIVE STATEMENT AS TO RESIDUES.

In respect to the use of chemical leavening agents in general, it may be said that they introduce an artificial process into bread making which is likely to produce results not entirely favorable to health, and, therefore, on general principles, this manner of bread making should not be given the preference. On the other hand, it seems perfectly certain that the occasional consumption of the small quantities of mineral residues left in loaves made by the leavening agents is in no wise prejudicial to a person in good health. The relative nocuousness of the residue left from alum and mixed baking powders is perhaps stated as fairly as possible in this bulletin, Part V, page 574, as follows:

(1) That form of alum powder in which sufficient phosphate is added to combine with all the aluminum present is a better form, and less apt to bring alum into the system than where alum alone is used.

(2) It must be expected that small quantities, at least, of alum will be absorbed by the digestive fluids where any form of powder containing it is used.

(3) Whether the absorption of small quantities of alum into the human system would be productive of serious effects is still an open question, and one that careful physiological experiments alone can decide.

For a more extended discussion of the residues, especially those containing alum in baking-powder breads, Part V of this bulletin, pages 562 and 575, may be consulted.

COMPOSITION OF BREAD.

By reason of the many different methods of bread making practiced throughout the United States, it is difficult, even from a large number of analyses, to determine what is the composition of the typical classes of the breads used in the United States. The most valuable data of this kind which can be obtained are those secured by actual baking experiments, in which the character of the wheat and flour are known, and in this way the composition of bread can be compared directly with that of the flour from which it is made. One of the most important points in studying the composition of bread is in determining the percentage of moisture which the normal bread contains. It is the object of bakers in general to make a loaf which contains a maximum content of water consistent with palatability and general porosity of the loaf. Extensive experiments in the study of the composition of bread have been made in England, and a full account of baking experiments made in London in 1882 is found in Bulletin No. 4 of this division, page 59 and following. An extensive series of baking experiments was also made in this laboratory under carefully controlled conditions, and the data obtained in these experiments are highly important as a basis for the scientific study and judgment of bread. It is found that the percentage of moisture which could be secured in the loaf could be easily changed by varying the conditions under which the dough is prepared. The baking experiments were carried on under the direction of Mr. Clifford Richardson, and the bread was made by an expert employed

COMPOSITION OF FLOUR AND BREAD.

for the purpose. The method pursued was a modification of the Vienna process, which, as is well known, gives bread of a most excellent quality. The dough was mixed in mass with pressed yeast, and the fermentation allowed to proceed under the ordinary conditions provided for the preliminary process until the outer pellicle began to crack. In this condition the dough was rekneaded, put into pans, and set in a warm place until it had risen to the proper point, when it was baked. The baking was carried on in a large gas stove, the oven of which could be kept at a very constant temperature. All the materials employed in making the dough, as well as the products obtained, were weighed on a delicate balance, and therefore the data secured can be regarded as determining in a very certain manner the changes which take place during the process of baking.

The flours from which the breads were made had the following composition:

Composition of samples of flour.

No.	Name of flour.	Moisture.	Nitrogen.	Proteids. N × 6.25.	Gluten.	
					Moist.	Dry.
		Per cent.	Per cent.	Per cent.	Per cent.	Per cent.
1	Maryland Patent Flour	11.55	1.65	10.33	33.32	9.60
2	Maryland Straight	11.08	1.75	10.94	32.49	10.28
3	Maryland Low Grade	12.78	1.84	11.50	30.15	11.13
4	District of Columbia Patent	12.98	1.46	9.10	31.58	9.09
5	District of Columbia Straight	12.38	1.53	9.56	33.40	9.76
6	Straight Virginia	12.16	1.93	12.08	36.07	11.41
7	Low Grade Virginia	11.77	2.02	12.60	36.81	11.60
8	Roller Patent, Virginia	12.10	1.73	10.81	37.89	11.08
9	Ohio Patent	12.85	1.70	10.62	29.63	10.47
10	Indiana Patent	12.33	1.59	9.94	33.60	10.03
11	Illinois Patent Flour	12.00	1.93	12.08	37.36	11.56
12	Wisconsin Straight	12.37	1.60	9.98	28.39	9.56
13	Roller Patent, Wisconsin	13.25	1.85	11.55	34.45	10.65
14	Best Minnesota Patent Process	12.82	1.90	11.90	39.18	11.98
15	Minnesota Low Grade	12.05	2.51	15.09	34.22	14.06
16	Minnesota Bakers'	11.77	1.95	12.19	30.71	11.71
17	Roller Patent, Missouri	12.04	1.67	10.44	32.24	9.23
18	New Process, Oregon	14.03	1.15	7.18	20.84	6.75

The quantity and kind of materials used in making the bread, temperature of baking, weight of the bread when cold and the percentage of the weight of bread compared with the weight of flour used are given in the following table:

Quantity and kind of materials for bread.

No. of sample.	Weight of flour.	Weight of milk.	Weight of water.	Weight of salt.	Weight of yeast.	Time of baking.	Temperature of oven.	Bread.	
								Weight, cold.	Per cent, cold, on weight of flour.
	Grams.	Grams.	Grams.	Grams.	Grams.	Min.	° C.	Grams.	
1......	2,032	500	650	25	10	45	....	2,729	134.4
2......	2,049	500	650	25	10	45	228	2,795	136.4
3......	2,014	500	650	25	10	45	....	2,754	136.7
4......	2,031	500	650	25	10	50	248	2,746	135.2
5......	2,024	500	650	25	10	45	243	2,740	135.4
6......	2,024	500	650	25	10	55	243	2,759	136.3
7......	2,073	500	650	25	10	45	236	2,754	132.9
8......	2,050	500	650	25	10	45	230	2,732	132.9
9......	2,045	500	650	25	10	45	245	2,757	134.8
10......	2,030	500	650	25	10	45	235	2,730	134.5
12......	2,044	500	650	25	10	45	....	2,792	136.6
13......	2,025	500	650	25	10	45	248	2,808	138.7
14......	2,032	500	650	25	10	45	247	2,785	137.1
15......	5,038	500	650	25	10	45	248	2,738	134.3
16......	2,034	500	650	25	10	45	248	2,733	134.4
17......	2,047	500	650	25	10	45	230	2,781	135.9
19......	2,110	500	650	25	10	50	....	2,840	134.6
20......	2,049	500	650	25	10	45	240	2,780	135.7
21......	2,008	500	650	25	10	50	230	2,772	134.0
22......	2,041	500	650	25	10	45	....	2,791	136.8
23......	2,043	500	650	25	10	45	232	2,754	134.8
24......	2,035	500	650	25	10	45	....	2,730	134.2
25......	2,031	500	650	25	10	45	245	2,728	134.3
26......	2,034	500	650	25	10	45	249	2,788	137.1
27......	2,040	500	650	25	10	45	234	2,745	134.1
29......	2,028	500	650	25	10	45	....	2,747	135.5
30......	2,024	500	650	25	10	45	242	2,784	137.6
31......	2,000	500	650	25	10	45	....	2,807	139.9
32......	2,029	500	650	25	10	45	234	2,786	137.3
33......	2,024	500	650	25	10	45	246	2,742	135.5
34......	2,031	500	650	25	10	45	238	2,803	138.0
35......	2,050	500	650	25	10	50	248	2,738	133.0
36......	2,042	500	650	25	10	45	242	2,746	134.5
37......	2,085	500	650	25	10	45	240	2,689	129.0
38......	2,087	500	650	25	10	45	240	2,753	132.0

In the foregoing table the samples of bread were made from the flours contained in the next preceding table, as follows:

Breads Nos. 1 and 2 were made from flour No. 1; breads Nos. 3 and 4 from flour No. 2; breads Nos. 5 and 6 from flour No. 3; breads Nos. 7 and 8 from flour No. 4; breads Nos. 9 and 10 from flour No. 5; breads Nos. 12 and 13 from flour No. 6; breads Nos. 14 and 15 from flour No. 7; breads Nos. 16 and 17 from flour No. 8; bread No. 19 from flour No. 9;

breads Nos. 20 and 21 from flour No. 10; breads Nos. 22 and 23 from flour No. 11; breads Nos. 24 and 25 from flour No. 12; breads Nos. 26 and 27 from flour No. 13; breads Nos. 29 and 30 from flour No. 14; breads Nos. 31 and 32 from flour No. 15; breads Nos. 33 and 34 from flour No. 16; breads Nos. 35 and 36 from flour No. 17, and breads Nos. 37 and 38 from flour No. 18.

TEMPERATURE OF BAKING.

The temperature of the oven in which the baking experiments were conducted showed an average of about 240°. The question is often raised regarding the temperature of the interior of the loaf. It is evident that a body containing as much water as a loaf of bread, often as much as 40 per cent, could not be subjected for a very long time to a temperature much above the boiling point of water without seriously altering the proportions between the water and solid bodies. It is quite evident, not only from the character of the finished loaf, but also from careful determinations which have been made, that the temperature of the interior of the loaf does not, as a rule, exceed that of boiling water, and is probably a little less. The high nonconductive properties of the dough render the penetration of the heat into the interior of the loaf somewhat slow, and the fact that the interior of the loaf is not darkened shows that the temperature necessary to the process of caramelization has not been reached.

In experimental determinations of the temperature in the interior of the loaf of bread conducted by Mallet[1] it was found that the range was from 197° to 212° F., never exceeding the latter. In a series of determinations of the temperature of the interior of a loaf, reported in the Journal de Pharmacie et de Chimie, series 5, vol. 27, page 16, it is shown that the temperature of the interior of a loaf as it leaves the oven is between 97° and 100°. It is never more than 100°, even after the baking has continued forty minutes. On the removal of the loaf from the oven, on account of the high nonconducting power of the crust, the temperature falls gradually, requiring from five to six hours for a loaf weighing two pounds to reach the temperature of the surrounding air. It is, therefore, just to conclude from the above data that a loaf of bread of medium size, baked in an oven where the temperature is about 240°, will not acquire in forty minutes, the usual maximum time for baking, a temperature above the boiling point of water in the interior of the loaf.

THE PERCENTAGE OF MOISTURE IN THE LOAF.

In the baking experiments made in this division it was found that the average percentage of moisture in the loaf was a little over 30. In a large number of samples of bread examined by Voorhees[2] at the Connecticut Station it was found that the average percentage of moisture in

---

[1] Chemical News, Nos. 1515 and 1516.
[2] Office of Experiment Stations Bulletin No. 35.

commercial samples of bread often rises above 40 per cent; in fact, in one instance reported by Voorhees the percentage of moisture was found to be over 49 per cent.

Lawes and Gilbert[1] have found that bread contains from 33 to 44 per cent of moisture, in accordance with the method of manufacture.

RELATION OF FLOUR TO MOISTURE IN BREAD.

It is doubtless true, as indicated before, that in breads made for sale, especially where the sale is based on the weight of the loaf and not subjected to legal restrictions, the natural tendency of the baker would be to incorporate as much water as possible in the loaf. It is not to be denied that loaves containing as much as 40 per cent of moisture may be perfectly palatable and porous and not have an excessive doughy constituence. The baker regards as a "strong" flour the one which will absorb and hold the most moisture in baking, and not the one which contains the greatest amount of nutritive materials. Again, it may be said that the percentage of moisture in the bread is often not under the control of the baker, but depends largely upon the nature of the flour employed. It is not possible, therefore, to give a rigid rule which would be applicable to all cases, inasmuch as in some instances a bread might be sticky and doughy, containing only 35 per cent of moisture, while with a different kind of flour a bread would be perfectly palatable and of a proper consistence, containing over 40 per cent.

RELATION OF MOISTURE TO SIZE AND SHAPE OF LOAF.

If the interior of the loaf be separated from the crust and examined, it will be found to contain a larger quantity of moisture. The interior of the bread will contain from 35 to 50 per cent of moisture and the crust from 16 to 25 per cent, according to the temperature to which it has been subjected in baking. In respect to nutritive value, therefore, a given weight of the crust represents more nutrition than the same weight of the crumb. There is, however, no definite relation existing between the quantity of moisture in the crust and crumb. It depends altogether upon the temperature and duration of baking and has little to do with the shape and size of the loaf or the character of the flour from which it is made. It is evident, however, that the total quantity of moisture in a loaf of bread depends somewhat upon its size and shape. Theoretically it is demonstrable that a perfectly spherical loaf of bread under similar conditions will contain more moisture than one of the same weight and of any other shape. It is also demonstrable that the flattest and thinnest loaves under conditions otherwise similar will contain the least quantity of moisture. This is illustrated by comparing the different percentages of moisture in thin biscuits prepared for the use of army rations and the ordinary soft loaves of the bakers.

---

[1] Composition of Wheat-grain, its Products in the Mill, and Bread, page 57.

SUMMARY OF OBSERVATIONS REGARDING MOISTURE.

In the breads purchased in the open market and examined in this division in connection with this research, it will be seen, by referring to the table of analyses given on page 1323, that the percentage of moisture varies from a minimum of 29.69 in No. 14401 to a maximum of 40.39 per cent in No. 14356. In the average composition of the different classes the minimum is found in class 4, viz, 32.99 per cent, and the maximum in class 1, 37.53 per cent. This is another illustration of the fact that the flour used in making the high-grade loaves known as Vienna rolls is a particularly strong flour, capable of absorbing and holding a large proportion of water.

Summarizing our knowledge of the subject of moisture in bread, it may be said that the ordinary yeast breads of commerce contain from 30 to 40 per cent of moisture, and the average loaf 35 per cent; that the quantity of moisture in a loaf depends upon many conditions, one of the most important of which is the nature of the flour. In bakers' parlance, a "strong" flour is one which has the capacity of absorbing and holding during the process of baking a maximum quantity of water. The percentage of moisture also depends upon the size and shape of the loaf, on the duration of the baking, and the temperature of the oven. The relative proportions of moisture in the crust and crumb vary with the conditions of baking, and are practically independent of the usual size and shape of the loaf and of the character of the flour, but the relative quantities of crust and crumb vary chiefly with the time and temperature of baking and the size and shape of the loaf.

LOSS DURING FERMENTATION.

The loss of solid matter during the fermentation and baking of the bread is due to the conversion of part of the solid matter into volatile substances and their evaporation during the process of baking. The only substances which are changed in any appreciable degree by this process are the sugars which the flour may contain. It is evident, therefore, that the loss in no case can be greater than is due to the fermentation of the sugars. It is not probable that any large quantity of sugar will be formed from the starch during the fermentation process. The quantity of fermentable sugar in a wheat flour is not usually greater than one-half of 1 per cent, rising in some instances to 1 per cent. The statements which are made by some authorities, therefore, that there may be a loss of from 3 to 6 per cent during fermentation, are evidently exaggerated. Jago places the loss of the solid matter during fermentation at about $2\frac{1}{2}$ per cent; but this seems to be also an extravagant estimate. Lawes and Gilbert are inclined to the opinion that the loss of solid matter during panary fermentation is less than 1 and probably less than one-half of 1 per cent, and this is doubtless very nearly correct. It must be admitted, moreover, that not all of the sugar which is present in a flour is decomposed during the process of fermentation, unless the period of raising the bread be prolonged beyond usual limits. In addition to this, it must be considered that it is difficult in the process of baking to expel all the products of the fermentation. A portion of the carbon dioxid and of the alcohol will undoubtedly remain entangled in the meshes of the loaf. Even, therefore, allowing for the fact that a portion of the starch may be converted into sugar and undergo a partial fermentation, it is not to be expected that the total loss in weight in dry matter in the loaf itself will be greater than the amount of sugar originally present in the flour. Of course, it is understood if the loaf be ground and dried for the purpose of a chemical determination of loss that the whole of the alcohol and carbon dioxid will be driven off, but in the loaf as it comes from the oven or as it is brought upon the table such a complete evaporation of the volatile products of fermentation is not found.

CHEMICAL CHANGES PRODUCED IN THE LOAF DURING BAKING.

In addition to the many changes mentioned above as due to fermentation, certain changes in the constitution of the materials of flour are produced by the combined action of heat and water. These changes, of course, are produced in the maximum degree in the crust of the bread, whereas the temperature of boiling water in the interior of the bread acts less vigorously in its effects upon the chemical constituents of the flour. In respect to the proteid matters, it is certain that all of the proteids of the material will be rendered insoluble by the temperature to which they are subjected. The proteid matters in the crust of the bread certainly undergo additional changes by reason of the high temperature to which they are subjected, the nature of which is not definitely known. The same is true of the fats or oils, which are oxidized to a certain extent by the action of the oxygen of the atmosphere at the high temperature to which the crust is subjected. It is probable, therefore, that a splitting up to some degree of the molecules of the glycerides composing the fat and oil takes place, especially in the crust of the loaf. In the interior of the loaf the carbohydrates probably undergo little change except a degradation of the starch grains and a slight tendency of the starch to be converted into dextrin. In the crust, however, in addition to those changes, there is a decided caramelization of the starchy particles, as is evidenced by the browning of the loaf. The effects of these changes in respect of nutritive properties can not be discussed in this place, but are more particularly the subjects of investigation where the digestive values of the different bodies are to be determined.

CLASSIFICATION OF THE BREADS OF COMMERCE.

In attempting to classify breads bought in the open market the same difficulty is encountered that was met in the classification of commercial flours. The only guide which is of any value in these cases is the appearance of the loaf and the description or name as furnished by the dealer or baker. When it is remembered that names are used somewhat indiscriminately in the description of commercial articles, it is easily seen that a classification based upon such information is not rigidly scientific. Nevertheless, for purposes of comparison it may be used, and guided by such data the breads which were bought in the open market have been divided into the six classes which follow, viz: Class 1, Vienna; class 2, homemade breads; class 3, Graham breads; class 4, rye breads; class 5, Quaker breads; class 6, miscellaneous breads.

It is evident at a glance from the above description that at least two of these classes, viz, homemade and Quaker, have no definite rank, and might with propriety be included in the miscellaneous class, reducing the number of classes from six to four. Inasmuch, however, as quite a number of samples were found on the open market sold under these names, it was deemed advisable to place them in a separate classification.

In the class "miscellaneous breads" are grouped all those varieties of bread purchased in the open market not included in the other five classes. It is evident that this class represents very well the ordinary miscellaneous breads sold by bakers and grocers, corresponding to the group of miscellaneous flours discussed under that subject. It may be remarked as a matter of surprise that no Indian-corn breads are found in the above list. This arises from the fact that the Indian-corn breads consumed in the United States are, in so far as I know, wholly produced in the home, and are not sold as breads by bakers and grocers. Although the use of Indian-corn breads is so general in the United States, I doubt if any purchaser could go into any bakery or grocery store, at least in the more populous Northern cities, and be able to purchase a loaf of Indian-corn bread. Inasmuch as it was not possible for the investigation to extend into the breads of domestic production, no samples of maize bread were purchased for examination.

DESCRIPTION OF SAMPLES ANALYZED.

The following table contains the name of each of the samples as given by the dealer, the name of the dealer, the name of the manufacturer, the price per loaf, and the weight of the loaf in grams. To convert the weight in grams into pounds, divide by 454. The data show that the loaves weigh approximately one pound each. Only in three instances, viz, Nos. 14384, 16020, and 16022 did a loaf weigh as much as an ounce less than a pound, while in many instances the excess was greater than an ounce. All were made in Washington.

1320 FOODS AND FOOD ADULTERANTS.

Description of breads bought in the open market.

Serial No.	Name.	Where bought.	Baker.	Price.	Fresh weight.
				Cents.	Grams.
14352	Vienna	N. W. Burchell, 1325 F street NW.	C. Schneider, 413 I street NW.	5	452
14353	Homemade	....do	....do	5	454.3
14354	Graham	....do	....do	5	449.1
14356	Quaker	....do	....do	5	451.9
14383	Old-time	A. A. Winfield, 215 Thirteen-and-a-half street SW.	Gross Bros., 411 Six-and-a-half street SW.	4	451
14384	Rye	....do	....do	4	425
14385	Havenner	....do	Havenner Baking Co., 472-476 C street NW.	5	462
14386	Blue Ribbon Bread	....do	Leary & Schneider, 119 First street SW.	5	487
14395	Vienna	W. Berens & Sons, 622 E street NW.	W. Berens & Sons, 622 E street NW.	5	469
14396	Rye	....do	....do	5	466
14397	Raisin	....do	....do	5	469
14398	Graham	....do	....do	5	442
14399	Homemade	....do	....do	5	408
14400	Quaker	....do	....do	5	490
14401	Cream	....do	....do	5	510
14402	Biscuit Loaf	....do	....do	5	480
14403	Chicago Split Loaf, Steam Bread.	....do	....do	5	484
15229	Butter	August Meier, C and Fourteenth streets SW.	August Meier, C and Fourteenth streets SW.	4	480
15230	Rye	....do	....do	4	515
15231	Quaker	....do	....do	4	466
15232	Biscuit	....do	....do	4	478
15984	Rye	George Klenk, 2122 L street NW.	George Klenk, 2122 L street NW.	8	916
15985	Graham	....do	....do	5	516
15986	Vienna	....do	....do	5	460
15987	....do	Patrick Stanton, 2315 L street NW.	Patrick Stanton, 2315 L street NW.	5	457
15988	Rye	....do	....do	5	468
15989	....do	A. Detterer, 2012 H street NW.	A. Detterer, 2012 H street NW.	5	511
15990	Graham	....do	....do	5	457
15991	Vienna	....do	....do	5	433
15992	....do	G. S. Krafft & Sons, Eighteenth and Pennsylvania avenue NW.	G. S. Krafft & Sons, Eighteenth and Pennsylvania avenue NW.	5	428
15993	Graham	....do	....do	5	458
15994	Rye	....do	....do	5	453
16019	Vienna	C. Schneider, 413 I street NW.	C. Schneider, 413 I street NW.	5	470
16020	Graham	....do	....do	5	419
16021	....do	C. Schwab, 1211 H street NW.	C. Schwab, 1211 H street NW.	5	466
16022	Vienna	....do	....do	4	418
16023	....do	A. Gassmann, Eighth and M streets NW.	A. Gassmann, Eighth and M streets NW.	5	440
16024	Graham	....do	....do	5	439
16025	....do	G. H. Schulze, 1751 I street NW.	G. W. Schulze, 1751 I street NW.	5	447
16026	Vienna	....do	....do	5	498

ANALYTICAL DATA.

In the following tables are given the data obtained from the analyses of the samples of bread purchased in the open market. On the receipt of the loaves of bread they were chopped into fine pieces and weighed without delay, placed in an oven and dried in bulk until the quantity of water was reduced to a small amount. The weight of the residue having been obtained, the total loss of the moisture was noted. In this condition the breads were ground to a fine powder and thereafter subjected to the usual analytical determinations. It is evident that there will be reckoned as moisture by this process all the substances volatile at the temperature at which the drying took place. Inasmuch as the quantity of alcohol, carbon dioxid, and oils lost in the drying process is extremely minute, the figures given may be taken as representing essentially the moisture present. The data are given first upon the sample as purchased, and afterwards calculated to dry substance.

ETHER EXTRACT.

In regard to ether extract, it may be said that the material which is separated from the residue by ether represents not only the fat and oil of the original flour, but also any fatty substance which may have been added during the process of baking. While it is not always customary to add fat to the dough, yet it is almost the universal custom to grease the pan or the surface of the loaf before baking, in order that the baked loaf may not stick to the pan. If milk be used in making bread, as is often the case, it is evident also that a portion of fat will be introduced with the milk. Attention will be called further on to the difficulty which is experienced in extracting all the fatty matter from bread. An inspection of the data, however, will show that there are great differences in the quantity of fat in different classes of breads, it being the least in the Vienna breads, and greatest in the so-called homemade breads. In the miscellaneous breads will be noted very wide variations in the quantity of fat, showing in some instances the addition of a large quantity of fat to the loaf before baking.

FIBER.

In regard to fiber, it is evident that the quantity found in the bread will be practically the same as that found in the flour. It is not surprising, therefore, to see the fiber in the case of the Graham breads larger than that of any other class, inasmuch as the Graham breads are presumably made of wheat flour from which the bran is only imperfectly removed.

The proteids of bread have been calculated by both the old and the new factors for obvious reasons. Inasmuch as nearly all previously recorded analyses of wheat flour and its products have had the proteids computed on the basis of nitrogen multiplied by 6.25, it is advisable to use this same factor for the sake of direct comparison. In the light of recent investigations, however, the product $N \times 5.70$ is more nearly correct for the proteid matter. In the table of carbohydrates, which are calculated by difference, the fiber is excluded, and the number for carbohydrates therefore represents the total carbohydrate bodies less the fiber given in the preceding column. The calculation has been made on the supposition that the proteids are represented by $N \times 5.70$, and are therefore about 1 per cent higher than would be obtained by calculation on the supposition that the proteids are represented by $N \times 6.25$.

The ash not only represents the mineral matter present in the flour, but also any salt or other mineral condiment or adulterant added in the making of the loaf.

COMPOSITION OF BREADS.

Composition of breads purchased in the open market.

CLASS I.

Serial No.	Moisture.	In the original substance.								In the dry substance.							Calculated calories of combustion.	Ascertained calories.
		Proteids N × 6.25.	Proteids N × 5.70.	Ether extract.	Crude fiber.	Ash.	Salt.	Carbohydrates excluding fiber N × 5.70.		Proteids N × 6.25.	Proteids N × 5.70.	Ether extract.	Crude fiber.	Ash.	Salt.	Carbohydrates excluding fiber N × 5.70.	Digestible albuminoids.		
	Per ct.	Per ct.	Per ct.	Per ct.	Per ct.	Per ct.	Per ct.	Per ct.		Per ct.	Per ct.	Per ct.	Per ct.	Per ct.	Per ct.	Per ct.	Per ct.		
14352	35.67	9.26	8.44	0.54	0.22	1.44	0.82	53.91		14.40	13.13	0.85	0.34	2.24	1.26	83.78	....	4,372	4,420
14995	39.38	8.10	7.40	0.09	0.40	1.10	0.42	52.03		13.37	12.19	0.15	0.67	1.81	0.69	85.85	66.83	4,339	4,381
15086	37.07	8.38	7.64	2.36	0.52	1.16	0.57	50.87		13.51	12.32	3.80	0.84	1.87	0.92	82.01	93.20	4,525	4,571
15087	39.07	9.70	8.85	1.11	0.74	1.13	0.67	49.24		16.08	14.66	1.84	1.23	1.87	1.11	81.63	92.16	4,404	4,494
15991	31.96	9.90	9.03	0.10	0.63	1.42	0.74	57.49		14.55	13.27	0.15	0.93	2.09	1.09	84.49	93.88	4,345	4,352
15992	33.84	9.14	8.34	1.66	0.68	1.16	0.68	55.00		13.84	12.62	2.51	1.03	1.76	1.03	83.11	88.26	4,409	4,477
16019	37.14	8.95	8.16	1.77	0.53	1.31	0.40	51.62		14.24	12.99	2.82	0.84	2.08	0.64	82.11	92.53	4,477	4,483
16022	36.54	9.46	8.63	0.72	0.38	0.86	0.26	53.25		14.91	13.60	1.14	0.60	1.36	0.41	83.90	93.05	4,432	4,460
16023	56.34	6.73	6.14	0.52	1.22	0.85	0.38	63.85		15.42	14.06	1.19	2.79	1.95	0.87	82.80	94.96	4,418	4,455
16026	38.54	9.06	8.26	1.72	0.86	1.50	0.70	49.98		14.75	13.45	2.80	1.40	2.44	1.29	81.31	93.39	4,510	4,483
Average	38.71	8.87	8.09	1.06	0.62	1.19	0.57	53.72		14.51	13.23	1.73	0.97	1.95	0.93	83.10	89.87	4,435	4,458

CLASS II.

Serial No.	Moisture.	Proteids N × 6.25.	Proteids N × 5.70.	Ether extract.	Crude fiber.	Ash.	Salt.	Carbohydrates excluding fiber N × 5.70.		Proteids N × 6.25.	Proteids N × 5.70.	Ether extract.	Crude fiber.	Ash.	Salt.	Carbohydrates excluding fiber N × 5.70.	Digestible albuminoids.	Calculated calories of combustion.	Ascertained calories.
14353	32.46	9.10	8.30	2.11	0.34	0.37	0.63	55.78		13.48	12.29	3.12	0.50	2.02	0.94	82.57	64.15	4,483	4,558
14599	33.58	6.78	6.18	1.79	0.14	0.72	0.49	57.73		10.21	9.31	2.69	0.21	1.08	0.74	86.92	43.30	4,450	4,436
Average	33.02	7.94	7.24	1.95	0.24	1.05	0.56	56.75		11.85	10.80	2.91	0.36	1.55	0.84	84.75	53.76	4,467	4,497

Composition of breads purchased in the open market—Continued.

CLASS III.

Serial No.	In the original substance.								In the dry substance.							Digestible albuminoids.	Calculated calories of combustion.	Ascertained calories.
	Moisture.	Proteids N × 6.25.	Proteids N × 5.70.	Ether extract.	Crude fiber.	Ash.	Salt.	Carbohydrates excluding fiber N × 5.70.	Proteids N × 6.25.	Proteids N × 5.70.	Ether extract.	Crude fiber.	Ash.	Salt.	Carbohydrates excluding fiber N × 5.70.			
	Per ct.	Per ct.	Per ct.	Per ct.	Per ct.	Per ct.	Per ct.	Per ct.	Per ct.	Per ct.	Per ct.	Per ct.	Per ct.	Per ct.	Per ct.	Per ct.		
14354	33.44	8.98	8.19	1.78	0.70	1.95	0.77	54.84	13.49	12.30	2.08	1.05	2.93	1.16	82.09	63.09	4,423	4,280
14308	33.73	8.15	7.43	0.56	0.63	1.16	0.76	57.12	12.30	11.22	0.85	0.95	1.76	1.15	86.17	74.32	4,300	4,370
15965	36.57	8.10	7.39	4.88	1.49	1.40	0.51	49.76	12.77	11.65	7.69	2.35	2.21	0.80	78.45	80.03	4,097	4,780
15990	35.21	9.49	8.65	0.40	1.54	1.63	0.67	54.11	14.65	13.36	0.62	2.38	2.52	1.03	83.50	93.35	4,353	4,347
15998	37.02	10.06	9.17	0.30	0.84	1.97	1.01	51.48	15.97	14.50	0.57	1.33	3.13	1.60	81.74	93.84	4,345	4,335
16020	35.33	8.96	8.17	1.94	0.56	1.40	0.74	53.16	13.86	12.64	3.00	0.87	2.16	1.12	82.20	88.44	4,477	4,444
16021	29.39	8.65	7.89	2.14	1.79	0.75	0.61	59.83	12.25	11.17	3.03	2.54	1.06	0.86	84.74	92.67	4,499	4,306
16024	35.39	9.57	8.73	3.47	1.78	1.28	0.31	51.13	14.81	13.51	5.37	2.70	1.98	0.48	79.14	92.28	4,596	4,560
16025	37.14	8.41	7.67	2.76	0.88	1.81	0.88	49.38	13.38	12.20	4.39	1.40	2.88	1.40	80.53	93.26	4,510	4,483
Average	34.80	8.93	8.15	2.03	1.13	1.59	0.69	53.40	13.72	12.51	3.13	1.74	2.29	1.07	82.06	86.01	4,473	4,434

CLASS IV.

14384	32.83	8.54	7.79	0.12	0.41	1.85	0.86	57.41	12.72	11.60	0.17	0.62	2.75	1.29	85.48	41.24	4,290	4,629
14396	33.69	7.78	7.10	0.08	0.42	1.40	0.60	57.73	11.73	10.70	0.11	0.63	2.10	1.04	87.90	58.00	4,299	4,230
15230	32.45	7.52	6.86	0.89	0.44	0.92	0.32	58.88	11.14	10.16	1.32	0.65	1.36	0.48	87.16	58.05	4,383	4,320
15984	29.58	10.34	9.43	0.57	0.60	2.70	1.60	60.72	13.92	11.87	0.72	0.76	3.40	2.01	84.01	91.61	4,295	4,320
15988	38.50	8.56	7.81	1.43	0.98	1.65	0.99	50.55	13.93	12.70	2.33	1.00	2.69	1.61	82.28	87.76	4,422	4,474
15989	35.83	9.07	8.27	0.34	0.99	2.68	1.65	52.88	14.13	12.89	0.53	1.54	4.18	2.57	82.40	87.07	4,271	4,323
15991	39.08	8.62	7.86	1.17	0.49	1.70	0.90	49.29	14.37	13.11	1.95	0.82	2.83	1.50	82.11	93.82	4,403	4,470
Average	33.42	8.63	7.88	0.66	0.62	1.84	1.00	56.21	13.91	11.86	1.02	0.95	2.79	1.50	84.38	74.06	4,338	4,395

COMPOSITION OF BREADS. 1325

CLASS V.

14356	40.39	8.35	7.62	0.78	0.28	1.28	0.73	49.93	14.01	12.78	1.31	0.47	2.15	1.22	83.76	62.52	4,394	4,110
14400	37.05	7.02	6.40	0.81	0.21	0.87	0.53	54.87	11.15	10.17	1.28	0.33	1.38	0.84	87.17	59.96	4,380	4,330
15231	31.05	7.98	7.28	1.83	0.29	1.04	0.49	58.80	11.57	10.55	2.65	0.42	1.50	0.70	85.30	55.64	4,452	4,461
Average	36.16	7.78	7.10	1.14	0.26	1.06	0.58	54.53	12.24	11.17	1.75	0.41	1.68	0.92	85.41	59.27	4,339	4,395

CLASS VI.

14383	40.80	7.19	6.56	0.12	0.33	0.75	0.22	51.77	12.14	11.08	0.20	0.56	1.27	0.37	87.45	78.96	4,345	4,243
14385	39.96	7.41	6.76	0.91	0.28	1.15	0.70	51.22	12.34	11.25	1.51	0.47	1.91	1.17	85.33	62.00	4,388	4,411
14386	37.34	6.99	6.37	1.81	0.25	1.02	0.48	53.46	11.16	10.18	2.88	0.40	1.03	0.76	85.31	43.90	4,451	4,493
14307	30.71	7.36	6.71	3.07	0.46	1.18	0.85	58.33	10.62	9.60	4.43	0.66	1.71	1.23	84.17	43.10	4,519	4,462
14401	29.69	6.54	5.98	1.94	0.22	1.03	0.51	61.38	9.30	8.48	2.76	0.31	1.47	0.73	87.29	46.89	4,123	4,407
14402	34.63	8.36	7.62	2.09	0.26	1.07	0.54	54.59	12.78	11.66	3.19	0.44	1.64	0.83	83.51	59.13	4,492	4,410
14403	33.16	9.03	8.24	0.82	0.24	0.76	0.38	57.02	13.51	12.32	1.23	0.35	1.14	0.57	85.31	67.92	4,424	4,457
15229	32.20	7.92	7.22	1.12	0.38	1.05	0.44	58.41	11.08	10.05	1.65	0.56	1.55	0.66	86.15	46.38	4,400	4,306
15232	31.17	7.58	6.91	1.43	0.25	1.02	0.35	59.47	11.01	10.04	2.08	0.36	1.48	0.50	86.40	58.95	4,415	4,418
Average	34.41	7.60	6.93	1.48	0.30	1.00	0.49	56.18	11.62	10.59	2.21	0.46	1.53	0.76	85.66	56.36	4,420	4,401

DISCUSSION OF ANALYTICAL DATA.

In the discussion of the analytical data of different classes of bread it would be advisable to compare them as far as possible with the different classes of flour. As has been intimated, however, such a comparison is not rigidly possible unless the bread be made from standard flour, samples of which can be analyzed in comparison with the bread itself. This is evidently impossible in the samples which are purchased in the open market. For this reason an attempt will be made only in a general way to compare the composition of the bread with that of the flour.

COMPARISON OF BREAD WITH FLOUR.

VIENNA BREAD, CLASS 1, COMPARED WITH HIGH-GRADE PATENT FLOURS, CLASS 1.

Calculating the average data of the high-grade patent flours to dry substance for uniformity with the calculations for bread, the following results are presented:

TABLE 1.—*Comparison of composition of bread and flour.*

Constituents.	Flour.	Bread.
	Per cent.	Per cent.
Proteids (N × 6.25)	11.95	14.51
Proteids (N × 5.70)	10.89	13.23
Ether extract	1.18	1.73
Ash	0.50	1.95
Crude fiber	0.22	0.97
Carbohydrates (N × 6.25), including fiber	86.36	81.82
Carbohydrates (N × 5.70), including fiber	87.41	83.10

The most marked variation which is seen here is found in the quantity of ether extract, which is considerably less than would be expected from the flour. The fiber in the bread is correspondingly larger than in the flour, the baking apparently rendering some of the carbohydrates insoluble in the ordinary reagents. This is probably due particularly to the partial caramelization which takes place in the crust. Ash, as would naturally be expected, is very much higher than in the flour, due to the added salt. The proteids are practically identical with those in the flour, and the carbohydrates in the bread are diminished by the fermentation of the sugar in proportion as the amount of ash has been increased. In the high-grade bread, therefore, we find practically no change from the flour in respect of the amount of proteids, but an increase in the amount of ash corresponding to the added salt and a diminution in the carbohydrates, corresponding to the added salt and the loss of sugar by fermentation.

BREADS OF CLASSES 2, 4, AND 5.

It will not be possible in these classes to compare them with any of the classes of flours given in the previous tables. The general remarks made in respect of the composition of breads of class 1 are applicable also to these three classes.

BREADS OF CLASS 3.

There are no flours with which the breads of class 3 can be directly compared, inasmuch as no Graham flours were bought for analysis. The chief difference to be expected in this class of breads would be in the increase in fiber, due to the leaving of a portion of the bran in the flour. In round numbers, the quantity of fiber in the Graham bread is about double that of ordinary breads. In computing the amount of salt which is present in the Graham bread the same factor was used as with the others, viz, 0.50 per cent, representing the percentage of ash in the flour. It is entirely probable that this is too small a factor for the Graham bread in which the ash of the flour would be presumably larger, so that the number given for the amount of salt added in this instance is probably too high.

BREADS OF CLASS 6.

The miscellaneous breads of class 6 may be properly compared with the miscellaneous flours contained in Table 4 of the flour analyses.

On calculating the average data of class 4, miscellaneous wheat flours, to dry substance, the following numbers are obtained:

TABLE 2.—*Comparison of composition of bread and flour.*

Constituents.	Bread.	Flour.
	Per cent.	Per cent.
Proteids (N × 6.25)	11.80	11.62
Proteids (N × 5.70)	10.75	10.59
Ether extract	1.22	2.21
Ash	0.56	1.53
Crude fiber	0.24	0.46
Carbohydrates (N × 6.25), including fiber	86.43	84.63
Carbohydrates (N × 5.70), including fiber	87.47	85.66

In comparing the numbers of class 6 with these data it will be noted in the first place that the ether extract of the breads is almost double that of the flours, showing that a considerable quantity of grease has been used in the baking. The fiber is also about double that of the flours, indicating, as in the case of the high-grade breads, that a considerable degree of change in baking, rendering a portion of the carbohydrate bodies insoluble, has taken place. The ash of the miscellaneous breads shows the addition of an average of about 1 per cent of salt in the preparation of the loaf for baking. The carbohydrates show a loss proportional to the increase in the amount of ash and fat, and a decrease due to the fermentation of the sugar. Comparison of the percentage of carbohydrates in the baked breads in all instances with those present in the flour show that the loss on fermentation amounts to scarcely 1 per cent of the total carbohydrate matter. It is evident, therefore, that the statements to which attention has been previously called, to the effect that the loss on fermentation varies from 2 to 6 per cent, are entirely too extravagant.

A TYPICAL AMERICAN HIGH-GRADE BREAD.

A typical American high-grade yeast bread made with the best flour and in the most approved manner has approximately the following composition:

	Per cent.		Per cent.
Moisture	35.00	Ash	1.50
Proteids (N × 5.70)	8.00	Fiber	.30
Ether extract	.75	Carbohydrates, other than fiber	54.45

Of the ash mentioned 0.50 per cent may be ascribed to the natural mineral ingredients of the flour, and 1 per cent to added salt. The chief variations from the typical composition are found in the moisture and ether extract. The moisture may rise to 40 per cent in breads made of the strongest flour, or sink to 30 per cent or less when inferior flours are employed. The quantity of ether extract depends chiefly on the amount of fat which is added to the bread during baking, or which is used to grease the exterior of the loaf or interior of the pan to prevent sticking during baking. When no fat is added the quantity of ether extract in the bread will be found uniformly less than that in the flour from which it is made, due to the fact that in the process of baking a portion of the fat is rendered difficultly soluble, either by reason of oxidation or by being mechanically surrounded by films of insoluble matter, probably incrustations of dextrin or proteid matter.

RYE BREAD.

In samples of rye bread examined in Norway the moisture varied from 35.3 to 46.1 per cent and the ash from 0.3 to 1.82 per cent. The means for a large number of analyses of rye bread are:

Quality of bread.	Moisture.	Proteids.	Ether extract.	Ash.	Crude fiber.	Carbohydrates.
	Per cent.	Per cent.	Per cent.	Per cent.	Per cent.	Per cent.
Best quality	40.00	6.40	0.25	0.60	0.38	52.37
Coarse	38.30	7.81	.55	.05	.93	51.46

An addition of mineral substances could not be found in either the bread or in the flour. During the winter, 1891-92, however, on account of the high price of rye, the flour was adulterated with wheat flour. The presence of small quantities of wheat flour are detected under the microscope by means of the hairs and the transverse cells. Wittmach has shown that the walls of the transverse cells of wheat are very much thicker than in rye. It is necessary, however, to take cognizance of the fact that rye sometimes contains a small amount of wheat. In Hungarian rye there was found as much as 3 per cent.[1]

DETERMINATION OF FAT IN BREAD.

Analysts have long observed the difficulty which is encountered in extracting the fat from bread. It has been observed repeatedly that the quantity of material extracted by anhydrous ether from bread is considerably less than that contained in the materials of which the bread is made. It has also been observed in adding weighed quantities of fat to the dough that less than the quantity added was secured by extraction in the bread. In general, it has been assumed that the process of baking oxidized the fat in such a way as to render it to some extent insoluble in anhydrous ether. The exact nature of this process has not been explained. It is evident that the particles of fat contained in the crust of the bread would be subjected to a sufficiently high temperature to oxidize them and to dispel all the volatile acids. It is thought, therefore, that the chief loss which the fat suffers must be in the crust. The temperature of the interior of the loaf, as has been shown before, is not sufficient to affect materially the composition of the fat. It has been claimed by other authors that the process of baking incrusts the fat globules with insoluble material, such as dextrin and proteids, and renders it impracticable to reach the fat particles by the solvent on subsequent extraction. In point of fact, it is probable that the deficiency of fat, as shown by the extraction of the bread with anhydrous ether, is due partly to each of the causes assigned. There is doubtless an oxidation of the fat, especially in the exterior parts of the loaf, and a loss of volatile constituents. It is probably also true that particles of fat become entangled in the insoluble particles of the loaf itself, and thus are protected from the action of the solvents subsequently applied.

IMPERFECTION OF METHOD FOR EXTRACTING FAT.

Instead of extracting the ground dried bread directly with anhydrous ether, it has been proposed by Weibull[2] previously to treat the bread with reagents which will dissolve the supposed incrusting matters. For this purpose from 1 to 3 grams of the powdered bread are placed in a small beaker with from 15 to 30 c. c. of water, which has been acidified with 10 drops of sulphuric acid. The mass is then boiled for at least an hour, stirring frequently. It is then slowly and completely neutralized with powdered chalk or marble and spread on fat-free paper, which is suspended by wires in a drying oven. The very last portions may be removed from the beaker with fat-free cotton. After drying at

---

[1] Ztschr. Nahr.-Unters., Hyg. u. Waarenk., vol. 8, 134.
[2] Zeitschrift für angewandte Chemie, 1892, vol. 15, p. 450.

100° for two or three hours the paper is completely dry, and can then be extracted in a Soxhlet apparatus in the usual manner, the extraction being complete in eight hours.

The boiling with dilute sulphuric acid dissolves the starch and dextrin and frees the fat, which collects in large drops and is afterwards easily extracted. Anhydrous ether must be used, as other ether will dissolve small quantities of dextrose and a constant weight can not be obtained. The gluten in the bread also tenaciously incloses the fat and yields it to the action of the acid.

This process of fat extraction from bread has been thoroughly tried in this Department and found to be imperfect. Only a slightly greater quantity of fat was secured by the treatment proposed than by the direct extraction of the finely powdered dry bread with anhydrous ether. At the present time there is no method of extraction known which will secure from the bread as large a quantity of fat bodies as is contained in the material composing it. The presence of unextracted fat in a bread is not only to be considered from the point of view of its composition, but also must be taken into consideration in calculating the heat of combustion. Any nonextracted fat will evidently be classed by difference with the nonnitrogenous matters, having a combustion value much less than that of the fat itself. The natural result of this would be that in calculating the calorimetric equivalent of bread a small portion of the fat might be reckoned as carbohydrates, and thus the calculated value of the sample would be less than that actually obtained by combustion in oxygen.

FAT USED IN GREASING PANS.

The bakers employ the term "bread oil" to designate an oil used to grease bake pans. For this purpose it is customary to use oleomargarine, lard, or olive oil, or sometimes olive oil or poppy oil of the first pressing. A dealer in Saxony, however, has been selling an oil under the name of "patent bread oil," which he stated to be American palm oil. Upon analysis it proved to be a mineral oil, such as is commonly used as a lubricant.[1] In three cases a large number of persons were made severely ill by the consumption of baker's goods prepared with this oil, which is wholly undigestible. The use of the oil was prohibited by an ordinance of the city government of Dresden on October 10, 1893.

USE OF ALUM IN BREAD.

Alum is sometimes added to flour in the preparation of bread for the purpose of making a whiter loaf. According to the statement in the Millers' Journal (vol. 12, page 32), the whitening action of the alum is due to its action on cerealine and an organized ferment contained

---
[1] Pharm. Centralhalle (n. F.), vol. 14, p. 405; abs. in Chem. Centralblatt, 1894, vol. 1, p. 94.

chiefly in the bran of the wheat. This ferment when in action produces lactic acid, and it is due to its activity that the dark coloration which the alum is added to correct arises.

Alum in bread is usually detected by a tincture of logwood, which is formed by digesting 5 grams of partially chipped logwood in 100 c. c. of alcohol. In the application of the test to flour 10 grams are intimately rubbed up with 10 c. c. of water and treated with 1 c. c. of the tincture of logwood and the same quantity of a saturated solution of ammonium carbonate. After thorough mixing, if alum be present the color soon changes to lavender or blue. The blue color should be persistent when the sample is heated to the temperature of boiling water for an hour. When no alum is present in the flour the resulting tint is only a slight pink. The activity of logwood in this respect probably resides in the hæmatoxalyn which it contains. Hæmatoxalyn itself, it is claimed by some authors, may be substituted for the logwood in the test for alum. When applied to bread it is recommended that 5 c. c. of the tincture of logwood be mixed with an equal quantity of the saturated ammonium carbonate and 80 c. c. of water. The whole of this mixture should be poured over 10 grams of the bread in a fine powder. After standing for five minutes the excess of liquid is poured off. After washing the residuum slightly with water it is placed in an oven and heated to the temperature of boiling water. If alum be present a lavender or dark-blue color is produced, which is intensified on drying. Bread which contains no alum first attains a light red tint which fades into a buff or light brown. Bread which is sour, soggy, old, or acid in its character may give a logwood test by the above process when no logwood is present. This coloration is probably due to the phosphate of alumina, which is slightly soluble in dilute acetic acid. The logwood test for bread, therefore, can not be considered reliable unless it is applied to the fresh loaf or one in which no acidity has been developed.

THE ACIDITY OF BREAD.

The acidity of bread is very important both with regard to hygiene and palatability. Flour contains probably no acids in a free state, and the acidity of bread is caused during its preparation by the ferments present. An examination of bread made by the usual methods of fermentation discloses acetic acid, acid potassium phosphate, an acid soluble in water and ether, probably lactic acid, and an acid insoluble in ether. Quantitatively the acids are present in the proportion of 20 parts volatile acids, 5 parts nonvolatile acids soluble in ether and water, and 4 parts of an acid soluble in ether but not in water. The free organic acids amount to from 40 to 60 per cent of the total acidity. It has been shown that bread has a greater nutritive value when used in connection with meat, and that in this case sour bread is better than neutral. In order to discover if the acidity of the bread has any influence on the poisonous effect of some foreign vegetable substances which are sometimes found in bread, Lehmann[1] mixed sour dough with cockle seed and it was found that a highly acid bread neutralized the poison.

ADULTERATIONS.

Of 815 flours examined in the Food-Control Station at Vienna, 107, nearly 14 per cent, contained bran, cowpeas, cockle seed, *lolium temulentum* (darnel), and traces of *tiletia caries*.

Twenty-six samples of ginger cakes were colored with eosin, safranin, and fuchsin. In one case the yellow color contained distinct traces of lead.

Various pastry was colored red with eosin, violet with anilin violet; a yellow color contained lead chromate. A sample of pastry containing beaten white of egg contained alum, which was undoubtedly added to permit the use of spoiled eggs.

One sample of flour and the noodles prepared from it had bluish-green spots, due to an aniline color. An apple dumpling and the corresponding flour contained large quantities of zinc oxide. Two samples of Graham bread were spoiled by mold.

From September 1, 1892, to August 31, 1893, ten breads and breadstuffs were examined, of which two were confiscated. One was a cheap bread made from a poor quality of rye and wheat flours together with foreign seeds. The other was moldy.

Cakes were found to be colored with aniline dyes, and several poisonous ones were found to be colored with such as Martius yellow, fuchsin, and lead chromate.

Forty-six flours were examined, of which ten were declared unfit for use or adulterated. A number contained foreign seed, others were moldy, and one rye flour had been made from germinated grains. A cheap flour contained 16.5 ash, mostly sand; an American flour was maize flour with 5.32 per cent ash, of which 0.41 per cent was alum and the rest magnesia, probably derived from magnesium carbonate. One sample of flour contained 1.77 per cent zinc white.

ANALYSES OF RUSSIAN "HUNGER" BREAD.[2]

During the Russian famine of 1891–92 several bread substitutes were used. Five of these were analyzed, namely:

1. Bread made from the chaff of rye and oats with buckwheat, and a red grass the scientific name of which is not known.
2. Bread from the seed of Chenopodium.
3. Bread from rye flour, Chenopodium seeds, and potatoes.
4. Bread from rye flour, Chenopodium seeds, and red grass.
5. Bread consisting of 75 per cent Chenopodium seeds, 12.5 per cent potatoes, and 12.5 per cent rye flour.

---

[1] Ztschr. Nahr.-Unters., Hyg. u. Waarenk., Vol. VII, No. 12, p. 199.
[2] Op. cit., No. 10, p. 168.

The analyses gave the following data:

Analytical data.

No.	Proteids.	Ether extract.	Starch, dextrin, and sugar.	Crude fiber.	Ash.
	Per cent.	Per cent.	Per cent.	Per cent.	Per cent.
1	10.25	0.94	36.55	32.05	20.21
2	11.30	3.89	42.95	25.72	16.14
3	15.35	2.27	58.31	16.64	7.61
4	13.75	1.10	45.59	26.31	13.25
5	15.30	2.18	46.89	27.34	8.09
6[1]	12.75	1.12	78.86	2.71	2.63

[1] The common bread baked by the Russian peasants.

CHARACTER OF SUBSTITUTES FOR FLOUR IN BREAD.

The nineteenth century records the greatest number of famines, namely, 47 in the Russian Empire and 43 in other parts of Europe. These famines are, however, no longer so terrible in character as in the preceding centuries, when the people satisfied their hunger with the meat of dogs and cats and even of their fellow beings. Bread substitutes have been introduced probably on account of the old theory that the quality of a food is to be judged simply by its chemical composition. Now, however, when the digestibility of a food determines its value, it is self-evident that the bread substitutes only temporarily lengthen life and finally are instrumental in destroying it. Attempts to substitute other substances for bread date from the earliest times. An examination of the bread substitutes used during the last Russian famine, made by Hefanowsky,[1] gave sufficient proof of the above statements. The "hunger bread" collected contained oats, buckwheat, acorns, various papilionaceæ, potatoes, straw, bark, earth, barley, etc.

The samples were examined in the following manner:

1. For a preliminary chemical examination, 1 gram of the powdered sample was mixed in a test tube with 10 c. c. distilled water and 5 c. c. 10 per cent sodium hydroxid solution and boiled. A rose-red coloration of the foam indicated the presence of flour of the leguminosæ (pease, beans, etc.).

2. One gram of the substance was boiled with 10 c. c. of distilled water, filtered, and the filtrate tested with ferrous sulphate solution. A dark-brown color indicated the presence of acorns or of some bark.

3. The sample was then examined microscopically, the various constituents being separated by Schulze's method—i. e., by means of nitric acid and potassium carbonate.

The samples were then compared with two genuine breads, one a better kind of rye bread baked in Kasan, the other a peasants' bread from western Russia. In external appearance, color, and odor these

[1] Ztschr. Nahr.-Unters., Hyg., u. Waarenk., Vol. VII, No. 20, p. 358.

substitutes had little in common with the normal bread. Some varieties were very rich in nitrogen and contained three times as much cellulose as the genuine bread. Others again were poor in nitrogen. In all cases the high amount of cellulose present made them very indigestible. Some samples showed a high percentage of fat, which is derived from the substances used.

Those substances which are of the greatest importance to nutrition were present in much smaller quantities than in genuine breads. This all proves that hunger bread can not serve as nutriment, but only condemns the body to a chronic hunger and is followed by serious complications.

COMPARATIVE CHEMICAL EXAMINATION OF BISCUIT MADE FROM RYE, AND FROM RYE AND WHEAT.

It often happens that the price of wheat is lower than that of rye. It thus becomes an object of some commercial importance to mix wheat flour with rye flour in those countries where rye bread is in great demand. It has been found that biscuit made from rye and wheat could be substituted for those made from rye. A chemical examination of the Russian mixed biscuit by Wilbouschewitz is given below.[1] The samples examined were as follows:

DESCRIPTION OF SAMPLES.

1. Rye biscuit with 12½ per cent wheat.
2. Rye biscuit with 25 per cent wheat.
3. Pure rye biscuit.
4. Pure rye biscuit.
5. Pure rye biscuit.

Analytical data.

No. of sample.	Proteids.	Sugar.	Starch and dextrin.	Crude fiber.	Free acids.
	Per cent.	Per cent.	Per cent.	Per cent.	Per cent.
1	15.45	1.65	75.48	3.47	0.86
2	16.36	1.79	75.13	3.15	0.89
3	12.75	2.36	78.51	3.54	1.18
4	16.48	3.07	73.32	3.75	0.66
5	14.94	4.62	73.03	3.97	0.89

The article notes that the Russian biscuit have a higher percentage of proteids than the German soldier bread, but are less digestible, on account of the higher percentage of cellulose. The sugar is less in the biscuits containing wheat than in the pure rye biscuit, probably on account of diminished fermentation in the latter.

---

[1] Ztschr. Nahr.-Unters., Hyg., u. Waarenk., Vol. VII, No. 24, p. 371.

THE DETECTION OF EGG YOLK IN BREADSTUFFS.

In Europe the yolk of eggs is extensively employed in the manufacture of noodles. This substance may also be employed in making bread or cakes where a yellow color is desired. The following method of detecting the yolk may be used.

While trying to determine the amount of yolk used in making noodles, the Reinsch method was used on some known mixtures. Noodles were made containing 6, 2, and 4 eggs in 1,000, 1,000, and 900 grams of wheat flour, respectively. The noodles were finely powdered; extracted repeatedly with ether, the extracts incinerated with potassium nitrate, the ash dissolved in hot water, and the phosphoric acid determined in the solution. A blank was made with the flour. Assuming the Reinsch method as reliable and that eggs of approximately 30 grams weight with 10 grams of yolk were used, the above samples should have given, respectively, 0.0573 per cent, 0.0212 per cent, and 0.0442 per cent phosphoric acid, corresponding to 5.08 per cent, 1.88 per cent, and 3.92 per cent egg yolk. The results showed, however, that the method is not reliable, as the amount of undecomposed organic phosphorus compounds which will pass into the ether extracts depends very much on the method of preparing the noodles.[1]

THE INFLUENCE OF MOLD ON THE COMPOSITION OF BREAD.

Penicillium glaucum grows especially rapidly on bread. Bread contains all the nutritive material and the moisture necessary for the rapid growth of mold. Its growth decreases the percentage of carbohydrates in the substratum. Rye bread was examined fresh and then allowed to become moldy. The following figures were obtained by Dietrich:[2]

Effect of mold on bread.

Calculated to dry substance.	Fresh.	7 days (moldy).	14 days (moldy).
	Per cent.	Per cent.	Per cent.
Proteids	11.29	12.90	14.55
Ether extract	0.20	0.84	0.83
Ash	1.53	1.73	1.90

The per cent of proteids in a moldy bread can thus not serve as a judgment of the fresh bread, as it is increased by the corresponding decrease in carbohydrates.

Penicillium glaucum is the most dangerous mold on maize. It was found that its growth produced a phenol-like body which in large doses produced headache, vertigo, and even impaired the sight.[3]

---

[1] Ztschr. Nahr.-Unters., Hyg., u. Waarenk., Vol. VII, No. 10, p. 168.
[2] Op. cit., No. 5, p. 70.
[3] Op. cit., No. 21, p. 372.

BREAD MADE FROM THE WHOLE GRAIN.

The use of the whole grain of cereals for bread making is often urged for hygienic reasons. In Europe bread is made from the whole rye grain by a process[1] consisting in cleaning and softening the whole grain and then making dough directly from it by means of rollers without previously making a flour.

Three samples of bread thus prepared were analyzed with the following results:

Constituents.	Rye bread decorticated.	Wheat bread decorticated.	Rye bread not decorticated.
	Per cent.	*Per cent.*	*Per cent.*
Moisture	51.57	50.96	49.79
Proteids	12.03	9.89	11.81
Ether extract	0.47	0.36	0.57
Carbohydrates	34.18	35.99	35.14
Crude fiber	0.82	1.21	1.62
Ash	0.95	1.55	1.00

In this country bread is made from the whole wheat grain, which is subjected to a shredding process described below.

SHREDDED WHEAT BISCUIT.

This food product is unique in that it is a completely cooked whole wheat food. In its preparation the wheat grains are boiled in water until they are somewhat soft, then they are passed through a machine which reduces them to long filaments or threads, resembling in general appearance spaghetti or fine macaroni. These filaments as they come from the machine are laid lightly one upon another until they are built up to the requisite height, when they are formed into small loaves resembling biscuit and baked until brown. The baking process is followed by another process that subjects the biscuit for about five hours to a dry heat at a temperature sufficient to raise them to a desirable degree of lightness, the shredded whole wheat biscuit manifestly preserving the composition of the whole wheat berry, with the exception of the slight solubility of any of its outer constituents in the water which is employed. The lightness of the biscuit is secured without the use of yeast or baking powder and is short without lard or any substitute therefor. The following data show the relation between the sample of the shredded whole wheat biscuit and the typical wheat such as is described in Bulletin No. 45.

---

[1] Ztschr. Nahr.-Unters., Hyg., u. Waarenk., Vol. VII, No. 19, p. 336.

Comparison of wheat and shredded biscuit.

Constituents.	Shredded biscuit.	Typical wheat.
	Per cent.	Per cent.
Moisture	10.57	10.00
Proteids	12.00	12.25
Ether extract	1.03	1.75
Ash	2.65	1.75
Crude fiber	2.58	2.40
Carbohydrates other than fiber	71.11	71.25

From an inspection of the data it will be seen that there is remarkable agreement between the shredded wheat biscuit and typical wheat. The most marked departure is in the amount of ether extract and ash, the former being less and the latter more in the biscuit than in the typical wheat, while the biscuit differs from the average yeast bread in having about one-third as much moisture and considerably more ash.

In nutritive value it is seen that the shredded wheat biscuit contains all the principles and in almost exactly the same proportions, that are found in the whole wheat, changed only by the heat to which they are subjected in the process of preparation.

BREAD FROM WHOLE-WHEAT FLOUR.

A "flour of the entire wheat" is also made by the Franklin Mills Company, of Lockport, N. Y. This flour, however, is not made of the whole grain, as its name would imply, but is made from the grain after the removal of the outer envelope. It is claimed by the company that this outer husk is entirely removed in the manufacture of the "Flour of the Entire Wheat." According to the statements made in Bulletin No. 74 of the Agricultural Experiment Station of Alabama, the bread made from this flour is of a light-brown color, is more moist and richer in flavor than ordinary loaves. It is further stated that it lacks the dryness so characteristic of white bread, especially that made by bakers. The claim which is made, that the bread made from this flour contains the entire nutritious matter of the elements of the wheat is, however, open to an objection based on the fact that the outer bran is also composed of nutritious and mineral substances, and the name is therefore, to this extent, a misnomer. There is no doubt, however, of the fact that a bread made from wheat from which only the outer bran is removed contains more of the mineral ingredients than bread made from wheat flour from which a part (the bran), consisting of the outer coatings of the grain, have been entirely removed. The composition of the "Flour of the Entire Wheat" is shown in the table of flour analyses, serial No. 15262. As a comparison with the analytical data obtained here, those secured by Mr. B. B. Ross, State chemist of Alabama, are submitted:

Flour of the entire wheat.

Constituents.	Ross.	Wiley.
	Per cent.	Per cent.
Moisture	6.36	12.70
Proteids	14.19	13.39
Ether extract	1.51	1.61
Ash	0.91	1.03
Carbohydrates	77.03	71.27
	100.00	100.00

Of the carbohydrates in the data given for the analysis made in this laboratory 0.63 per cent was crude fiber, leaving a residue of 70.64 per cent for starch, sugar, and dextrin. The percentage of moisture found by Ross is exceptionally low.

ADULTERATION OF BREAD.

There is a sufficient number of instances of adulteration of bread to make a discussion of the subject important.

SOAP AS AN ADULTERANT.

It is not believed that bread is ever adulterated with soap in this country. Several instances of such adulterations abroad have been reported.[1]

The addition of soap is said to give a light soft bread, and when only small quantities are added it is difficult to detect the adulteration. In order to distribute the soap evenly in the dough it is, previous to its incorporation therewith, emulsified with olive or cotton oil, and in this condition can be intimately distributed throughout the mass. The soap probably suffers partial decomposition under the influence of fat-splitting ferments and of the lactic and acetic acids formed during the fermentation of the bread. The following method has been proposed for the detection of soap in bread.

The dried bread is coarsely pulverized and completely extracted in a Soxhlet apparatus with 92 per cent alcohol, the alcohol evaporated, the extract dried and weighed. It is then dissolved in hot water and the acidity determined with decinormal soda. The residue from the alcohol extraction is dried and extracted with ether. This extract contains the unchanged fat derived from the flour, milk, and butter used and the oil, which, according to Crispo, is used to emulsify the soap before it is added to the bread.

Another portion of bread is incinerated, the ash treated with water,

---

[1] Rev. Internat. des fals., 1893, No. 7, p. 139.

filtered, and the filtrate titrated with decinormal oxalic acid. The solution must be filtered, so as to remove the earthy phosphates, as only the alkalinity of the alkaline bases present is desired.

No instance of an adulteration of bread with soap has ever been observed in this country, and the above method has not been submitted to trial in this laboratory. It is not probable that any American chemist will be called upon to investigate an adulteration of this kind.

GYPSUM AS AN ADULTERANT.

The use of gypsum, terra alba, or other inert white earthy powders has never been detected as an adulteration in flour or bread in the samples examined in this laboratory. No authentic record of such an adulteration in the United States is at hand. Many adulterations of this kind are reported in foreign countries.[1]

In one instance a wheat flour was reported to contain 53.50 per cent of gypsum. In 9 flours examined in Grätz, one was found which contained 39 per cent of gypsum.[2]

In the report of an examination of 66 breads in another citation 3 samples were found which contained traces of copper, and 1 a trace of zinc and arsenic.[3] It should be remembered, however, that traces of metals of this kind may naturally exist in wheat and other cereals when grown upon soil containing them. In the same report it is stated that one sample of barley flour contained 0.3 per cent of sand.

STANNOUS CHLORID AS AN ADULTERANT.

In the reports of the food control station in Vienna the following instances of adulteration are noted:[4]

A sample of spiced bread examined in the municipal laboratory of Paris[5] contained 1 per cent of tin. Smaller, yet weighable quantities were found in several other samples.

It seems to be established that the tin is added in the form of stannous chloride, and that it is used to render a product made of poor rye or wheat flour and molasses similar in appearance and texture to the genuine product made from good flour and honey. Such a mixture without this addition would be heavy and have little porosity.

This adulteration, of Belgian origin, has recently extended into Northern France, where it makes it impossible for honest manufacturers of this product to compete with those using this fraudulent process.

In the writer's opinion, the use of tin for this purpose should be prohibited, even if not injurious in itself, since it permits the substitution of inferior materials for good ones.

---

[1] Ztschr. Nahr.-Unters., Hyg., u. Waarenk., Vol. VII, No. 1, p. 14.
[2] Op. cit., Vol. VII, p. 27.
[3] Op. cit., Vol. VII, No. 8, p. 134.
[4] Ztschr. Nahr.-Unters., Hyg., u. Waarenk., Vol. XX, p. 354; and Vol. VII, pp. 13, 27, 44, 63, and 375.
[5] M. A. Riche, in Revue internationale des falsifications, 1892, vol. 6, p. 35.

The writer states that he has been making experiments for several years to determine the action of tin salts on the animal economy.

Bayess, Charlard, and Proust regarded tin as harmless, and considered the cases of food poisoning of their day to be due to lead.

Dr. Guersant cites a case of poisoning by food which was inadvertently salted with stannous chloride instead of common salt. The disagreeable flavor of the preparation prevented most of the guests eating it. Those who ate even small quantities of it suffered from diarrhea.

Orfila has made the following observations on the results of experiments made by him: Stannous chloride, taken into the stomach, has an irritating action on its tissue and has an especially noticeable action on the nervous system. When the salt is injected into the veins it appears to act on the lungs.

Many scientists in different countries—Wagner, Hals and Löbisch, Menke and Hehner, Ungar and Bodlander, Sachs, Sadgewick, Beckurts, Nehring, Blarez, Bettink, Van Hamel Roos, Kayser, Weber, etc.—have examined the question of tin in its relations to preserved foods, and all their works seem to lead to the conclusion that tin can not be considered harmless.

PARTIALLY PREPARED OR BREAKFAST FOODS.

Partially prepared or so-called breakfast foods are common articles of diet in American families. They consist of the partially baked or softened cereals prepared in different ways, or sometimes eaten practically whole, as in the case of cracked wheat. Nearly all the cereals are represented in these partially prepared or breakfast foods. Oats probably occupies the first rank, and oatmeal in some form of preparation is almost a constant article of diet on the breakfast table. Wheat and maize are not far behind, and these products are also used to a very large extent as breakfast diets. There is not place here to describe the methods of preparing these foods in general. Many of them have been subjected to a high temperature, by which the starch grains are softened and formed into a kind of paste. The hulls and skins are removed from other cereals, so that the product does not represent the whole grain, but only a portion thereof. In some cases, as in the manufacture of cerealine, the germ is also removed, as well as a portion or all of the outer envelopes of the grain. One object in this manufacture appears to be the preparation of a food which can be made ready for the table in a few moments. It is probable, however, that too little time is consumed in the final cooking of these breakfast foods, and instead of using only a few moments in their preparation, their wholesomeness, palatability, and digestibility would be greatly improved by subjecting them for a longer time to the temperature of boiling water in the process of final preparation.

An attempt has been made to secure practically all the leading brands of these breakfast foods, but the impossibility of doing this without having agents in all parts of the United States is readily seen. Many brands of breakfast foods have only a local or a limited use, and those brands which are in common use in one part of the country may be almost wholly unknown in another. In purchasing all the brands which are on the markets which can be personally inspected by the employes of this division, it is not probable that nearly all of the breakfast foods are represented in the list which follows. It is believed, however, that the constitution of the different types of breakfast foods is very accurately shown in the average data of the tables which follow.

DESCRIPTION OF PARTIALLY PREPARED CEREALS AND BREAKFAST FOODS.

14358. Granula, prepared and sold by Our Home Granula Company, Dansville, N. Y., sole manufacturers of Dr. J. C. Jackson's Granula.

14359. Shredded Whole Wheat Biscuit. Manufactured by The Cereal Machine Company; office and factory, 55-63 Jackson street, Worcester, Mass.

14360. Imperial Granum. The Imperial Granum Company, shipping depot, John Carle & Sons, New York, U. S. A.

14361. Foulds' Wheat Germ Meal, Daverio Process. Prepared from choice winter wheat by the Foulds' Milling Company, Cincinnati, Ohio. "Prepared from the glutinous portion of wheat."

14363. Whole Wheat Gluten. Health Food Company, 61 Fifth avenue, New York.

14364. Cooked Gluten. Health Food Company, 61 Fifth avenue, New York. "This is the crude gluten of wheat perfectly cooked and subsequently transformed into a dry flour or meal."

14366. Wheatlet. The Franklin Mills Company, Lockport, N. Y. "A delicate and delicious breakfast food. A complete natural product of the whole of the wheat."

14368. Germea. Prepared from the choicest California white wheat. The John T. Cutting Company, San Francisco and New York.

14369. Pettijohns Breakfast Gem. Manufactured by C. S. Laumeister, 203-207 Mission street, San Francisco, Cal. Prepared in California from the best selected and thoroughly cleaned California white wheat.

14370. Leggett's Cracked White Wheat. Francis H. Leggett & Co., packers of farinaceous products, West Broadway, Franklin and Vesey streets, New York.

14371. F. F. V. Breakfast Malt Food. Manufactured by Refined Food Company, New York City. "F. F. V. Malt Breakfast Food is made according to a formula which is the result of many years of experiment and actual tests in the practice of Dr. Fillmore Moore. All the woody and nonnutritious substances are removed and the insoluble starch is made soluble or converted into maltose by diastase, a digestive ferment. F. F. V. Breakfast Food is manufactured from wheat, barley, and Southern corn.

14372. Granulated Barley. Health Food Company, 61 Fifth avenue, New York.

1342   FOODS AND FOOD ADULTERANTS.

14375. Breakfast Pearl Hominy. Made by the Washington Pearl Hominy Mills, Washington, D. C.

14376. Quaker Rolled White Oats. Manufactured by the American Cereal Company, Chicago, Ill., U. S. A.

14377. Hornsby's Steam Cooked Oatmeal, H-O. The H-O Company, New York, U. S. A. Product manufactured and guaranteed by "The Clover Mills," Buffalo, N. Y. "Prepared by cooking with steam, which converts the starch into digestible sugar, making the product easily assimilable."

14378. Parched Rolled Oats, Quail Brand. Nebraska City Cereal Mills, Nebraska City, Nebr., U. S. A.

14379. Fleischmann's Vienna Bread Crumbs from The Edelheim Company (incorporated). Proprietors of Fleischmann's Vienna Model Bakery, 233–259 North Broad street, Philadelphia, Pa.

14387. Pates Alimentaires de Choix. (Vermicelli Taganrock Choix.) Laroze et Cie., Lyons, France, fabricants.

14389. Durkee's Pearl Tapioca. F. R. Durkee & Co., importers and manufacturers of choicest quality food products, New York. "Tapioca is the product of a plant variously known in the tropical countries in which it is cultivated as cassava, cassada, manipot cannabina, mandioca, tapioca, etc."

14390. Ceylon Spice Company's McKinley's Protection Brand Instantaneous Tapioca. The Ceylon Spice Company, sole proprietors and manufacturers, Front and New streets, Philadelphia, Pa.

14391. Finely Granulated Rio Tapioca. Parrish Brothers, Baltimore, Md. "Selected with great care. Dissolves instantly."

14392. Smith's Homemade Egg Noodles. Manufactured only by S. R. Smith Company, Harrisburg, Pa. "Made from fresh eggs and high-grade flour only."

14393. L'Etoile Egg Noodles. Vernier et Freres, Bordeaux, France.

15253. Cerealine Flakes. The Cerealine Manufacturing Company, sole manufacturers, Columbus, Ind.

15256. Pearl Hominy. John Outcalt, Spotswood, N. J.

15257. Pearl Breakfast Hominy. Manufactured by Baltimore Pearl Hominy Mills, Baltimore, Md.

15265. Wheatena. Health Food Company, 61 Fifth avenue, New York. "Made from peeled wheat. The best quality of white wheat is selected, the bran coats are removed, and the pure food of the kernel reduced to a granular form."

15266. ABC Oatmeal (Crushed White Oats), Hulled, Steam Cooked, and Desiccated. The Cereals Manufacturing Company, 83 Murray street, New York.

15267. ABC White Wheat, Hulled, Steam Cooked, and Desiccated. The Cereals Manufacturing Company, 83 Murray street, New York.

15271. Eli Pettijohn's Best. Made from best selected Pacific coast white wheat. Eli Pettijohn Cereal Company, Minneapolis, Minn.

15273. Pearl Samp. Made by Baltimore Pearl Hominy Mills, Baltimore, Md.

15275. Hecker's Farina. Manufactured at Hecker Mills, 203 Cherry street, New York.

15276. Granulated Rio Tapioca. Imported by E. C. Hazard & Co., New York.

15277. Kingsford's Oswego Corn Starch (known also as prepared corn). Manufactured expressly for food by T. Kingsford & Son, Oswego, N. Y.

15278. Hill's East Indian Manioca. Manioca Company, Rowland F. Hill, New York.

15279. Durkee's Rice Flour. E. R. Durkee & Co., importers and manufacturers of choicest quality food products, New York.

15280. Extra Quality Flake Tapioca. Put up by Francis H. Leggett & Co., New York.

15281. Roasted Oats, Onderdonk's Patent. American Cereal Roasting Company, 6 Harrison street, New York.

15282. Pates Extra Taganrok Superieur. (Vermicelli.) Santelli et Cie, Lyons, France.

15284. Petites Pates Extra, Lettres et Chiffres. Vve. Garres Jne. et Fils, Usine street, Nicolas, Bordeaux, France.

15283. Spaghetti. La Favorita, Valence, Bordeaux, New York. Fabrica di Paste Sopraffine D'Ogni Qualita, Alexis Godillot Jeune, Bordeaux, France.

15320. Graham Flakes or Granulated Graham. Francis H. Leggett & Co., New York.

15321. Spaghetti Senza. John di Cola, established 1861, Manufacturing House of Superior Maccaroni, Termini Imerese, Sicily.

15322. Pates Extra Taganrok Superieur. Santelli et Cie., Lyons, France.

15323. Pates Alimentaires Taganrok Superieur Extra. Santelli et Cie., Lyons, France.

15325. Ralston Health Club Breakfast Food, indorsed by Ralston Health Club, Martyn College, Washington, D. C. Manufactured by Robinson-Danforth Company, proprietors, Purina Mills, St. Louis, Mo. "A perfect food made from selected wheat, rich in gluten."

15326. Granose Flakes. Manufactured solely by the Sanitarium Health Food Company, Battle Creek, Mich. "Represents the entire wheat berry undeteriorated by any milling process and thrice cooked, whereby the starch is largely converted into dextrin."

15329. Granulated Rye. Manufactured by Health Food Company, 61 Fifth avenue, New York. "Made from the best rye, hulled by the wet process and reduced to a granular meal without the injurious heating of millstone grinding."

15331. F-S Granulated Hominy. Manufactured by The American Cereal Company, at the Schumacher Mills, Akron, Ohio, U. S. A.

15332. **Friends Rolled White Oats** (kiln dried). Manufactured only by Muscatine Oat Meal Company, Muscatine, Iowa.

15333. **Parched Farinose.** Manufactured by The American Cereal Company, at the Schumacher Mills, Akron, Ohio, U. S. A. Prepared from Ohio's best amber wheat. "Rich in gluten, germ, nitrates, fat, and phosphates."

15335. **Granola.** Manufactured by Sanitarium Health Food Company, Battle Creek, Mich. "Wheat and Oats. An invalid food prepared by a combination of grains so treated as to retain in the preparation the 'highest degree of nutrient qualities,' while eliminating every element of an irritating character."

15336. **Superior Scotch Pinhead Oatmeal.** Carr & Co., Millers and Biscuit Manufacturers, Carlisle, England.

Composition of breakfast and partially prepared foods.

CLASS I.—INDIAN CORN PRODUCTS.

Serial No.	In the original substance.						In the dry substance.					Digestible proteids.	Calculated calories of combustion.	Estimated calories.
	Moisture.	Proteids, N×6.25.	Ether extract.	Crude fiber.	Ash.	Carbohydrates other than fiber.	Proteids, N×6.25.	Ether extract.	Crude fiber.	Ash.	Carbohydrates other than fiber.			
	Per ct.	Per ct.	Per ct.	Per ct.	Per ct.	Per ct.	Per ct.	Per ct.	Per ct.	Per ct.	Per ct.	Per ct.		
14375	12.79	6.31	0.77	0.71	0.33	79.80	7.24	0.88	0.81	0.38	91.50	8.87	4,375	4,202
15253	10.98	9.06	.99	.62	2.33	76.60	10.18	1.11	.70	2.65	86.06	47.57	4,348	4,413
15256	11.90	8.25	.15	.60	.23	79.47	9.36	.17	.68	.26	90.21	4.49	4,384	4,346
15257	13.05	8.31	.60	.63	.42	77.62	9.56	.69	.72	.48	89.27	15.76	4,408	4,387
16273	11.45	8.25	.81	1.03	.25	79.26	9.31	.91	1.16	.28	89.50	17.45	4,442	4,374
15331	13.84	7.31	.17	.43	.37	78.31	8.48	.20	.50	.43	90.87	54.99	4,356	4,318
Average	12.33	7.92	.58	.67	.66	78.51	9.02	.66	.76	.75	80.57	24.86	4,385	4,300

Composition of breakfast and partially prepared foods—Continued.

CLASS II.—WHEAT PRODUCTS.

Serial No.		In the original substance.						In the dry substance.						
	Moisture.	Proteids, N×6.25.	Proteids, N×5.70.	Ether extract.	Crude fiber.	Ash.	Carbohydrates other than fiber, N×5.70.	Proteids, N×6.25.	Proteids, N×5.70.	Ether extract.	Crude fiber.	Ash.	Carbohydrates other than fiber, N×5.70.	Digestible proteids.	Calculated calories of combustion.	Estimated calories.
	Per ct.	Per ct.	Per ct.	Per ct.	Per ct.	Per ct.	Per ct.	Per ct.	Per ct.	Per ct.	Per ct.	Per ct.	Per ct.	Per ct.		
14361	9.91	9.75	8.89	1.49	1.01	1.03	78.76	10.82	9.87	1.65	1.12	1.14	87.34	69.23	4,404	4,302
14363	11.09	14.38	13.11	3.26	2.53	2.04	70.50	16.17	14.75	3.67	2.85	2.29	76.39	62.17	4,542	4,544
14364	6.81	12.75	11.63	.71	.85	1.01	79.84	13.68	12.48	.76	.91	1.08	85.66	54.90	4,406	4,432
14366	11.78	11.38	10.38	1.51	1.06	1.12	73.21	13.00	11.80	1.71	1.22	1.27	85.16	55.54		4,445
14368	10.28	8.75	7.98	1.88	1.17	1.18	78.68	9.75	8.89	2.10	1.30	1.32	87.69	54.29	4,403	4,376
14369	8.99	9.25	8.44	2.20	1.88	1.69	77.08	10.28	9.38	2.44	2.09	1.88	86.30	76.97	4,405	4,453
14370	10.44	10.50	9.58	1.59	1.88	1.65	76.74	11.72	10.69	1.78	2.10	1.84	85.69		4,395	4,557
15265	9.65	13.44	12.26	3.45	1.39	1.54	73.10	14.88	13.57	3.82	1.54	1.71	80.90	84.15	4,577	4,947
15267	10.97	13.94	12.71	1.64	1.95	1.79	72.89	15.66	14.28	1.84	2.19	2.01	81.87	35.87	4,644	4,337
15271	11.28	9.75	8.89	1.68	1.77	2.19	75.96	10.99	10.02	1.89	2.00	2.47	85.62	67.89	4,447	4,429
15320	8.45	14.38	13.11	1.10	2.36	1.22	76.12	15.71	14.33	1.20	2.58	1.33	83.14	63.49	4,449	4,522
15325	11.01	12.56	14.45	1.71	.88	.99	74.84	14.11	12.87	1.92	.99	1.11	84.10	76.11	4,532	4,416
15326	10.08	15.50	14.19	1.25	1.42	3.35	71.13	17.30	15.78	1.39	1.58	3.73	79.10	46.98	4,449	4,452
15331	9.35	11.81	10.77	1.73	.57	.87	77.28	13.03	11.88	1.91	.63	.96	85.23	64.52	4,471	4,482
Average	10.08	12.01	10.96	1.80	1.48	1.55	75.62	13.36	12.19	2.01	1.65	1.73	84.08	62.47	4,402	4,482

BREAKFAST FOODS. 1347

CLASS III.—OAT PRODUCTS.

Serial No.	Moisture.	In the original substance.						In the dry substance.					Digestible proteids.	Calculated calories of combustion.	Estimated calories.
		Proteids, N×6.25.	Proteids, N×6.31.	Ether extract.	Crude fiber.	Ash.	Carbohydrates other than fiber, N×6.31.	Proteids, N×6.25.	Proteids, N×6.31.	Ether extract.	Crude fiber.	Ash.	Carbohydrates other than fiber, N×6.31.			
	Per ct.	Per ct.	Per ct.	Per ct.	Per ct.	Per ct.	Per ct.	Per ct.	Per ct.	Per ct.	Per ct.	Per ct.	Per ct.	Per ct.		
14376	7.86	16.06	16.22	8.23	1.25	1.62	66.07	17.43	17.60	8.93	1.36	1.76	71.71	53.30	4,928	4,670
14377	8.92	16.06	16.22	6.89	1.11	1.62	66.16	17.64	17.82	7.56	1.22	2.00	72.53		4,802	4,800
14378	8.74	14.94	15.09	7.10	0.90	1.91	67.16	16.37	16.53	7.78	0.99	2.09	73.60	38.89	4,832	4,544
15266	8.21	15.69	15.85	7.14	1.69	1.63	67.17	17.09	17.26	7.78	1.84	1.78	73.18	77.69	4,893	4,728
15281	6.46	14.13	14.27	6.96	1.23	1.95	70.36	15.11	15.26	7.74	1.31	2.08	75.22	42.96		
15332	6.97	16.56	16.73	7.39	1.23	1.71	67.20	17.80	17.98	7.94	1.90	1.84	72.24	47.16	4,907	4,696
15336	6.45	13.81	13.95	8.55	0.98	1.91	69.14	14.76	14.91	9.14	1.05	2.04	73.91	46.56	4,878	4,587
Average	7.66	15.32	15.48	7.46	1.20	1.79	67.61	16.60	16.77	8.08	1.38	1.94	73.20	51.09	4,875	4,671

CLASS IV.—STARCH AND TAPIOCA.

Serial No.	In the original substance.						In the dry substance.					Calculated calories of combustion.	Estimated calories.
	Moisture.	Proteids, N×6.25.	Ether extract.	Crude fiber.	Ash.	Carbohydrates other than fiber, N×6.25.	Proteids, N×6.25.	Ether extract.	Crude fiber.	Ash.	Carbohydrates other than fiber, N×6.25.		
	Per ct.	Per ct.	Per ct.	Per ct.	Per ct.	Per ct.	Per ct.	Per ct.	Per ct.	Per ct.	Per ct.		
14389	11.46	0.38	0.09	0.09	0.12	87.95	0.43	0.10	0.10	0.14	99.33	4,210	4,025
14390	12.13	.19	.07	.19	.10	87.51	.22	.08	.11	.11	99.59	4,212	4,140
14391	11.62	.38	.01	.11	.09	67.90	.43	.01	.12	.10	99.46	4,208	4,050
15276	11.38	.25	.00	.12	.02	88.35	.28	.00	.14	.02	99.70	4,228	4,244
15277	11.65	.44	.00	.23	.43	87.48	.50	.00	.26	.49	99.01	4,179	4,209
15278	10.54	.50	.05	.01	.14	88.77	.56	.06	.01	.16	99.22	4,206	4,240
15280	10.28	.56	.00	.19	.10	89.06	.62	.00	.21	.11	99.27	4,110	4,215
Average	11.29	.39	.03	.13	.14	88.15	.43	.04	.15	.16	99.37	4,193	4,160

Composition of breakfast and partially prepared foods—Continued.

CLASS V.—NOODLES, SPAGHETTI, AND MACARONI.

Serial No.	In the original substance.					In the dry substance.							Calculated calories of combustion.	Estimated calories.
	Moisture.	Proteids, N×6.25.	Ether extract.	Crude fiber.	Ash.	Carbohydrates other than fiber, N×6.25.	Proteids, N×6.25.	Ether extract.	Crude fiber.	Ash.	Carbohydrates other than fiber, N×6.25.	Digestible proteids.		
	Per ct.	Per ct.	Per ct.	Per ct.	Per ct.	Per ct.	Per ct.	Per ct.	Per ct.	Per ct.	Per ct.	Per ct.		
14387	10.69	11.38	0.38	0.49	0.90	76.05	12.74	0.43	0.55	1.01	85.82	76.89	4,354	4,290
14392	10.62	11.69	1.48	.35	1.40	74.72	13.08	1.66	.39	1.66	83.60	56.80	4,434	4,300
14393	10.73	11.69	.53	.25	.44	76.61	13.10	.50	.28	.49	85.82	70.13	4,424	4,275
15262	10.05	11.69	.25	.80	.66	76.35	13.14	.28	.90	.74	85.84	85.03	4,444	4,385
15283	11.13	13.25	.08	.71	.62	74.92	14.91	.09	.79	.70	84.30	87.20	4,462	4,399
15284	.88	12.19	.10	.69	.65	86.09	12.30	.19	.70	.70	86.85	80.58	4,420	4,351
15321	10.84	11.19	.24	.47	.71	77.02	12.55	.27	.53	.80	86.38	76.50	4,416	4,344
15322	10.26	12.44	.34	.60	.84	76.12	13.86	.38	.73	.93	84.83	87.46	4,447	4,364
15323	10.76	12.69	.27	.61	.69	75.59	14.26	.30	.68	.78	84.66	86.21	4,454	4,373
Average	0.66	12.02	.42	.56	.78	77.12	13.33	.47	.62	.86	85.34	80.53	4,428	4,342

CLASS VI.—BARLEY.

Serial No.	In the original substance.					In the dry substance.							Calculated calories of combustion.	Estimated calories.
	Moisture.	Proteids, N×6.25.	Proteids, N×5.82.	Ether extract.	Crude fiber.	Ash.	Carbohydrates other than fiber, N×5.82.	Proteids, N×6.25.	Proteids, N×5.82.	Ether extract.	Crude fiber.	Ash.	Carbohydrates other than fiber, N×5.82.	Digestible proteids.		
	Per ct.	Per ct.	Per ct.	Per ct.	Per ct.	Per ct.	Per ct.	Per ct.	Per ct.	Per ct.	Per ct.	Per ct.	Per ct.		
14372	10.92	7.50	6.98	0.89	0.67	0.86	80.35	8.42	7.84	1.00	0.75	0.97	90.19	30.20	4,344	4,365

CLASS VII.—MISCELLANEOUS.

Serial No.	In the original substance.						In the dry substance.					Digestible proteids.	Calculated calories of combustion.	Estimated calories.
	Moisture.	Proteids, N×6.25.	Ether extract.	Crude fiber.	Ash.	Carbohydrates other than fiber. N×6.25.	Proteids, N×6.25.	Ether extract.	Crude fiber.	Ash.	Carbohydrates other than fiber. N×6.25.			
	Per ct.	Per ct.	Per ct.	Per ct.	Per ct.	Per ct.	Per ct.	Per ct.	Per ct.	Per ct.	Per ct.	Per ct.		
14358	3.76	12.00	1.33	2.39	1.91	81.00	12.47	1.38	2.48	1.98	84.17	41.66	4,399	4,385
14360	4.54	15.06	0.25	0.28	0.44	79.71	15.78	0.20	0.29	0.46	83.50	24.44	4,462	4,485
14371	8.57	11.63	1.75	0.73	1.05	77.00	12.72	1.91	0.80	1.15	84.22	69.91	4,465	4,470
15335	8.75	12.56	0.86	0.55	0.83	77.00	13.76	0.94	0.60	0.91	84.39	72.13	4,460	4,502
Average	6.41	12.81	1.05	0.99	1.06	78.68	13.68	1.12	1.04	1.13	84.07	52.04	4,449	4,460

STUDY OF THE ANALYTICAL DATA.

The analytical data are given as computed for the original substance, and also for the water-free substance. Where the factor for the proteids determined by recent analyses differs sensibly from 6.25, the old normal factor, the proteids have been calculated by both methods in order to give not only the data of comparison with old analyses, but also to secure a method of computing the total carbohydrates present by difference, as determined by the new factor. The variations produced by these two computations are seen chiefly in wheat and barley, where the new factor for the calculation of proteids is considerably lower than the old number. The variations in the case of Indian corn are so slight, between 6.25 and 6.22, as to render a separate calculation unnecessary. In the oat products the difference is also very little, namely, 6.25 and 6.31, but in this case the results calculated by the new factor are given. Where two series of factors have been given, the appropriate headings indicate the one which has been employed, namely, $N \times 6.25$ for the old factor, and $N \times$ the number expressing the new factor. In the calculation of the carbohydrates, where two factors are given for the proteids, the one which has been used for the calculation of the carbohydrates is placed above the column so as to avoid confusion, as, for instance, in class 2, wheat products, the carbohydrates are calculated on the basis of the factor of $N \times 5.70$, as indicated at the top of the column. A study of the analytical data reveals in the averages given the character of the products which are used for breakfast foods.

CLASS I.—INDIAN CORN PRODUCTS.

In this class it is seen that quite uniformly the germ has been extracted before the preparation has been made. In some cases the extraction has been quite perfect, as in No. 15256 and in No. 15231. In other instances a considerable quantity of oil has been left in the product, as is shown by No. 15253. The quantity of fiber shows a pretty thorough separation of the flour from the bran in all cases except No. 15273, where a considerable quantity of fiber has been left in the meal. The ash is normal in all cases except No. 15253, where it is evident that some mineral matter—probably common salt—has been added to the preparation. The mean percentage of proteids is what would be expected from Indian-corn products from which the germ and a considerable quantity of the envelope rich in protein has been removed. The carbohydrate column represents the starches, sugars, pentosans, and all other carbohydrate matters not included under fiber. The numbers in each case are obtained by subtracting the sum of the other ingredients from 100. The percentage of moisture in the products represents very nearly the normal percentage in the fresh grains.

CLASS II.—WHEAT PRODUCTS.

Wheat is used to a very large extent in the preparation of breakfast foods, and the number of samples purchased in the open market derived from wheat was greater than that obtained from any other cereal.

The ether extract shows that the wheat germs, as a rule, were not removed in the process of the preparation of the material. In a few instances the quantity of ether extract indicates that the product was a mixture of wheat and oatmeal. The samples containing an excess of oil for wheat products are Nos. 14363, 14369, and 15265. In two of these instances the large quantity of proteids also indicates the admixture of oatmeal, while in the third one, namely, No. 14369, the low quantity of proteids would lead to the supposition that the substance used for mixing was Indian-corn meal from which the germ had been removed instead of oatmeal.

The fiber is abnormally high in two instances, namely, Nos. 14363 and 15320. In these cases it must be supposed that the bolting of the product was not carried to the full limit, and that a large portion of bran remained in the flour.

In regard to the ash there is one instance where it is evident that there was a mixture of mineral matter, probably common salt. In two other cases the quantity of ash appears to be rather high, namely, Nos. 14363 and 15271. The increase, however, is not sufficiently great to warrant the assumption of the introduction of extraneous mineral matter.

The mean percentage of the proteids is what would be expected from the average composition of wheaten flours. The variations are also within the limits of various kinds of wheat, although No. 14368 falls very low, even for a wheat poor in proteids. A high content of proteids is found in Nos. 14363, 15320, and 15326.

Class III.—Oat Products.

The oat products are quite characteristic of oatmeal from the whole grain. It is evident that the germ has not been removed, as the quantity of oil is fully up to, if not in excess of, that usually present in the oats. Fiber, ash, and proteids are also normal. The quantity of oil and proteids being so high, causes a corresponding depression in the carbohydrate matter. It is evident in the analyses which are given that there was no adulteration practiced in the case of the oat products examined. The high nutritive value of the oatmeal, in respect of both its content of fat and of proteids, is fully illustrated by the analytical data obtained.

Class IV.—Tapioca.

The class of partially prepared foods which bears the general name of tapioca is represented in this place. Often ordinary starches are employed for breakfast foods and would be included in this class. Tapioca proper is derived from starches produced in tropical regions. It is made chiefly from the semiliquid starches or juices of the cassava plant. The sweet cassava grown in Florida also yields an excellent article of tapioca.[1]

Strictly speaking, tapioca would not be considered in bulletins devoted to cereals and their products, but inasmuch as cereals are often used as substitutes for tapioca, it is thought proper that it should find a place in this bulletin. Analytical data show that the starches and tapiocas examined were, from a chemical point of view, composed almost exclusively of pure starch and water. The quantities of starch, ether extract, fiber, and proteids are only such as would be expected in starches which had not been purified with particular care.

Class V.—Macaroni, etc.

Noodles, spaghetti, and macaroni are names for products which are essentially similar in their character and chemical composition. They are made from flour rich in gluten, molded into threads, solid or tubular. They form an important item of diet in Italy and are used to a large extent in this country. The analytical data reveal only the characteristics of a good wheat flour. Only in one instance does an excess of mineral matter, presumably common salt, occur, namely, in No. 14392. In this instance also oil of some kind seems to have been used in the manufacture. All the other samples are evidently made of pure wheat flours without any additions or adulterations of any description.

Class VI.—Barley Products.

Only one sample of a barley breakfast food was met with in the purchases which were made in the open market. The proteids in this sample were rather low and the carbohydrates correspondingly high. In other respects the analytical data do not merit further discussion.

Class VII.—Miscellaneous Products.

In this class were collected all the varieties of breakfast foods which could be purchased, and whose origin, that is, the nature of the cereal employed in whose manufacture, it was not possible to obtain from any description on the packages. There is nothing in the analytical data which tends to reveal the nature of the origin of these products, with the exception of the percentage of proteids which, taken in conjunction with the rather low ether extract, indicates that they are almost uniformly derived from wheat or wheat products. In the case of No. 14360, where the percentage of proteids would indicate that the sample might be derived from oats, the low percentage of ether extract removes the possibility of this being so. In samples No. 14358 and No. 14371, where the rather high content of oil might indicate the use of Indian corn, the high percentage of proteids excludes also that possibility. All of the miscellaneous breakfast foods appear to have been derived from wheat.

---

[1] See Bulletin No. 44, of this division.

BISCUITS.

A large variety of cereal foods are offered for sale to which the common term "biscuits" can be applied. All hard, brittle cakes which are unleavened may be considered under this head, with the possible exception of those which contain sugar. When biscuits contain added sugar they properly belong to the next category of cereal foods to be considered, viz, cakes. This class of bodies is sold under a great variety of names, as will be seen by inspecting the column headed "Trade name" of the appended description. They are often sold under the name of "crackers," but this latter name is not to be preferred, although it is in quite general use.

PREPARATION.

Biscuits are made almost exclusively of wheat flour, and the requisite degree of toughness of the dough is secured by a long preliminary working or beating, by means of which the conversion of the glutenin and gliadin into gluten is made very complete, and the dough assumes an elastic, rubber-like consistence. The more prolonged the preliminary working or beating of the dough the firmer and more brittle the finished products become. The addition of chemicals in the form of bicarbonate of soda or other similar materials is not to be recommended in the preparation of biscuit, although certain varieties are sold as soda biscuit or soda crackers. The trade name of the product is not always a sure index of the character of the compound. In the form of biscuit the bread made from wheat flour can be more conveniently transported and longer preserved than in almost any other form, and for this reason many forms of biscuit are found in the ration of soldiers, especially when on the march. A very hard, large biscuit was in extensive use during the late war, and is known as "hard-tack." In this form the greatest amount of nourishment can be carried at the least expense of transportation.

In the grouping of the samples which have been purchased in the open market in Washington it is possible that some may have been incorporated which do not properly belong under the general definition of biscuit given above. An attempt was made to eliminate all biscuits which contained any added sugar. It is evident, however, from an inspection of the analytical data, that many of the samples contained a considerable quantity of added mineral matter, which in most cases was found to be common salt. The analytical data follow.

17498—No. 13——13

FOODS AND FOOD ADULTERANTS.

Description of biscuits.

Serial No.	Trade name.	Name of dealer.	Name of manufacturer.	Price per pound.
				Cents.
14722	Split Boston Crackers.	N. W. Burchell, 1325 F street NW.	The Kennedy Biscuit Co., New York, N. Y.	16
14723	Saltines	...do...	J. D. Mason & Co., New York, N. Y.	18
14724	Water Thins	...do...	Holmes & Coutts, New York, N. Y.	18
14726	Graham Wafers	...do...	The New York Biscuit Co., New York, N. Y.	18
14727	Cream Blossom, or Egg Biscuit.	...do...	Mason & Co., Baltimore, Md	40
14728	Cream Lunch	...do...	The New York Biscuit Co., New York, N. Y.	14
14729	Mushrooms, or Egg Biscuit.	...do...	Mason & Co., Baltimore, Md	20
14730	Cream Crackers	...do...	...do...	14
14731	Dinner Biscuit	...do...	Huntley & Palmer, Reading, England.	36
14732	Educators (Dr. Johnson's).	...do...	The New York Biscuit Co., New York, N. Y.	16
14733	Water Crackers	...do...	Bent & Co., Milton, Mass	18
14734	Alberts (water crackers).	...do...	Holmes & Coutts, New York, N. Y.	20
15002	Baby Oyster Crackers.	...do...	The New York Biscuit Co., New York, N. Y.	10
15006	Sea Shells	...do...	...do...	40
15007	Animal Crackers	...do...	Mason & Co, Baltimore, Md	16
15009	Pretzellettes	...do...	The New York Biscuit Co., New York, N. Y.	18
15016	German Zwieback	...do...	Holmes & Coutts, New York, N. Y.	25
15020	Graham Crackers (Forget-Me-Nots).	...do...	The New York Biscuit Co., New York, N. Y.	[1]25
15254	Delicacy	John H. Magruder & Co., 1417 New York avenue NW.	C. D. Boss & Son, New London, Conn.	[1]25
15255	Lunch Milk Biscuit	...do...	...do...	12
15260	Keystone Cream Biscuit.	...do...	Marvin & Co., New York, N. Y	10
15263	Cracker Meal	...do...	C. D. Boss & Son, New London, Conn.	12
15264	Seaside Wafers	...do...	...do...	20
15269	Zephyrette (Larrabee's).	...do...	The New York Biscuit Co., New York, N. Y.	[1]25
15270	London Cream Biscuit.	...do...	Young & Larrabee, Syracuse, N. Y.	12
15272	Sardine Oat Cakes	...do...	John Walker & Co., Glasgow, Scotland.	[1]50
15274	Reception Flakes	...do...	Havenner's Bakery, Washington, D. C.	[1]25
15286	Sea Foam Wafers	...do...	The New York Biscuit Co., New York, N. Y.	18
15287	Cream Crackers	...do...	Havenner's Bakery, Washington, D. C.	12
15294	Saltines	...do...	The Kennedy Biscuit Co., New York, N. Y.	18
15296	Fort Pitt Butter Crackers.	...do...	Marvin & Co., New York, N. Y	10

[1] Per box.

BISCUITS, OR "CRACKERS."

Description of biscuits—Continued.

Serial No.	Trade name.	Name of dealer.	Name of manufacturer.	Price per pound.
				Cents.
15297	Brownie Pretzels (Schwab's).	John H. Magruder & Co., 1417 New York avenue NW.		15
15299	X-Ray Crackers	..... do	Marvin & Co., New York, N. Y	18
15302	Zephyr Pilot............	..... do	The Kennedy Biscuit Co., New York, N. Y.	15
15303	Jeff. Davis Water Crackers.	..... do	The New York Biscuit Co., New York, N. Y.	10
15307	3A Soda Crackers.....	..... do	..... do	10
15313	Water Crackers	G. G. Cornwell & Son, 1412-1414 Pennsylvania avenue NW.	Carr & Co., England.................	25
15318	Cracker Meal..........	..... do	Bent & Co., Milton, Mass............	15
15320	Graham Flakes........	..... do	Francis H. Leggett & Co., New York, N. Y.	15
15327	Wilson's Health Biscuit.	..... do	The New York Biscuit Co., New York, N. Y.	12
15330	Water Thin Biscuit ..	..... do	Medlar & Co., Philadelphia, Pa.....	25
15337	University (Plain) Biscuit.	..... do	Huntley & Palmer, Reading, England.	35
15339	Bath Oliver Biscuit...	..... do	..... do	30
15340	Grist Mill Crackers...	..... do	Potter & Wrightington, Boston, Mass.	15
15343	Breakfast Biscuit.....	..... do	Huntley & Palmer, Reading, England.	60
15344	Nursery Biscuit	..... do	..... do	40
15346	Petit-Beurre	..... do	..... do	35
15347	Luncheon Biscuit.....	..... do	Bent & Co., Milton, Mass...........	25

1356 FOODS AND FOOD ADULTERANTS.

Composition of biscuits.

Serial No.	Moisture.	In the original substance.							In the dry substance.						Digestible proteids.	Calculated calories of combustion.	Estimated calories.
		Proteids, N×6.25.	Proteids, N×5.70.	Ether extract.	Crude fiber.	Ash.	Salt.	Carbohydrates N×5.70.	Proteids, N×6.25.	Proteids, N×5.70.	Ether extract.	Crude fiber.	Ash.	Salt.	Carbohydrates, N×5.70.			
	Per ct.	Per ct.	Per ct.	Per ct.	Per ct.	Per ct.	Per ct.	Per ct.	Per ct.	Per ct.	Per ct.	Per ct.	Per ct.	Per ct.	Per ct.	Per ct.		
14722	6.84	11.31	10.31	7.11	0.79	1.43	0.57	74.31	12.14	11.07	7.63	0.85	1.54	0.61	79.76	51.90	4,592	4,791
14723	4.59	8.94	9.07	12.79	0.58	2.81	----	70.74	10.42	9.50	13.41	0.61	2.95	----	74.14	55.93	4,922	4,673
14724	5.41	10.44	9.52	10.09	0.21	1.25	0.53	73.73	11.04	10.07	10.67	0.22	1.32	0.56	77.94	34.77	4,862	4,750
14726	3.14	7.44	6.79	10.87	----	1.42	0.29	77.78	7.68	7.00	11.22	----	1.47	0.30	80.31	59.68	4,829	4,027
14727	5.42	12.44	11.35	11.93	0.34	0.84	0.04	70.46	13.16	12.00	12.62	0.36	0.89	0.04	74.49	64.79	5,010	4,167
14728	4.06	8.56	7.81	11.98	0.30	1.99	0.31	73.29	9.01	8.22	12.61	0.32	2.10	0.33	77.07	69.23	4,895	4,736
14729	6.37	12.81	11.68	16.05	0.51	1.16	0.04	64.74	13.68	12.48	17.14	0.54	1.24	0.04	69.14	41.45	5,234	4,821
14730	4.28	9.88	9.01	13.77	0.80	1.38	0.53	71.56	10.32	9.41	14.30	0.84	1.44	0.55	74.76	55.11	5,014	4,841
14731	5.05	10.63	9.69	8.03	0.24	2.55	1.65	74.68	11.20	10.21	8.46	0.25	2.69	1.74	78.64	62.37	4,092	4,643
14732	5.19	11.06	10.09	0.61	0.88	0.88	0.04	83.23	11.67	10.64	0.64	0.93	0.93	0.04	87.79	63.83	4,374	4,327
14733	6.58	11.88	10.83	0.21	0.29	0.49	0.02	81.89	12.72	11.60	0.23	0.31	0.52	0.02	87.65	77.86	4,387	4,358
14734	4.69	11.69	10.66	4.55	0.20	2.03	1.33	78.07	12.27	11.19	4.77	0.21	2.13	1.40	81.91	64.16	4,544	4,422
15002	6.51	11.19	10.21	9.19	0.21	3.07	2.27	71.02	11.97	10.92	9.83	0.22	3.28	2.43	75.97	78.19	4,749	4,720
15006	5.72	6.50	5.93	8.61	0.09	0.54	0.23	79.20	6.89	6.28	9.13	0.10	0.57	0.24	84.02	51.85	4,748	4,752
15007	5.42	9.25	8.44	8.37	0.48	0.65	0.04	77.12	9.78	8.92	8.85	0.51	0.69	0.04	81.54	70.97	4,774	5,003
15009	8.10	10.31	9.40	3.85	0.30	3.24	3.10	75.41	11.33	10.33	4.23	0.40	3.56	3.41	81.88	55.77	4,442	4,458
15016	7.73	10.31	9.40	9.12	0.30	0.83	0.20	72.92	11.17	10.19	9.88	0.33	0.90	0.22	79.03	66.05	8,842	4,638
15020	5.24	8.25	7.52	12.04	0.59	1.18	0.35	74.02	8.71	7.94	12.71	0.62	1.25	0.37	78.10	59.88	4,721	4,760
15254	11.82	9.94	9.07	11.32	0.02	3.53	2.65	64.26	11.27	10.28	12.84	0.02	4.00	3.01	72.88	68.51	4,802	4,994
15255	8.87	8.94	8.15	12.47	0.37	1.15	0.37	69.36	9.81	8.95	13.68	0.41	1.26	0.41	76.11	46.87	4,197	4,976
15260	8.43	8.86	8.10	10.79	1.10	2.33	1.66	70.35	9.70	8.85	11.78	1.20	2.54	1.81	76.83	60.59	4,855	4,738
15263	9.24	9.63	8.78	11.32	0.12	1.66	----	69.00	10.61	9.68	12.47	0.13	1.83	----	76.02	67.50	4,924	5,091
15264	7.89	10.00	9.12	10.82	0.35	3.01	2.64	70.12	10.86	9.90	11.75	0.38	2.23	2.87	76.12	65.00	4,874	4,692
15269	8.40	9.56	8.72	13.07	0.83	1.35	0.84	70.46	10.21	9.90	13.96	0.89	1.44	0.90	75.20	63.39	5,010	5,015
15270	8.72	10.00	9.12	11.67	0.22	1.57	0.93	68.92	10.96	10.00	12.78	0.24	1.72	1.02	75.50	43.70	4,950	4,978
15272	7.83	13.13	11.97	8.54	1.86	2.33	0.05	66.33	14.25	13.00	9.27	2.02	2.53	0.05	72.20	49.50	4,788	4,730

BISCUITS, OR "CRACKERS."

15274	9.53	9.19	8.38	13.01	0.30	2.09	1.38	66.99	10.16	9.27	14.38	0.33	2.31	1.53	74.04	84.98	4,994	5,052
15286	7.53	9.94	9.07	10.17	0.39	1.44	0.98	71.79	10.75	9.80	11.00	0.42	1.56	4.30	77.64	82.39	3,849	3,891
15287	7.92	9.25	8.43	10.66	0.39	1.10	0.61	71.89	10.04	9.16	11.58	0.42	1.19	0.66	78.07	70.97	4,896	4,943
15291	6.70	11.19	10.21	12.68	0.34	2.28	1.74	68.86	11.99	10.93	13.59	0.36	1.66	1.87	73.82	74.89	5,009	4,820
15296	9.48	11.19	10.21	8.79	0.27	2.51	2.25	69.01	12.36	11.27	9.71	0.30	2.77	2.49	76.25	60.86	4,770	4,665
15297	11.05	0.06	8.26	3.88	0.53	4.93	3.92	73.34	10.06	9.72	4.36	0.00	3.89	4.11	82.03	76.49	4,426	4,420
15299	8.72	7.13	6.50	12.90	0.32	1.63	1.72	70.35	7.81	7.12	14.02	0.35	1.79	1.88	77.07	65.78	5,361	4,948
15302	8.18	10.44	9.52	10.22	0.27	0.91	0.40	71.17	11.37	10.37	11.13	0.29	0.99	0.44	77.51	68.30	4,902	4,743
15303	9.40	12.19	11.12	3.37	0.46	0.75	0.17	75.20	13.46	12.28	3.72	0.50	0.83	0.19	83.17	62.50	4,564	4,599
15307	8.43	9.75	8.89	7.68	0.25	2.04	1.28	72.96	10.65	9.71	8.39	0.27	2.23	1.40	78.67	66.05		
15313	7.37	11.50	10.49	4.40	0.82	0.76	0.47	76.96	12.42	11.33	4.75	0.89	0.82	0.51	83.10	63.57	4,597	4,619
15318	9.25	12.25	11.17	0.57	0.35	0.47	0.05	78.54	13.50	12.31	0.63	0.39	0.52	0.06	86.54	78.53	4,420	4,448
15320	8.45	14.38	13.11	1.10	2.36	1.22		76.12	15.71	14.33	1.20	2.58	1.33		83.14	63.49	4,440	4,429
15327	7.77	9.13	8.33	10.23	0.13	0.97	1.59	72.70	9.90	9.03	11.09	0.14	1.05	1.67	78.83	75.35	4,875	4,902
15330	4.67	12.56	11.45	7.36	0.41	2.05	0.46	74.47	13.18	12.02	7.72	0.43	2.15	0.49	78.11	61.15	4,708	4,754
15337	6.96	11.38	10.38	7.10	0.61	1.40	0.76	74.26	12.22	11.14	7.62	0.65	1.50	0.80	79.74	64.85	4,715	4,742
15339	5.54	10.19	9.29	11.56	0.74	1.39	0.02	72.22	10.79	9.84	12.24	0.78	1.47	0.68	76.45	55.25	4,930	4,783
15340	9.16	12.38	11.29	0.48	0.70	1.76	0.46	77.31	13.63	12.43	0.53	0.87	1.94	0.49	85.10	61.63	4,357	4,399
15343	6.14	10.81	9.86	8.75	0.32	1.20	0.08	74.05	11.52	10.51	9.32	0.34	1.28	0.09	78.89	43.29	4,630	4,661
15314	6.72	9.56	8.72	3.54	0.42	0.02	0.46	80.40	11.49	10.49	3.80	0.45	0.66	0.44	85.97	88.91	4,529	4,574
15346	5.20	8.38	8.55	7.99	0.40	1.11	0.42	77.15	9.89	9.02	8.43	0.42	1.17	0.54	61.38	79.42	4,734	4,606
15347	7.58	9.03	8.78	10.68	0.32	1.43	0.59	71.53	10.42	9.50	11.56	0.35	1.55		77.39	47.46	4,846	4,844
Average	7.13	10.34	9.43	8.67	0.47	1.57	0.99	73.17	11.16	10.18	9.33	0.53	1.70	1.08	78.79	65.81	4,755	4,697

DISCUSSION OF THE ANALYTICAL DATA.

In the study of the analytical data the most remarkable fact which presents itself is found in the large quantity of ether extract. When the difficulty of extracting the fat from baked bread is considered it must be admitted that the actual amount of fat present is probably considerably greater than that which is shown by the ether extract. The mean percentage of fat, as determined by analysis, is nearly 9, which shows the addition of from 9 to 15 per cent of fat in the preparation of the dough. This large percentage of added fat is one of the most constant characteristics of the class of cereal foods known as biscuits. In the 48 samples examined only 4 were free of added fat. The maximum amount of fat found by extraction with ether was 16.05 per cent in No. 14729, which would indicate that nearly 20 per cent of fat had been added in the mixing of the dough. This large percentage of fat, of course, adds to the nutritive value of the biscuits when considered from the point of view of condensation as favoring transportation. The natural consequence of the addition of the fat would be a diminution in the content of the other nutritive ingredients, and consequently the percentage of carbohydrates and of proteids is much less than in a straight bread or a biscuit made from a straight flour without the addition of fat. The mean percentage of proteids is 9.43 and of carbohydrates 73.17. The highest content of carbohydrates is found in those samples where no addition of fat was practiced, but the same can not be said of the proteids; for instance, the sample which contains the largest amount of fat contains also an amount of proteids far above the average, viz, 11.68 per cent, showing that the material was made from a flour extremely rich in gluten. Inasmuch as a stiff dough is highly essential in the manufacture of biscuits, it is evident that flours which contain a large percentage of gluten are to be preferred, and this is shown in the general analytical data. Only in a few instances do the proteids fall to a remarkably low percentage, viz, in No. 15299 and in No. 15020. The highest percentage of proteids is found in No. 15320, a sample which also, on account of its low percentage of ether extract, may be regarded as having received no additional fat in the dough, but probably a little from the greasing of the oven.

The above data are those found in the table of the original substance, and not the data calculated to dry matter, which are given also in the preceding table. It is evident from a study of the digested proteids that the method of kneading, the addition of large quantities of fat, and the hard baking, tend to diminish the digestibility of the proteid matter, as determined by artificial means. The average digestibility of proteid matter present was a little less than 66 per cent, which is far below that of ordinary cereal proteids. This fact should not be lost sight of in considering the nutritive value of the biscuits. It will be granted without argument that the artificial digestion does not in all cases, probably in very few, represent the actual digestibility of these proteids in the human stomach. In general it may be stated that in the form of biscuits wheat flour possesses its maximum practical degree of concentration as a food product. Biscuits contain a large percentage of fat, which adds to that extent to the nutritive value, but tends to diminish to a certain degree the artificial digestibility of the proteids. The general conclusion from a study of the analytical data is that biscuits may be used in ordinary life as a delicacy, in army life as a convenient means of transporting concentrated food, but that they should not be employed to the entire exclusion of bread, on account of their low coefficient of digestibility.

ROLLS.

By the term "rolls" is meant a kind of bread often eaten warm, and which differs to a certain extent from an ordinary loaf mostly in size, and from biscuits in having, as a rule, a leavening matter. Warm rolls in this country are a common article of diet on the breakfast table. They may be made by fermentation with yeast, or more commonly the leavening is produced by means of a baking powder. Warm rolls of this kind are usually, but improperly, known as biscuits. In the following table has been collected a number of samples of bread which are included under the general term of rolls. Their names vary greatly, as will be seen from the "trade name" column in the table. One of these, No. 14436, might very properly be included in the preceding table. It is a kind of a hard roll which is very common in the State of Maryland, from which it is named, and occupies a mean position between an ordinary roll and a true biscuit. It is usually eaten cold, and in its fabrication the method employed in the ordinary baking of biscuits is used. On account of the uncertainty of its classification it has been included in the following instead of the preceding table. Slightly sweetened and sometimes spiced rolls are often known by the name of "buns," samples of which are found also in the appended list. In the case of No. 14359 we have a sample of a roll which is made from the whole shredded wheat and which also might more properly be included in the preceding table or among the breakfast foods. This roll is light and spongy, but this is secured without the aid of leavening bodies by the mechanical condition of the material which is used in its preparation. The shreds of the whole wheat resemble the fibers of spaghetti. On account of their shape they do not lie close together, and when baked in the form of rolls or biscuits the resulting product is porous and spongy. The whole-wheat biscuit differs in other respects from the true biscuit in the method of its manufacture, no kneading being practiced except that which is produced in the manufacture of the shreds by the machines after the wheat grains have been softened in hot water. These whole wheat biscuits are made without the addition of any mineral matter, or without the addition of any fat, except what is necessary to grease the pans. They represent, therefore, very nearly the nutritive properties of the whole wheat grain. Following is a description of the rolls and breads of this classification, together with their composition, as determined in the original substance and calculated to dry matter:

Description of rolls.

Serial No.	Trade name.	Name of dealer.	Name of manufacturer.	Price per doz.	Weight per doz.
				Cents.	Grams.
14355	Pan Rolls	N. W. Burchell, 1325 F street NW.	C. Schneider	10	909
14359	Shredded Whole Wheat Biscuit.	....do	The Cereal Machine Company, Worcester, Mass.	15	....
14381	Rolls	A. A. Winfield, 215 Thirteen-and-a-half street SW.	Havenner's Bakery	10	860
14382	Rolls	....do	Berens & Sons, 622 E street NW.	8	928
14433	French Rolls	Berens & Sons, 622 E street NW.	....do	10	564
14434	Kaiser Rolls	....do	....do	12	838
14435	Hearth Bake	....do	....do	12	782
14436	Maryland Biscuit	....do	....do	10	575
14437	Vienna Rolls	....do	....do	10	820
14663	Currant Buns	....do	....do	10	420
15243	Buns	A. Meier, C and Fourteenth streets SW.	A. Meier, C and Fourteenth streets SW.	10	793

Analytical data.

Serial No.	Moisture.	In the original substance.							In the dry substance.						Digestible proteids.	Calculated calories of combustion.	Estimated calories.
		Proteids, N×6.25.	Proteids, N×5.70.	Ether extract.	Fiber.	Ash.	Salt.	Carbohydrates, N×5.70.	Proteids, N×6.25.	Proteids, N×5.70.	Ether extract.	Fiber.	Ash.	Salt.	Carbohydrates, N×5.70.			
	Per ct.	Per ct.	Per ct.	Per ct.	Per ct.	Per ct.	Per ct.	Per ct.	Per ct.	Per ct.	Per ct.	Per ct.	Per ct.	Per ct.	Per ct.	Per ct.		
14355	34.04	9.21	8.40	1.08	0.21	1.72	0.90	54.76	13.96	12.74	1.64	0.36	2.61	1.46	83.01	64.99	4,391	4,065
14359	7.21	9.58	8.72	1.29	2.28	2.18	......	80.60	10.30	9.40	1.39	2.46	2.35	......	86.06	56.17	4,298	4,253
14381	27.65	8.57	7.82	3.96	0.30	1.39	0.81	59.18	11.85	10.81	5.47	0.41	1.92	1.12	81.80	79.13	4,582	4,486
14382	28.43	9.12	8.32	1.39	0.25	1.18	0.62	60.68	12.74	11.62	1.94	0.35	1.65	0.87	84.79	62.57	4,427	4,366
14433	31.92	7.98	7.28	2.73	0.31	1.18	0.59	56.89	11.72	10.69	4.01	0.46	1.73	0.87	83.57	58.26	4,514	4,561
14434	31.47	7.87	7.18	3.61	0.46	1.54	0.82	56.20	11.49	10.47	5.27	0.67	2.25	1.20	82.01	79.89	4,552	4,616
14435	33.85	9.00	8.21	0.43	0.19	1.16	0.50	56.35	13.61	12.41	0.65	0.29	1.75	0.76	85.19	57.90	4,371	4,336
14436	25.02	7.49	6.83	6.83	0.58	1.41	0.83	59.91	9.99	9.11	9.11	0.77	1.88	1.11	79.90	77.36	4,741	4,712
14437	31.75	8.47	7.72	2.18	0.43	1.12	0.64	57.23	12.41	11.31	3.19	0.63	1.64	0.94	83.86	74.72	4,466	4,473
14663	27.46	6.66	6.07	7.55	1.11	0.61	......	58.31	9.18	8.37	10.41	1.53	0.84	......	80.38	......	4,838	4,873
15243	28.96	6.31	5.75	6.45	0.42	0.92	0.43	57.92	8.88	8.09	9.08	0.59	1.30	0.60	81.53	77.83	4,740	4,550
Average	27.98	8.20	7.48	3.41	0.60	1.31	0.69	59.82	11.47	10.46	4.74	0.77	1.81	0.81	82.90	68.89	4,538	4,481

DISCUSSION OF THE DATA.

The analytical data show that some of these rolls are made without the use of added fat. In samples Nos. 14381, 14434, 14436, 14663, and 15243 it is evident that a fat or oil has been used in the preparation of the dough. The percentage of ash shows that no mineral matter has been added to the flours in the manufacture of the rolls with the exception of a little salt. No. 14359, which represents the whole wheat, has the higher amount of mineral matter than any of the other samples and contains no salt, showing that this mineral matter is derived exclusively from the natural ash of the wheat. The artificial digestibility of the proteids is not as high as would be expected with this class of bodies. The caution, however, which has been given before in regard to the results of artificial digestion holds good in this class. It is more than probable that we do not secure in artificial digestion anything like so perfect a solution of the proteid matter as is accomplished by the natural digestive ferments of the alimentary canal.

CAKES AND LIKE GOODS.

By the term "cake" is generally understood a loaf containing a large quantity of added sugar. The trade name of cakes is almost legion, as will be seen by inspecting the column headed "trade name" of samples. We have included in this category all loaves, biscuits, buns, and other materials made of wheat or other cereal flours which have been artificially sweetened. These materials were purchased in the open market, and represent quite well the character of goods exposed for public sale. In private houses the baking of sweetened cakes is constantly practiced, and the composition of these cakes is essentially the same as those which are offered for public sale. In the manufacture of sweet cakes the flour is mixed with egg and sugar, or other saccharine matter, and butter to the proper consistence, and leavened generally with a baking powder instead of a yeast. The cakes are baked in all kinds of sizes and shapes, and are either plain or built up in layers with jelly, marmalade, or some other preserve between them. The exterior is often frosted with a mixture of white sugar beaten up with the white of an egg. The method of mixing the ingredients of these cakes, as well as the methods of frosting, are so varied that it would not be possible to undertake any minute description of them; only the general principles of their manufacture can be stated, as outlined above.

Cakes in general are baked in the oven or a skillet, the same as a loaf of bread. Some forms, however, are fried in hot grease, as is the case with doughnuts, crullers, or other similar substances. For flavoring matter various materials are employed, as strawberry, vanilla, and other flavoring substances, either the natural products or the artificial ethers resembling them. The cake or sweet cake is a very common ingredient of the dessert which is served after dinner. The ordinary cane sugar of commerce is the sweetening material which is usually employed, either in the pure state, as granulated sugar; or very often the lower grades of yellow sugar are employed where a white cake is not desired. Honey and glucose are not much used in private families

CAKES AND LIKE GOODS.

in this country in the manufacture of sweet cakes, but glucose as an ingredient of sirups is used to a considerable extent where molasses or sirups are present as the sweetening agent. In the manufacture of the variety known as ginger cake, the old-fashioned New Orleans open kettle molasses has been a standard ingredient. The difficulty of obtaining this variety of molasses at the present time has resulted in the substitution of the commercial sirups in the manufacture of this kind of goods. Inasmuch as these commercial sirups are often made chiefly of the glucose of commerce, much of the sweetening material in such instances may be from this source.

In the determination of the sugars they were first removed by alcohol from the finely ground dry mass after previous extraction with ether. The sucrose in the solution was determined by polarization before and after inversion. In most cases the only sugar found was sucrose. In a few cases the residual polarization represented small quantities of glucose—that is, commercial liquid starch sugar. When this sugar is present in an appreciable quantity, it is represented by data in foot notes of the analytical table which follows.

Description of cakes and similar goods.

Serial No.	Trade name of sample.	Name of dealer.	Name of manufacturer.	Price.
				Cents.
14664	Macaroons	Berens & Sons, 622 E street NW.	Berens & Sons, 622 E street NW., Washington, D. C.	[1]10
14665	Sugar Cakes	....do	....do	[1]10
14666	Doughnuts	....do	....do	[1]10
14667	Lady Fingers	....do	....do	[1]10
14725	Ginger Snaps	N.W. Burchell, 1325 F street NW.		[2]8
15003	Vanilla Wafers	....do	J. D. Mason & Co., Baltimore, Md	[2]20
15004	Puff Jumbles	....do	The New York Biscuit Co., New York, N. Y.	[2]20
15005	Fruit Crackers	....do	J. D. Mason & Co., Baltimore, Md	[2]16
15008	Butter Scotch	....do	The New York Biscuit Co., New York, N. Y.	[2]20
15010	Rose Jumbles	....do	E. S. Marvin & Co., New York, N. Y.	[2]20
15011	Oxfords	....do	....do	[2]20
15012	Bicycle Cakes	....do	J. D. Mason & Co., Baltimore, Md	[2]16
15013	Pineapple Puffs	....do	The American Biscuit Co., New York, N. Y.	[2]40
15014	Fig Biscuits	....do	E. S. Marvin & Co., New York, N. Y.	[2]20
15015	Strawberry Wafers	....do	Bent & Co., Milton, Mass	[2]25
15017	Vanilla Sugar Wafers	....do	Holmes & Coutts, New York, N. Y.	[2]50
15018	Ginger Wafers	....do	....do	[2]25
15019	Five o'clock Tea Biscuit.	....do	The New York Biscuit Co., New York, N. Y.	[2]25
15021	Violet Biscuit	....do	....do	[2]25
15022	Famous Extra Toast	....do	Holmes & Coutts, New York, N. Y.	[2]12
15233	Horse Cakes	August Meier, C and Fourteenth streets SW.	August Meier, C and Fourteenth streets SW., Washington, D. C.	[1]10
15234	Lady Fingers	....do	....do	[1]10
15235	Scotch Cakes	....do	....do	[2]20
15236	Fruit Cake	....do	....do	[1]10

[1] Per dozen. [2] Per pound. [3] Per box.

FOODS AND FOOD ADULTERANTS.

Description of cakes and similar goods—Continued.

Serial No.	Trade name of sample.	Name of dealer.	Name of manufacturer.	Price.
				Cents.
15237	Diamond Cakes	August Meier, C and Fourteenth streets SW.	August Meier, C and Fourteenth streets SW., Washington, D. C.	[1]10
15239	Coffee Cake	....do	....do	[2]5
15240	Ginger Bread	....do	....do	[2]3
15241	Cup Cakes	....do	....do	[1]10
15242	Macaroons	....do	....do	[1]10
15244	Drop Cakes	....do	....do	[1]10
15245	Doughnuts	....do	....do	[1]10
15246	Sugar Cakes	....do	....do	[1]10
15247	Jumbles	....do	....do	[1]10
15252	Morning Glory Wafers	John H. Magruder & Co., 1417 New York avenue NW.	Crosier, Stauffer & Co., Philadelphia, Pa.	[3]20
15256	Maize Wafers	....do	C. D. Boss & Sons, New London, Conn.	[3]25
15261	Cocoanut Macaroons	....do	Vanderveer and Holmes Biscuit Co., New York, N. Y.	[3]25
15268	Golden Snap	....do	C. D. Boss & Sons, New London, Conn.	[3]15
15285	Vanilla Wafers	....do	Crosier, Stauffer & Co., Philadelphia, Pa.	[3]20
15288	....do	....do	Havenner's Bakery, Washington, D.C.	[4]20
15289	Jamaica Nuts	....do	The New York Biscuit Co., New York, N. Y.	[4]10
15290	Apricot Tarts	....do	Havenner's Bakery, Washington, D.C.	[4]20
15291	Pilot Bread	....do	....do	[4]10
15292	Ginger Snaps	....do	....do	[4]10
15293	Iced Coffee Cakes	....do	The New York Biscuit Co., New York, N. Y.	[4]15
15295	Java Coffee Cakes	....do	E. S. Marvin & Co., New York, N. Y.	[4]12
15298	Rifle Nuts	....do	Havenner's Bakery, Washington, D.C.	[4]18
15300	Almond Macaroons	....do	The New York Biscuit Co., New York, N. Y.	[4]30
15304	Social Tea Cakes	....do	....do	[4]20
15305	Cream Blossoms	....do	....do	[4]10
15306	Fancy Ginger Snaps	....do	....do	[4]12
15308	Butter Scotch	....do	Havenner's Bakery, Washington, D.C.	[4]20
15309	Animal Crackers	....do	....do	[4]15
15311	Cornhills	G. G. Cornwell & Son, 1412-1414 Pennsylvania avenue NW.	The New York Biscuit Co., New York, N. Y.	[4]12
15312	Vanilla Wafers	....do	Kennedy Biscuit Co., New York, N. Y.	[4]20
15314	Café Noir	....do	Carr & Co	[4]25
15315	Cream Bars	....do	The New York Biscuit Co., New York, N. Y.	[4]20
15317	Sultana Cakes	....do	....do	[4]12
15334	Cigarette Wafers	....do	Krietsch's Würzen Biscuit Manufactories, Germany.	[2]45
15338	Homemade Ginger Snaps.	....do	Bent & Co., Milton, Mass	[2]25
15341	Raspberry Wafers	....do	Krietsch's Würzen Biscuit Manufactories, Germany.	[2]25
15345	English Fruit Cake	....do	The New York Biscuit Co., New York, N. Y.	[2]25

[1] Per dozen.   [2] Per cake.   [3] Per box.   [4] Per pound.

CAKES AND LIKE GOODS.

Composition of cakes and similar goods.

Serial No.	Moisture.	In the original substance.									In the dry substance.								Calculated calories of combustion.	Estimated calories.
		Proteids, N×6.25.	Proteids, N×5.70.	Ether extract.	Fiber.	Ash.	Salt.	Sugar.	Carbohydrates other than fiber and sugar, N×5.70.	Proteids, N×6.25.	Proteids, N×5.70.	Ether extract.	Fiber.	Ash.	Salt.	Sugar.	Carbohydrates other than fiber and sugar, N×5.70.	Digestible proteids.		
	Per ct.	Per ct.	Per ct.	Per ct.	Per ct.	Per ct.	Per ct.	Per ct.	Per ct.	Per ct.	Per ct.	Per ct.	Per ct.	Per ct.	Per ct.	Per ct.	Per ct.	Per ct.		
14664	27.55	5.41	4.93	9.57	0.57	0.40	0.06	33.74	23.24	7.47	6.81	13.21	0.79	0.55	0.08	46.57	32.07	85.75	4,812	4,624
14665	10.19	6.90	6.29	10.52	0.61	0.61	0.02	23.69	48.00	7.68	7.00	11.71	0.68	0.68	0.02	26.38	53.55	65.53	4,823	4,486
14666	21.61	6.73	6.14	19.33	0.60	0.40	0.03	1.28	50.64	8.59	7.83	24.66	0.77	0.51	0.04	1.61	64.60	80.82	5,529	5,452
14667	12.93	9.22	8.41	4.43	0.43	0.60	0.05	39.78	33.12	10.59	9.66	5.09	0.49	0.69	0.05	45.60	38.38	48.19	4,411	4,373
14725	4.98	6.06	5.53	15.44	0.79	1.82	0.47	28.66	42.90	6.37	5.81	16.23	0.83	1.91	0.49	30.12	45.10	71.12	4,971	4,921
15003	6.30	6.34	5.33	14.92	0.12	0.78	0.37	20.72	44.77	6.76	6.33	15.93	0.13	0.83	0.40	28.54	47.81	44.00	5,021	4,661
15004	12.40	7.07	7.27	10.89	0.23	1.34	0.68	21.04	46.63	8.10	8.30	12.43	0.21	1.53	0.78	24.02	53.51	50.67	4,831	4,783
15005	3.18	6.13	5.59	4.27	0.66	1.78	0.08	9.48	75.94	6.33	5.77	4.41	0.68	1.84	0.08	9.79	77.51	36.70	4,421	4,523
15008	7.51	0.15	5.01	15.49	0.48	1.48	0.52	26.15	43.28	6.65	6.06	16.75	0.52	1.60	0.56	28.27	46.80	70.22		
15010	6.74	7.88	7.19	12.70	0.35	0.65	0.10	29.02	43.35	8.45	7.71	13.62	0.38	0.70	0.11	31.12	46.47	68.02		
15011	5.21	8.60	7.93	9.41	0.26	0.62	0.21	25.04	51.53	9.17	8.36	9.93	0.27	0.65	0.22	26.42	54.37	74.11		
15012	5.48	7.50	6.84	8.99	0.14	0.65	0.21	23.40	54.50	7.93	7.23	9.51	0.15	0.68	0.22	24.76	57.67	53.33		
15013	17.94	4.23	3.86	1.75	0.29	0.41	0.03	43.34	32.44	5.16	4.71	2.13	0.32	0.50	0.04	52.82	39.52	60.17		
15014	17.86	4.50	4.16	6.01	1.73	1.11	0.15	19.00	49.53	5.55	5.06	8.05	2.11	1.35	0.18	23.13	60.30	76.64	4,905	4,748
15015	7.04	7.63	6.96	11.16	0.17	1.24	0.51	25.38	48.05	8.21	7.49	12.00	0.18	1.33	0.55	27.30	51.70	81.90	4,541	4,463
15017	6.38	7.81	7.12	8.37	0.30	1.54	0.23	24.77	53.46	8.34	7.61	8.80	0.28	1.64	0.25	26.46	57.21	77.50	4,720	4,606
15018	5.40	6.31	5.75	10.46	0.57	2.31	0.92	19.33	56.18	6.68	6.09	11.06	0.60	2.44	0.97	22.43	50.38	82.00	4,835	4,606
15019	4.19	8.50	7.75	10.44	0.28	1.11	0.57	21.32	54.91	8.87	8.09	10.90	0.29	1.16	0.59	22.25	57.31	74.94	4,917	4,700
15021	4.77	9.81	8.95	11.89	0.25	1.76	0.29	21.24	51.14	10.30	9.39	12.49	0.26	1.85	0.30	22.30	53.70	69.39		4,777
15022	8.21	9.63	8.78	11.51	0.18	1.20	0.71	2.74	67.58	10.25	9.35	12.54	0.20	1.31	0.77	29.85	46.75	51.58	4,990	4,860
15233	10.82	6.98	6.37	4.79	0.38	0.68	0.08	127.07	49.89	7.83	7.14	5.37	0.43	0.76	0.09	231.36	44.04	66.94	4,515	4,430
15234	21.72	6.80	6.20	3.11	0.10	0.49	0.03	449.10	19.28	8.68	7.92	3.97	0.12	0.61	0.04	462.72	24.64	62.00	4,415	4,327
15235	7.84	5.84	5.33	10.08	0.43	2.20	1.21	45.72	28.31	6.34	5.79	10.94	0.47	2.48	1.31	249.61	39.71	80.19	4,065	4,728

[1] Sucrose, 17.50 per cent; glucose, 10.41 per cent. [3] Sucrose, 30 per cent; glucose, 19.10 per cent. [5] Sucrose, 32.23 per cent; glucose, 13.44 per cent.
[2] Sucrose, 19.69 per cent; glucose, 11.67 per cent. [4] Sucrose, 38.32 per cent; glucose, 24.40 per cent. [6] Sucrose, 35.03 per cent; glucose, 14.58 per cent.

Composition of cakes and similar goods—Continued.

Serial No.	Moisture.	Proteids, N×6.25.	Proteids, N×5.70.	Ether extract.	Fiber.	Ash.	Salt.	Sugar.	Carbohydrates other than fiber and sugar, N×5.70.	Proteids, N×6.25.	Proteids, N×5.70.	Ether extract.	Fiber.	Ash.	Salt.	Sugar.	Carbohydrates other than fiber and sugar, N×5.70.	Digestible proteids.	Calculated calories of combustion.	Estimated calories.
	Per ct.	Per ct.	Per ct.	Per ct.	Per ct.	Per ct.	Per ct.	Per ct.	Per ct.	Per ct.	Per ct.	Per ct.	Per ct.	Per ct.	Per ct.	Per ct.	Per ct.	Per ct.		
15236	24.47	4.56	4.16	12.35	0.09	0.54	0.19	¹46.02	13.56	6.04	5.51	16.35		0.67	0.24	*50.78	16.98	50.61		
15237	19.57	4.31	3.93	14.19	0.61	1.04	0.52	5.59	52.86	5.37	4.90	17.60	0.11	1.35	0.67	7.24	68.50	50.64	5,056	5,150
15239	22.83	7.24	6.60	10.47	0.81	1.55	0.28	9.48	52.40	9.38	8.56	13.57	0.79	1.97	0.36	12.07	66.83	73.07	4,903	4,720
15240	21.49	6.25	5.70	8.42	0.90	1.21	0.34	32.48	30.89	7.96	7.26	10.72	1.15	1.43	0.40	38.13	36.25	68.76	4,757	4,662
15241	14.81	5.24	4.78	15.56	0.27	0.82	0.07	58.77	10.18	6.15	5.61	18.27	0.32	0.89	0.08	68.92	12.93	77.23	5,073	4,887
15242	8.06	6.67	6.08	12.97	1.41	0.22				7.26	6.62	14.11	1.53	0.03				82.61	4,835	4,799
15244	04.82	3.19	2.83	5.67	0.08	0.23	0.01			8.81	8.03	10.12	0.23		0.04			84.95		
15245	25.52	6.69	6.10	18.15	0.83	0.87	0.37	0.92	47.61	8.98	8.19	24.94	1.11	1.17	0.50	1.24	63.35	72.11	5,559	5,368
15246	13.28	6.48	5.91	4.76	0.27	0.61	0.11	27.27	47.90	7.47	6.81	5.49	0.31	0.70	0.13	31.44	55.25	58.28	4,511	4,442
15247	13.34	7.62	6.95	14.79	1.04	0.97	0.39	¹10.00	46.31	8.98	8.19	17.47	1.23	1.15	0.41	¹19.61	52.35	79.41	5,133	4,992
15252	8.52	10.44	9.52	14.67	0.30	2.93	2.30	0.56	63.50	11.41	10.41	16.04	0.33	3.20	2.51	0.61	69.41	74.81	5,059	5,016
15258	5.25	7.81	7.12	10.82	0.49	2.20	1.23	18.11	56.01	8.24	7.51	11.42	0.52	2.32	1.30	19.11	59.12	61.50	4,772	4,227
15261	6.95	3.13	2.95	21.55	0.67	1.03	0.13	44.67	22.18	3.30	3.06	23.16	0.72	1.11	0.14	48.01	23.98	80.97	5,227	5,231
15268	8.01	6.06	5.53	8.35	0.33	1.91	0.43	26.44	49.43	6.59	6.01	9.08	0.36	2.08	0.47	28.70	53.77	88.61		4,800
15285	0.33	5.65	5.15	12.87	0.40	1.05	0.49	29.66	41.54	6.23	5.68	14.20	0.44	1.16	0.54	32.71	45.81	82.71	4,891	
15258	7.70	6.37	5.81	19.61	0.10	1.27		30.79	34.66	6.90	6.29	21.25	0.17	1.38		33.30	37.55	71.22	5,270	5,109
15289	9.79	6.90	6.29	7.85	0.40	1.38	0.21	26.95	47.34	7.65	6.98	8.70	0.44	1.53	0.23	29.88	52.47	74.13		
15290	12.96	6.40	5.84	10.31	0.28	0.90	0.02	27.52	42.13	7.35	6.70	11.85	0.32	1.10	0.71	31.62	48.41	73.02	4,813	4,756
15291	9.91	10.50	9.58	0.55	0.27	1.13	0.01	0.30	79.26	11.66	10.63	.01	0.30	1.25	0.68	0.33	86.88	81.99		
15292	9.60	7.18	6.55	2.30	0.87	1.98	0.15	26.01	52.60	7.95	7.25	2.55	0.96	2.19	0.16	28.80	58.30	75.10	4,292	4,520
15293	11.01	4.95	4.51	4.67	0.18	0.61	0.17	¹37.16	41.80	5.56	5.07	5.25	0.20	0.69	0.18	⁴41.76	47.03	84.94	4,444	4,380
15295	12.70	6.45	5.88	9.07	0.62	0.91	0.32	¹22.80	47.84	7.40	6.75	10.40	0.71	1.04	0.40	¹26.24	54.86	91.17		
15298	10.59	6.32	5.76	5.42	0.29	1.78	0.28	20.09	55.47	7.07	6.45	6.06	0.32	2.04	0.31	23.14	61.99	72.05	4,475	4,382
15300	5.94	10.60	9.67	17.60	1.81	1.04	0.10	53.62	10.32	11.27	10.28	18.71	1.92	1.11	0.11	56.30	11.08	85.99	5,126	5,132

15304	7.48	8.97	8.18	9.77	0.24	1.12	0.48	21.59	51.62	9.70	8.85	10.56	0.26	1.21	0.52	22.75	55.37	66.98	4.779	4,603
15305	8.60	13.13	11.97	10.63	0.43	0.74	0.08	5.90	61.73	14.37	13.11	11.63	0.47	0.81	0.09	6.40	67.52	67.80	.....	.....
15306	8.24	6.65	6.06	7.12	0.74	2.57	0.69	22.01	53.26	7.25	6.61	7.76	0.81	2.80	0.75	22.99	58.03	67.80	.....	4,942
15308	9.26	6.37	5.81	8.02	0.18	1.07	0.88	31.59	44.07	7.02	6.40	8.84	0.20	1.18	0.97	34.81	48.57	78.74	4.621	4,618
15309	7.59	8.50	7.75	7.94	0.38	0.37	0.04	16.16	59.81	9.20	8.39	8.59	0.41	0.40	0.04	17.49	64.72	61.06	4.720	4,523
15311	6.78	10.25	9.35	5.12	0.42	1.18	0.72	10.76	66.39	11.00	10.13	5.49	0.45	1.27	0.77	11.54	71.12	65.85	4.570	4,523
15312	4.85	6.13	5.59	14.77	0.29	1.27	0.55	28.28	44.95	6.44	5.87	15.52	0.30	1.33	0.58	29.12	47.86	.....	4.963	4,872
15314	4.87	4.56	4.16	7.06	0.24	0.40	0.06	45.24	38.03	4.79	4.37	7.42	0.25	0.42	0.06	47.56	39.98	83.55	4.517	4,443
15315	6.64	7.09	7.01	8.23	0.40	0.84	0.59	23.00	52.88	8.24	7.51	9.89	0.43	0.90	0.63	24.64	50.93	78.74	4.733	4,660
15317	13.97	.....	.....	7.42	0.65	1.61	0.08	9.15	.....	.....	.....	8.62	0.75	1.87	0.09	10.42	.....	.....	.....	.....
15334	6.48	9.44	8.61	2.53	0.44	0.56	0.06	29.40	51.98	10.09	9.20	2.71	0.47	0.60	0.06	31.44	55.58	76.17	4.391	4,431
15338	6.76	7.31	6.67	9.19	0.30	2.66	1.21	14.48	59.88	7.84	7.15	9.86	0.39	2.85	1.30	15.53	64.22	66.62	4.506	4,570
15341	5.58	8.38	7.64	3.75	0.38	0.88	0.04	32.16	49.61	8.89	8.11	3.97	0.40	0.93	0.04	34.06	52.53	62.65	.....	.....
15345	20.22	.....	.....	8.85	2.32	1.79	0.32	0.78	.....	.....	.....	11.10	2.01	2.25	0.40	8.48	.....	.....	.....	.....
Average	11.65	0.91	6.29	9.81	0.50	1.17	0.39	24.57	46.01	8.00	7.29	11.41	0.57	1.30	0.44	27.64	51.59	71.17	4,805	4,729

[1] Sucrose, 33.86 per cent; glucose, 14.16 per cent.
[2] Sucrose, 42.15 per cent; glucose, 17.63 per cent.
[3] Sucrose, 19.34 per cent; glucose, 7.93 per cent.
[4] Sucrose, 22.30 per cent; glucose, 9.14 per cent.
[5] Sucrose, 29.06 per cent; glucose, 8.10 per cent.
[6] Sucrose, 32.65 per cent; glucose, 9.10 per cent.
[7] Sucrose, 11.89 per cent; glucose, 11 per cent.
[8] Sucrose, 13.63 per cent; glucose, 12.61 per cent.

DISCUSSION OF THE ANALYTICAL DATA.

An inspection of the analytical data shows that large quantities of fat are used in preparing these cakes. In private families butter is the fat which is generally employed for this purpose. It is probable that butter is also largely used by the public bakeries, but in addition to butter, lard is also often used, both in private families and the bakeries. It is not probable that any kind of fat except the two mentioned is extensively used. The presence of a large quantity of sugar, in addition to the amount of fat, naturally diminishes the content of proteids and carbohydrates to a minimum amount found in any of the cereal products. An inspection of the table of percentage of digestibility, however, shows that the addition of sugar does not influence in a deleterious way the action of the artificial digestive ferments. The general impression, to the effect that these cakes are unwholesome and indigestible is doubtless founded on erroneous notions. On account of their palatability, in the case of children who are allowed free access to them, these cakes are eaten to the exclusion of other kinds of foods, and hence the digestive apparatus may be deranged. In the case of adults the cakes are usually eaten after a very full meal, when no other food is necessary, and the evil effects which are produced thereby are more likely caused by an excess of food than by the character of the excess. There is no reason for supposing that a mixture containing wholesome fat, pure sugar, egg, and wheat flour would produce a loaf which would be either unpalatable or indigestible.

In a few instances, on account of the small quantity of sugar present, it is evident that the samples might, with more propriety, be placed in some other category. These samples were bought as sweet cakes, or under the supposition that they were sweet cakes, and therefore are included in the list. Out of the whole number purchased only four would be excluded by reason of deficient content of sugar. The proportion of sugar in the cakes, as will be seen by an inspection of the table, varies greatly. The quantity of sugar is a matter of taste and habit. Often the sweet bread or cake contains very little sugar—only enough to indicate to the taste the addition, at least, of a certain amount. In other cases the amount of sugar may approximate or exceed half of the whole weight of the loaf. In such matters no definite rule of guidance is laid down, but each cook is allowed to follow his own inclination or the recipe he happens to have on hand.

In regard to the quantity of moisture the widest variations are seen. In some cases the amount of moisture found was more than one-half of the whole weight, while in other instances the amount was one-third or one-quarter of the whole. These latter cases represent nearly the ordinary average loaf of bread. In most cases, however, the percentage of moisture which was found was very much less than that which exists in normal bread. In some cases the content of moisture descends to the level of the biscuit; indeed this is true of the majority of samples.

The average moisture in all the samples was a little less than 12 per cent, only about one-third of that which would be found in the case of bread. Some of the sweet cakes were remarkably dry, as, for instance, No. 15005, which contained a little over 3 per cent of water, and Nos. 15314 and 15315, containing nearly 5 and 7 per cent, respectively. This wide variation in the percentage of water, combined with small variations in the percentage of sugar, renders any comparison of the proteids and carbohydrates of little use. A better comparison will be found in the data calculated to the dry substance, but here also the varying elements of the sugar content causes the widest discrepancies in the comparison of the proteid and carbohydrate bodies.

STANNOUS CHLORID IN GINGER CAKE.

Moynier de Villepoix[1] found stannous chlorid in almost every sample of cakes examined by him. He found that it was used in combination with potassium carbonate for coloring purposes. The coloring was formerly done by using honey or molasses, but since these have been replaced by glucose the baker uses the above combination to obtain a yellow color.

---

[1] Rev. internat. des fals., 1893, 85. Ztsch. Nahr.-Unters., Hyg. u. Waarenkunde, Vol. VII, No. 3, p. 37.

INDEX.

A.

	Page.
Alum in bread	1330
Araban	1196
Ash, composition of cereal	1209, 1212
difficulties in procuring, for analysis	1210
importance in nutrition	1213

B.

Baking, loss	1317
powders	1303
alum	1307
containing more than one acid ingredient	1309
phosphate	1306
tartrate	1305
temperature	1315
Barley	1172
composition of unhulled	1173
flour	1282
products, composition	1348
Biscuit	1353
composition	1356
description of samples	1354
shredded wheat	1336
Bran, composition	1226
Bread, acidity	1331
adulteration	1330, 1333, 1338
alum	1330
American high-grade	1328
and flour, comparison	1326
baking, chemical changes	1318
loss	1317
temperature	1315
composition	1312, 1323, 1332
crude fiber	1321
description of samples	1319
ether extract	1321
fermentation, loss	1317
from flour of the entire wheat	1337
"hunger," composition	1332
influence of mold on the composition	1335
leavening	1298
making and baking	1296
materials used	1314
moisture	1315
rye	1328
salt-rising	1301
substitutes	1333
varieties	1297
Breakfast foods	1340
composition	1345
Buckwheat	1174
flo·	1282

C.

	Page.
Cakes and like goods	1362
composition	1365
stannous chlorid	1369
Calories, comparison of, calculated and ascertained	1249, 1369
of carbohydrates	1245
cereal oils	1247
cereals and cereal products	1243
ether extract	1247
vegetable proteids	1246
Carbohydrates, calories	1245
comparative nutritive value	1293
in flour	1261
insoluble	1192
of cereals	1192
soluble	1202
wheat, insoluble	1198
Cellulose group	1195
quantitative separation	1197
separation	1200
Cereal grains, composition	1171
Cereals, grinding	1219
preparation for food	1219
Chop, composition	1226
Corn flour, detection in wheat flour	1287
Crude fiber in bread	1321

D.

Dextran	1196
Dextrin	1205
Diastase	1209
Dough, viscosity	1269

E.

Enzymes	1208
Ergot in rye flour	1281
Ether extract in bread	1321, 1329
flour	1260

F.

Farinometer, Kedzie's (*see also* Gluten tester)	1269
Knais	1271
Ferments	1208
Flour, action of sulphur dioxid	1293
adulteration	1285
American, typical	1263
and bread, comparison	1326
bakers'	1264
carbohydrates	1261
classification	1237
combustion, heat. (*See* Calories.)	
common market wheat	1264
composition	1232, 1233, 1254, 1313
of wheat	1236, 1254, 1313
débris	1275
description of samples	1238
ether extract	1260
examination	1295
French	1266
gluten	1235, 1259
grades	1234
grading	1274
heat of combustion	1243
microscopic examination	1275
miscellaneous	1265
moisture	1257

INDEX. 1373

	Page.
Flour, of the entire wheat	1235
patent high grade	1264
preference of bakers	1236
properties affecting commercial value	1236
proteids	1258
self-raising	1266
substitutes	1285
sulphured, bread making	1295
nutritive properties	1293

G.

Galactan	1196
in cereals	1205
Gluten	1259
modification in sulphured flour	1294
separation of constituents	1191
tester (*see also* Farinometer)	1272

H.

Hemicellulose	1196

I.

Indian corn. (*See* Maize.)

Invert sugar in cereals	1205

L.

Leavening by already formed carbon dioxid	1302
baking powders	1303
spontaneous fermentation	1301
yeast	1299
of bread	1298
salt-rising bread	1301
Lignin	1196

M.

Macaroni, composition	1348
Maize	1175
and wheat, relative nutritive properties	1290
flour, composition	1279
use of, as wheat flour adulterant	1286
grinding	1277
meal, microscopic examination	1278
Mannan	1196
Meal, substitutes	1285
Middlings, composition	1226
Milling of maize	1277
wheat	1219
Mill, products from roller process	1222
Mineral hunger	1217
matters, excess	1216
importance in nutrition	1213
use as flour substitute	1289
Moisture in wheat flour	1257
Mold, influence on the composition of bread	1335

N.

Nitrogenous bases	1207
Noodles, composition	1348
Nutritive value of carbohydrates	1293
maize and wheat	1290
sulphured flour	1293

O.

Oat products, composition	1347
Oats	1178
Oils, calories of cereal	1247

P.

	Page.
Partially prepared foods	1310
composition	1345
Pentosans	1202
Potatoes, use in adulterating cereal products	1288
Prefatory note	1169
Proteids, barley	1173
calories of vegetable	1246
maize	1177
oat	1181
rice	1183
rye	1184
wheat	1190, 1258

R.

Raffinose	1207
Reducing sugars in cereals	1205
Rice	1181
Roller process	1219, 1222
Rolls	1359
composition	1361
Rye	1183
Rye flour, composition	1281
ergot	1281
Rye meal, production	1280

S.

Shorts, composition	1226
Spaghetti, composition	1348
Starch	1192
appearance with polarized light	1194
barley	1194
buckwheat	1194
composition	1347
deportment with enzymes	1195
maize	1193
oat	1194
rice	1194
rye	1194
wheat	1193
Sucrose, in cereals	1204

T.

Tapioca and starch, composition	1347

W.

Wheat	1185
and maize, relative nutritive properties	1290
composition	1186, 1226
kernel, structure	1220
milling	1219
nutritive properties	1290
products, composition	1316
screenings, composition	1226
shredded	1336
water soluble substances	1206
Wood, use as flour substitute	1289

X.

Xylan	1196

Y.

Yeast, fermentation	1299

Z.

Zymogen	1208

www.ingramcontent.com/pod-product-compliance
Lightning Source LLC
Chambersburg PA
CBHW021828230426
43669CB00008B/900